Y0-CAZ-385

From JERUSALEM to ZARAHEMLA

RELIGIOUS STUDIES CENTER PUBLICATIONS

BOOK OF MORMON SYMPOSIUM SERIES

The Book of Mormon: The Keystone Scripture
The Book of Mormon: First Nephi, the Doctrinal Foundation
The Book of Mormon: Second Nephi, the Doctrinal Structure
The Book of Mormon: Jacob Through Words of Mormon, To Learn with Joy
The Book of Mormon: Mosiah, Salvation Only Through Christ
The Book of Mormon: Alma, The Testimony of the Word
The Book of Mormon: Helaman Through 3 Nephi 8, According to Thy Word
The Book of Mormon: 3 Nephi 9–30, This Is My Gospel
The Book of Mormon: Fourth Nephi Through Moroni, From Zion to Destruction

MONOGRAPH SERIES

Nibley on the Timely and the Timeless
Deity and Death
The Glory of God Is Intelligence
Reflections on Mormonism
Literature of Belief
The Words of Joseph Smith
Book of Mormon Authorship
Mormons and Muslims
The Temple in Antiquity
Isaiah and the Prophets
Scriptures for the Modern World
The Joseph Smith Translation: The Restoration of Plain and Precious Things
Apocryphal Writings and the Latter-day Saints
The Pearl of Great Price: Revelations From God
The Lectures on Faith in Historical Perspective
Mormon Redress Petitions: Documents of the 1833–1838 Missouri Conflict
Joseph Smith: The Prophet, the Man

SPECIALIZED MONOGRAPH SERIES

Supporting Saints: Life Stories of Nineteenth-Century Mormons
The Call of Zion: The Story of the First Welsh Mormon Emigration
The Religion and Family Connection: Social Science Perspectives
Welsh Mormon Writings from 1844 to 1862: A Historical Bibliography
Peter and the Popes
John Lyon: The Life of a Pioneer Poet
Latter-day Prophets and the United States Constitution
View of the Hebrews: 1825 2nd Edition
Book of Mormon Authors: Their Words and Messages
Prophet of the Jubilee
Manuscript Found: The Complete Original "Spaulding Manuscript"
Latter-day Saint Social Life: Social Research on the LDS Church and its Members
From Jerusalem to Zarahemla: Literary and Historical Studies of the Book of Mormon

OCCASIONAL PAPERS SERIES

Excavations at Seila, Egypt

OTHER

Christopher Columbus: A Latter-day Saint Perspective
Church History in Black and White: George Edward Anderson's Photographic Mission to Latter-day Saint Historical Sites
California Saints: A 150-Year Legacy in the Golden State
A Woman's View: Helen Mar Whitney's Reminiscences of Early Church History

From JERUSALEM *to* ZARAHEMLA

Literary and Historical Studies of the Book of Mormon

S. Kent Brown

Volume Thirteen
in the Religious Studies Center
Specialized Monograph Series

Religious Studies Center
Brigham Young University
Provo, Utah

Library of Congress Catalog Card Number: 98-68060

ISBN 1-57008-560-9

First Printing, 1998

Distributed by
BOOKCRAFT, INC.
Salt Lake City, Utah

Printed in the United States of America

Contents

Introduction

Prompted by the Lord, Lehi and Sariah plunged their family into the desert of Arabia, opening a family saga that would continue for a thousand years but would remain unknown to the world for almost two and one-half millennia. This family story, along with that of others chronicled in the pages of the Book of Mormon, reveals civilizations transplanted from the ancient Near East to the Americas. As is the case with all known early societies, one reads of eras characterized by high achievement in government and commerce as well as those fraught with war and debilitating conflict. Like other ancient cultures, those represented in the Book of Mormon carry an important religious component. But unlike others, Book of Mormon peoples enjoyed a defining visit from the resurrected Jesus as well as centuries of prophecy anticipating that visit. In this respect, only the Bible matches the Book of Mormon as a religious record.

Even so, a reader could be excused for asking the question, Why another book on the Book of Mormon? After all, a number of works by Latter-day Saints have appeared in recent years that offer fresh perspectives on the Book of Mormon, particularly in the wake of President Benson's stress on studying this book.[1]

My reply comes in two parts. First, I have come to the study of the Book of Mormon from the world of the Bible. I have found that asking questions of the text of the Book of Mormon, much as one asks questions of the text of the Bible, often yields both unexpected and insightful answers. Why? Because the work has its origin in the world of the Bible and is a genuinely ancient product.[2] As a result, it bears the inner markings of a composition written by ancient authors in real situations, situations that have influenced the manner in which they have composed and compiled the records that make up the Book of Mormon. In this connection, one has to be impressed—not put off—by the mushrooming number of studies that have taken this point of view and as a consequence have yielded important results.[3]

The second reason grows out of my observation that every time I push against the Book of Mormon text—asking hard questions, usually because I have noticed something of interest—the pushing brings results. For instance, more than twenty years ago I noticed in Nephi's early writing an oft-repeated phrase, "my father dwelt in a tent" (1 Ne. 2:15; 10:16; etc.). Becoming curious, I began to ask, Why does this phrase appear in these passages? I was mildly surprised—although subsequent reflection has told me that I should not have been—to find myself staring at fundamental building blocks of Nephi's composition in his efforts as both author and compiler. A published study resulted wherein I detailed a major source that Nephi drew on when compiling his own record, namely the record of his father, Lehi. That study, slightly revised, appears in this volume as "Recovering the Missing Record of Lehi."

Pursuing the Exodus pattern in the Book of Mormon has offered an opportunity to explore a substantial piece of the fabric of this work. The exploration has led to discoveries that reach far beyond those initial finds when I began to stumble onto pieces of the Exodus story. Others, before me and after me, have also noted elements here and there in the text that tie back to the experience of the Israelites under Moses' leadership.[4] As evidence began to grow more or less of its own accord, I wanted to see whether it all hung together when scrutinized. In my view, the Book of Mormon text has withstood the initial tests, portraying an extraordinarily rich tapestry of tradition and memory as well as scriptural interpretation and application. I have set out some of the dimensions of the Exodus theme in two essays, "The Exodus Pattern in the Book of Mormon" and "Moses and Jesus: The Old Adorns the New."

Two of my most satisfying studies look at the teachings of two prominent Book of Mormon figures, Alma the Younger and Samuel the Lamanite. Everyone is familiar with the accounts of Alma's dramatic conversion (Mosiah 27; Alma 36). I wanted to trace the impact of that experience on his speeches. I was not disappointed. I learned that all of his recorded sermons exhibit influences from that event. The results of my study appear in "Alma's Conversion: Reminiscences in His Sermons."

The one recorded sermon of Samuel the Lamanite offered a different kind of discovery. Because I was familiar with personal and communal laments in the biblical Psalms, I stumbled onto laments in Samuel's address, laments which present features in common with the Psalms. What is significantly different is the prophetic dimension of these laments, a dimension not shared by the Psalms, as well as the fact that Samuel uttered his two poetic laments at the height of his condemnation of his hearers. I have entitled my study, "The Prophetic Laments of Samuel the Lamanite."

Three of the first four pieces in the collection represent fresh studies, all growing out of 1 Nephi. The first, "What Were Those Sacrifices Offered by Lehi?" seeks to uncover the kinds of sacrifices offered by Lehi and the reasons why Lehi made those particular offerings, including the need to atone for sin. The second study suggests Nephi's personal reasons for including Isaiah 48–49 in his first book, reasons that go back to Nephi's feelings for Jerusalem and to his belief that Isaiah's prophecies spoke about the journey of his family to the New World. I have called this piece, "What is Isaiah Doing in First Nephi?" The third study—number four in the collection—consists of an examination of the meanings of certain terms in the Book of Mormon, terms that can refer to servitude in the Bible. Not surprisingly, these terms also seem to point to servile situations among Book of Mormon peoples. This study carries the title, "Sojourn, Dwell, and Stay: Terms of Servitude."

A fourth new study focuses on thorny legal and social issues that arose when the renegade priests of king Noah abducted Lamanite women and obliged them to become their wives. In my view, the complexities generated by the incident—which ruptured a treaty—can best be understood in light of biblical law and custom. Such a conclusion should not surprise us because the people involved had descended from families who came from Jerusalem and had treasured a record which contained the Mosaic law. This study bears the title, "Marriage and Treaty in the Book of Mormon: The Case of the Abducted Lamanite Daughters."

One of my earliest studies of a Book of Mormon issue attempted to determine the approximate date of the visit of the risen Jesus to the Nephites and Lamanites in the city of Bountiful. Latter-day Saint artists generally depict Jesus' visit as immediately following the terrible storm and the three days of darkness which were associated with Jesus' death (3 Nephi 8–10). But it seemed to me that in light of 3 Ne. 10:18, which speaks of Jesus' visit happening "in the ending of the thirty and fourth year," a substantial period of time intervened between the visit and the earlier storm, which began "in the thirty and fourth year, in the first month, on the fourth day of the month" (3 Ne. 8:5). Once I began to dig around, evidence appeared in the text to support a view that Jesus did not come to the assembled people in Bountiful until many months after his resurrection. Now slightly revised, I have titled this piece, "When Did Jesus Visit the Americas?"

A word is now in order about what these studies are and are not. They represent, on the one hand, attempts to set out the dimensions and complexities of the Book of Mormon record. They are not, on the other, attempts to finalize what can or cannot be known about a subject. One must keep in mind that students are somewhat handicapped because the English translation of Joseph Smith is effectively the *Urtext*, the original document, to which we must address all questions. We do not possess the ancient text from which Joseph Smith worked. Because that text is not available, there are limitations as to how far we can pursue certain issues. For instance, a verbal phrase frequently used in the Exodus account is "bring out" or "bring forth." One can, of course, readily check the Hebrew term in the Bible. But we are limited to supposing that the same or a similar ancient term underlies these English phrases in Exodus-like settings described in the Book of Mormon.[5] Hence, in some ways—though not all—these studies must be considered provisional, not definitive.

NOTES

1. Ezra Taft Benson, "The Book of Mormon—Keystone of Our Religion" *Ensign*, October 1986, 4–7.

2. Two collections of essays that argue for the antiquity of the Book of Mormon have been edited by Noel B. Reynolds: *Book of Mormon Authorship* (Provo, Utah: Religious Studies Center, Brigham Young University, 1982), and *Book of Mormon Authorship Revisited: The Evidence for Ancient Origins* (Provo, Utah: F.A.R.M.S., 1997). Not all agree. Among those who view the

Book of Mormon as a modern production, one finds Thomas F. O'Dea, *The Mormons* (Chicago: University of Chicago Press, 1957). A more ingenious but nonetheless unpersuasive view of the Book of Mormon as a mixture of ancient and modern elements is that of Blake T. Ostler, "The Book of Mormon as a Modern Expansion of an Ancient Source," *Dialogue: A Journal of Mormon Thought* 20, no. 1 (spring 1987): 66–123.

3. A substantial number of contributions to the volumes edited by Monte S. Nyman and Charles D. Tate Jr., under the title *The Book of Mormon* and published by the Religious Studies Center at Brigham Young University, exhibit the kind of interest that I have noted. In addition, several articles under the title "Book of Mormon" in the *Encyclopedia of Mormonism* bring together in brief form evidence that arises from the text. Moreover, the Foundation for Ancient Research and Mormon Studies (F.A.R.M.S.) has published a growing list of titles, both books and article-length studies, that argue for an ancient provenance for the book itself, including the *Journal of Book of Mormon Studies,* which began to appear in 1992.

4. See, for instance, Noel B. Reynolds, "Nephi's Political Testament," in *Rediscovering the Book of Mormon,* ed. John L. Sorenson and Melvin J. Thorne (Salt Lake City: Deseret Book, 1991), 228–29; David R. Seely, "The Image of the Hand of God in the Book of Mormon and the Old Testament," *ibid.,* 140–46; Terrence L. Szink, "Nephi and the Exodus," *ibid.,* 38–51; George S. Tate, "The Typology of the Exodus Pattern in the Book of Mormon," in *Literature of Belief,* ed. Neal E. Lambert (Provo, Utah: Religious Studies Center, Brigham Young University, 1981), 245–62.

5. Moroni writes that "we have written this record . . . in the characters which are called among us the reformed Egyptian," but, had room allowed, "we should have written in Hebrew; but the Hebrew hath been altered by us" (Morm. 9:32–33; cf. 1 Ne. 1:1; Mosiah 1:4). Hence, one is never on completely solid linguistic ground.

What Were Those Sacrifices Offered by Lehi? 1

The opening chapters of the Book of Mormon mention sacrifices offered by Lehi. Some are called "burnt offerings," others simply "offering" or "sacrifice." By examining the sacrifices of ancient Israel noted in the Bible, we come to an understanding of Lehi's sacrifices—their meaning and their purpose. In short, Lehi made offerings for the safe return of his sons and for purging serious sins.

Twice in the desert, Lehi's party offered "sacrifice and burnt offerings" while giving "thanks unto . . . God." Each set of offerings came after the return of Lehi's sons from extended trips back to Jerusalem. They first ventured forth to obtain the plates of brass (1 Ne. 5:9) and later to persuade, successfully, the family of Ishmael to join their modest-sized exodus to a new land of promise (7:22). But on a prior occasion, when Lehi's family initially set up its base camp not far from the shore of the Red Sea (2:5–6), Lehi "built an altar of stones" and thereafter "made an offering . . . and gave thanks unto the Lord" (2:7).[1] In this case, Nephi mentions no burnt offerings. Why not? What was the difference?

The difference is the presence of sin, real or perceived. But the sin stands in relief only when we notice the common elements peeking out of all the accounts. In each of the three instances—the family's move to the base camp, the return of the sons with the brass plates, and their later return with Ishmael's family—the common factors are a safe journey and the subsequent giving of thanks. We then ask, How much do these observations tell us about the sacrifices? A lot.

Peace Offerings

For a safe journey, according to Psalm 107, a person was to "sacrifice the sacrifices of thanksgiving" (107:22) for safety in travel, whether through the desert or on water (107:4–6, 19–30). What were those "sacrifices of thanksgiving"? They consisted of peace offerings, known from Leviticus 3. In fact, the second common feature—the family giving thanks—secures the interpretation that these sacrifices were indeed peace offerings serving as thanksgivings to the Lord.

At this juncture it is important to note three characteristics of peace offerings. First, the Hebrew term which is translated "peace offering" in the King James translation properly means an offering for well-being,[2] thus its tie to safety in traveling. This observation leads to a second one, that the peace offering served many purposes, only one of which was thanksgiving.[3] Third, and not incidentally, in all of its forms this offering was an occasion for rejoicing, a happy state that Nephi highlights for us when recounting the mood of Lehi's sacrifice after the sons returned with the brass plates: "Their joy was full" (1 Ne. 5:7).[4] This last observation tightens the knot on the conclusion that in every instance Lehi's sacrifices consisted of a peace offering used for expressing thanksgiving.

Notably, peace offerings were "the most common type of sacrifice," an offering accompanied by a "covenant meal" in which worshipers enjoyed "fellowship with one another and their God." Truly such occasions were to be a time of rejoicing.[5] Furthermore, the sacrifice itself was to be an animal—either "male or female" in this case—from the flock or herd (Lev. 3:1, 6, 12), accompanied by unleavened baked goods (7:12–13). In this light, one has to assume either that among the "provisions" moved by Lehi's family from Jerusalem were animals intended for sacrifice (1 Ne. 2:4) or, more probably, that Lehi's baggage bore goods that the family could exchange with local people for sacrificial animals.[6] According to Leviticus, the resulting foods for the feast, including the sacrificed animal, were to be "eaten the same day that [they were] offered" so that nothing of the sacrifice remained to the following morning (Lev. 7:15).[7] Thus the banquet and celebrating would continue into the night.

Burnt Offerings

Thus far, we have established that the sacrifices made by Lehi were peace offerings, an observation made firm through details in the account, such as Lehi's party giving thanks and taking the occasion for rejoicing.[8] Contributing also is the fact that under the Mosaic law it was customary that one offer a sacrifice when one safely completed a journey.[9] We now turn to the need for the burnt offerings.

Why, one may ask, did Lehi offer this other kind of sacrifice? In response we note that according to Leviticus 1 a burnt offering was made for atonement—and more specifically, purging—after one had committed sin.[10] "If any man of you bring . . . a burnt sacrifice . . . it shall be accepted for him to make atonement" (1:2–4). In the case of burnt offerings, the animals for sacrifice might come from a herd or flock, or they might be birds (1:3, 10, 14). If the animals, only males in this instance, came from a herd or flock, then, as with the peace offerings, Lehi's family would have either brought them from Jerusalem—unlikely in light of Nephi's description of what they took from home ("provisions")—or purchased them locally. If Lehi offered birds, he likely bought them from someone in the area of the base camp who raised domesticated fowl.[11]

The more important issue, of course, has to do with sin, real or suspected, and how one transferred it away.[12] For sacrifices offered at the temple in Jerusalem, the priests were under daily obligation to sacrifice burnt offerings on the chance that someone in ancient Israel had sinned. Naturally, the priests could not realistically check in every corner of the land for sinning, but they could safely assume that every day someone had committed some sin, thus justifying the burnt offerings. Hence, the offerings were intended to cover all possible bases, whether the sin was known or not.[13]

In the case of Lehi's burnt offerings, sin stood close by. In a couple of instances, of course, one might question whether family members had really committed sin. But one must remember that Lehi was proceeding as if he were a priest offering sacrifices at the temple just in case.

Lehi's Offerings

Let us take up the two instances wherein Lehi offered burnt offerings, but in reverse order. The second time that Lehi sacrificed burnt offerings came after the return of his sons with the family of Ishmael (1 Ne. 7:3–22). Where was the sin? It springs quickly into view. The brothers' long journey to Jerusalem seems to have gone well, since Nephi does not comment on it. But during the return trip to the camp, a quarrel erupted when the older brothers, along with members of Ishmael's family, announced that they had decided to return to the city instead of continuing to the camp. Nephi, not shy in expressing his feelings about his brothers' "rebellion," became embroiled in a heated exchange of words that eventually provoked his angry brothers into tying him up "with cords" so "that they might leave [him] in the wilderness to be devoured by wild beasts" (7:7, 16). Only the miraculous intervention of the Lord and the poignant pleading of certain women in the company softened the hearts of the brothers so that "they did cease striving to take away [Nephi's] life" and sought his forgiveness (7:17–20). Even though Nephi "did frankly forgive them all that they had done" (7:21), there still remained the necessity to purge their sin from themselves. After the brothers sought Nephi's forgiveness, Nephi then records that "I did exhort them that they would *pray unto the Lord* their God *for forgiveness*" (7:21, emphasis added). At the very least, Nephi saw sin. As a result, after the party reached the camp, Lehi found it necessary to "offer . . . burnt offerings" to the Lord (7:22). There was no reason to take a chance.

An earlier scene recounts the trip of Lehi's sons back to Jerusalem to obtain the plates of brass. In this case, one does not need to look far to find sin. It poked its head up even before the sons left camp, as soon as Lehi asked them to bring the brass plates from Laban's custody to himself. Disappointedly, Lehi confided to Nephi that "thy brothers murmur, saying it is a hard thing which I have required of them; but . . . it is a commandment of the Lord" (3:5). Lehi's choice of the verb *to murmur* clearly ties the attitude of his older sons to that of the resisting Israelites during the Exodus from Egypt,[14] a stance that Nephi later characterized as "revil[ing] against Moses and against the true and living God"

(17:30). Such complaining on its own constituted mild rebellion. But there is more.

After arriving in the city, Nephi and his three brothers made two unsuccessful attempts to acquire the brass plates, once by persuasion and the other time by an offer to purchase them, the latter occasion presenting to Laban an opportunity to falsely accuse the brothers of theft. As a result, the two older brothers, Laman and Lemuel, decided to take matters into their own hands and began to "smite [their younger brothers] even with a rod." This action was cut short by the unexpected intervention of "an angel of the Lord" who scolded the two oldest brothers for their conduct (3:28–29), emphasizing the fact that their behavior defied the Lord's purposes. Even then, the brothers continued "to murmur" (3:31; 4:4).

In addition to the complaints and ill-behavior of the older brothers, one discovers that Lehi's wife, Sariah, had complained at length to her husband during the month-long absence of her sons.[15] She feared that her sons must have "perished in the wilderness" and that because Lehi was "a visionary man," an expression that must have carried pejorative meaning,[16] "we [shall] perish in the wilderness" far "from the land of our inheritance" (5:2). Of course, when her sons returned to camp, she immediately changed her tune, rejoicing and becoming "exceedingly glad" (5:1). But what is more important, she thereafter affirmed her testimony in the divine guidance received by her husband: "Now I know of a surety that the Lord hath commanded my husband to flee into the wilderness; yea, and I also know of a surety that the Lord hath protected my sons" (5:8). Even so, her sin had to be purged both from herself and from the camp.

While these occurrences may seem mild, involving complaints and a family scuffle, another one was not, for it involved what some might have considered a homicide. Nephi killed Laban (4:4–18), creating a need for sacrifice. To be sure, Nephi assures us that he had been impelled to this deed by the promptings of the Spirit—three times in fact, the last coming in an audible voice[17]—and he had stubbornly resisted. After all, he had just been admiring the workmanship of Laban's sword in the moonlight,[18] as the latter lay drunk in the street, when the Spirit interrupted his thoughts with the horrifying impression that Nephi use the sword on Laban. Struggle as Nephi might, he could not shake the persisting feelings, growing stronger by the minute, that he take Laban's life.

Although the Lord clearly placed Laban among "the wicked" (4:13) and although Nephi knew Laban's failings because "he had sought to take away [Nephi's] life" and "also had taken away our property" (4:11), Nephi "shrunk and would that I might not slay" Laban (4:10). In the end, however, Nephi "did obey the voice of the Spirit, and . . . I smote off [Laban's] head with his own sword" (4:18), thus creating the deepest need for Lehi to "offer . . . burnt offerings unto the Lord" to purge any vestiges of uncleanness that might have clung to Nephi (5:9).[19]

Conclusion

The three recorded occasions of Lehi offering sacrifices, when measured against sacrificial law in the Bible, become immediately understandable in light of the family's situation. When Lehi "made an offering unto the Lord, and gave thanks" (1 Ne. 2:7; also 5:9; 7:22), he was sacrificing a peace offering which served as a thanksgiving for safety in travel, whether for oneself or for others. In each instance, members of the family had safely completed a long journey.[20] When he offered "burnt offerings unto the Lord" (5:9; also 7:22), Lehi was bringing to the altar sacrifices that would atone for sin, sin that would stain the camp and those within it. And in each case, one can readily detect sin in the prior behavior of family members, whether it took the form of complaining, family jousts, or the taking of human life. Here, Lehi sought to free his extended family from the taint of unworthiness so that he and they would be able to carry out the purposes of the Lord.

NOTES

1. The phrase "altar of stones" derives from Mosaic Law (see Ex. 20:24–25; Deut. 27:5–7). On the character of Lehi's altar, Hugh Nibley has pointed out—rightly in my view—that in accord with the law of Moses, it must have been of unhewn field stones; *Lehi in the Desert, The World of the Jaredites, There Were Jaredites* (Salt Lake City: Deseret Book and F.A.R.M.S., 1988), 62–63.

2. Hebrew *zebaḥ šelamîm*, "sacrifice of well-being." Jacob Milgrom, *Leviticus 1–16*, Anchor Bible 3 (New York: Doubleday, 1991), 204, 217.

3. The biblical forms include the thanksgiving offering (e.g., Lev. 22:29), the freewill offering (e.g., Num. 15:3), and the sacrifice for a vow (e.g., Prov. 7:14); see Milgrom, *Leviticus 1–16*, 218–19. In a much later era, without acknowledging other purposes, Josephus would call these simply "thank offerings" (*Antiquities* 3.9.2).

4. See Deut. 27:7; also Milgrom, *Leviticus 1–16*, 218.

5. Nathaniel Micklem, *The Book of Leviticus*, The Interpreter's Bible, ed. G. A. Buttrick (New York: Abingdon, 1953), 2:21–22.

6. That there must have been many people living in the area of Lehi's base camp cannot be doubted, since the incense trail passed through the region, and local people were needed to service the caravans at their stops. For a review of the civilizations that existed in Arabia during the mid-first millennium B.C., see Gus W. van Beek, "South Arabian History and Archaeology," in *The Bible and the Ancient Near East*, ed. G. Ernest Wright (New York: Doubleday, 1965), 300–26.

7. See Milgrom, *Leviticus 1–16*, 219.

8. The burnt offering, under certain circumstances, could also bring a time for rejoicing; see Milgrom, *Leviticus 1–16*, 175; cf. 219, 758.

9. Nibley, in *Lehi in the Desert*, 62–63, has pointed out that Arabs also perpetuated such a custom.

10. The Hebrew term is *'olâ*, the oldest known propitiatory offering. See Milgrom, *Leviticus 1–16*, 175–77, 267–68, 858.

11. One issue is whether a person could offer a sacrifice of birds snared in the wild. The answer is yes. While the law specifies "turtledoves, or . . . young pigeons" (Lev. 1:14), which were the birds most frequently domesticated, one could presumably also offer wild ones. See Milgrom, *Leviticus 1–16*, 168–69.

12. In the ceremony of the burnt offering, before slaughtering the sacrificial animal, the petitioner placed a "hand upon the head of the burnt offering" (Lev. 1:4), thus transferring guilt to the animal. See Milgrom, *Leviticus 1–16*, 150–53.

13. See Ex. 29:38–46; Lev. 1:7; 6:12–13; also Milgrom, *Leviticus 1–16*, 146—"it is the first sacrifice [and last] each day"; see also 157, 387.

14. See Terrence L. Szink, "Nephi and the Exodus," in *Rediscovering the Book of Mormon*, ed. John L. Sorenson and Melvin J. Thorne (Salt Lake City: Deseret Book and F.A.R.M.S., 1991), 38–51.

15. The length of a one-way trip to Jerusalem from the camp, which lay sixty or so miles south of modern Aqaba, a journey of "three days" from the northeast tip of the Red Sea (1 Ne. 2:6), would have been almost 250 miles, a distance that would require nine or ten days for young men to walk. See D. Kelly Ogden's study, the last of many to calculate this distance, "Answering

the Lord's Call," in *Studies in Scripture, Vol. 7: 1 Nephi to Alma 29*, ed. Kent P. Jackson (Salt Lake City: Deseret Book, 1987), 17–33. For observations on the possible location of the camp, see Lynn M. and Hope A. Hilton, "In Search of Lehi's Trail, Part 2: The Journey," *Ensign*, October 1976, 43–45. The outlook of the Hiltons that matches a journey of "three days" beyond Aqaba is more compelling than that of Paul Hedengren, *The Land of Lehi* (Provo, Utah: Bradford & Wilson, 1995), 3–4, even though Hedengren has identified a year-round source of water just a few miles south of Aqaba, which he identifies as the river Laman. Lehi and his family could have reached this water source after only one day's trek.

16. This sense must be correct, because Lehi felt the need to turn Sariah's phrase into a more positive view: "I know that I am a visionary man; for if I had not seen the things of God in a vision I should not have known the goodness of God, but had tarried at Jerusalem, and had perished with my brethren" (1 Ne. 5:4).

17. Cf. "When I, Nephi, had *heard* these words" (1 Ne. 4:14, emphasis added).

18. Nephi had gone into the city "by night," and thus there must have been moonlight which allowed him to examine the sword (1 Ne. 4:5, 9).

19. There are several treatments of Nephi's defense of his actions with Laban. See, for example, Noel B. Reynolds, "The Political Dimension of Nephi's Small Plates," *BYU Studies* 27, no. 4 (fall 1987): 15–37, especially 24; Eugene England, "Why Nephi Killed Laban: Reflections on the Truth of the Book of Mormon," *Dialogue: A Journal of Mormon Thought* 22 (fall 1989): 32–51, especially 40–45; and John W. Welch, "Legal Perspectives on the Slaying of Laban," *Journal of Book of Mormon Studies* 1 (fall 1992): 119–41. Even though laws existed that would protect Nephi until he received a fair hearing, as Reynolds points out, the killing of Laban potentially brought sin within Lehi's camp. In addition, because Laban's death allowed the sons to obtain the brass plates, this incident must have lived on in memory and stood behind the later Lamanite claim that Nephi had "robbed them" of the plates (Mosiah 10:16).

20. It is possible that without mentioning sacrifice directly, Nephi intended his readers to understand that there were other occasions when Lehi's party would have sacrificed peace offerings in order to conform to Mosaic requirements. Nephi repeats key words and phrases—already used in the three known instances—in connection with the family's comings and goings as well as preparations for continuing the journey. See 1 Ne. 16:32 ("did give thanks"), 17:6 ("exceedingly rejoiced"), 18:1 ("worship the Lord"), 18:4 ("humble themselves again before the Lord"), and 18:23 ("we did arrive"), coupled with the presence of clean animals in the promised land that could be sacrificed (18:25). The phrase "before the Lord" may also point in some of these instances to worship at an altar (16:32; 18:4).

What Is Isaiah Doing in First Nephi? Or, How Did Lehi's Family Fare so Far from Home? 2

The prophet Nephi incorporated words of Isaiah in his first book for both public and private reasons. Nephi openly declared that he intended to deepen people's faith in the Holy One of Israel while linking his family's experiences to prophecies concerning the scattering and gathering of Israel. Evidence in the Book of Mormon points also to the sorrow and estrangement which the family of Lehi and Sariah felt as they fled their home in Jerusalem and traveled across deserts and oceans to the New World. In Isaiah, Nephi found calming solace as well as evidence of prophetic fulfillment.

Nephi said, "We did take our tents and depart into the wilderness, across the river Laman" (1 Ne. 16:12). Evidently with purpose, Nephi tells us indirectly that the base camp of his father, Lehi, had been pitched on the bank of the river Laman that was nearer to Jerusalem. When the members of their party crossed that stream, they left Jerusalem behind forever, striking out into the desert and cutting themselves off from home.[1]

At first blush, the question about Isaiah seems to be out of place or, at the very least, out of focus. After all, Nephi assures us that Isaiah had been one of his favorite books, and his acquaintance with this work had led him to quote significant parts of it (e.g., 1 Ne. 19:23; 2 Ne. 11:8).[2] Moreover, Nephi supplies us with his reasons—public reasons, it turns out—why he had included chapters 48 and 49 of Isaiah at the end of his first book. I believe, however, that he kept other poignantly personal reasons largely to himself, allowing those reasons to be expressed principally by others. As it turns out, it is his younger brother Jacob who, writing after Nephi's death, allows us to see most clearly the acutely personal inducements for including these passages from Isaiah.[3] Most of them have to do with the grave challenges that the family encountered in the desert of Arabia.

To be sure, the public reasons that Nephi offers to us for his appeal to Isaiah stand within the larger prophetic message about the scattering and gathering of Israel, of which he and his family—the scattered—and their distant posterity—the gathered—were a part.[4] One does not look far to find that Isaiah's prophecies had a good deal to say about these events.[5] As a prime example, one reads a passage that both addresses the scattered remnants of Israel and—this next point is especially important—fits precisely the circumstance of the departure of Lehi's family: "Hearken . . . all ye that are broken off and are driven out because of the wickedness of the pastors of my people; yea, all ye that are broken off, that are scattered abroad, who are of my people, O house of Israel" (1 Ne. 21:1 = Isa. 49:1).[6] On the side of the gathering, one reads the tender assurance that the Gentiles "shall bring thy sons in their arms, and thy daughters shall be carried upon their shoulders. And [Gentile] kings shall be thy nursing fathers, and their queens thy nursing mothers" (1 Ne. 21:22–23 = Isa. 49:22–23). A third passage not only characterizes the Lord's loving care for his people at the time of the future gathering but, as in the first passage, mirrors his efforts to provide necessities for Lehi's party as they traveled in the desert, much as he had for the Hebrew slaves: "They thirsted not; he led them through the deserts; he caused the waters to flow out of the rock for them; he clave the rock also and the waters gushed out" (1 Ne. 20:21 = Isa. 48:21).[7] The allusions to manna (Ex. 16:14–15; etc.) and water provided by the Lord from a rock (Ex. 17:1–6; Num. 20:2–11), of course, need no comment.

In light of the first and third passages that can plainly point to aspects of the journey of Lehi's family, one notes that in Nephi's view the words of Isaiah in chapters 48–49 apparently anticipated the entire trip, from beginning to end, starting with the flight from Jerusalem and ending with the settlement in the promised land. In a word, Nephi is saying, "Isaiah spoke about us."[8]

But before turning to Nephi's announced reasons for appealing to Isaiah's book and then to the travel experiences, as well as Isaiah's words about such, we should observe that Nephi's thorough acquaintance with Isaiah is beyond challenge.[9] Throughout his work, Nephi's expressions brighten with phrases and terms that reflect an influence radiating from Isaiah.[10] For instance, borrowing a phrase from Isa. 29:14, Nephi speaks of "a marvelous work" which will "be of great worth unto our seed" (1 Ne. 22:8). In fact, the angel who accompanied Nephi during his vision used this same phrase, a hint that the angel knew of Nephi's acquaintance with it from Isaiah (14:7).[11] In addition, Nephi calls God "the Holy One of Israel" and "Savior," titles at home in Isaiah's works.[12] Further, Nephi employs expressions that find parallels in Isaiah, such as "Eat, drink, and be merry, for tomorrow we die"[13] and "the four quarters of the earth."[14] As a capstone of sorts, even the Spirit of God recognized Nephi's grasp of Isaiah's book and virtually quoted to him what must have been a line familiar from Isaiah about the Lord giving a sign[15]—in Isaiah's prophecy, the sign consisted of the virgin who gives birth—and then followed it almost immediately with the vision of the virgin (11:7; 11:13–20).

Nephi's Stated Reasons

Nephi's stated motives are straightforward and high-minded. In introducing chapters 48 and 49, he announces that his most important purpose—and I want to emphasize this purpose—is to "more fully persuade [his people] to believe in the Lord their Redeemer" (1 Ne. 19:23).[16] A companion motive appears in his introduction of the Isaiah chapters in his second book, "that whoso of my people shall see these words [of Isaiah] may . . . rejoice" (2 Ne. 11:8). Consistent with his first purpose of bringing others "to believe in the Lord," one observes that embedded in Isaiah 49 lies a clear prophecy about the future Messiah-king, portrayed as the "servant of the Lord" (Isa. 49:1–6 = 1 Ne. 21:1–6).[17] According to Isaiah, the Messiah-king will be called "from the womb" and, though his mouth will be "like a sharp sword," he will seemingly spend his "strength for nought" (Isa. 49:1, 2, 4). In the end, however, he will not only "bring Jacob again" to the Lord but more broadly will be "a light to the Gentiles" and become the Lord's "salvation unto the end of the earth" (49:5–6).[18]

The second most important reason that Nephi included Isaiah's prophecies appears in a much later passage, just before recording Isaiah 2–14. He reveals that in quoting Isaiah he seeks to bring comfort, even joy, to his people: "I write some of the words of Isaiah, that whoso of my people shall see these words may lift up their hearts and rejoice" (2 Ne. 11:8). While we shall return to this passage, and the implications therein that Nephi's people needed a rejuvenation of sorts, we note here that Nephi set out other reasons for his quotations from Isaiah. For example, he adds that he "read unto them that which was written by the prophet Isaiah . . . for our profit and learning" (1 Ne. 19:23). Further, immediately afterward, while addressing his people directly, he said first that Isaiah's words were written for "the house of Israel . . . who have been broken off" (19:24),[19] and second that since Isaiah was shown "concerning us" (19:21), Nephi wanted his people to "have hope" (19:24).

Nephi's Personal Reasons

When we turn to his more personal view, on the other hand, I suggest that as Nephi looked back on his family's experience in the desert of Arabia, he eventually came to see those events in poignantly personal terms. In a word, the desert formed a decisive moment for his extended family. Although, as we have noted, he himself was guarded in expressing how the desert experience had affected him and the others,[20] his younger brother Jacob was not. As a result, Jacob supplies an important set of clues about what the family's separation from home meant for them. In short, the separation was painful and the early generations did not feel completely at home in their adopted surroundings in the New World. Near the end of his life, Jacob spoke of the record on the small plates of Nephi, sighing, "I conclude this record, declaring that I have written according to the best of my knowledge, by saying that the time passed away with us, and also our lives passed away like as it were unto us a dream, we being a lonesome and a solemn people, wanderers, cast out from Jerusalem, born in tribulation, in a wilderness, and hated of our brethren, which caused wars and contentions; wherefore, we did mourn out our days" (Jacob 7:26). This mournful summary, in fact, cast in the language of lament, provides a key to the last chapters of 1 Nephi, including the personal reasons why Nephi inserted two chapters from Isaiah's book. How so?

Although Jacob was not born in Jerusalem, nor did he ever set foot in the city, he faithfully reflects the feelings of other family members about the harsh necessity of leaving their home, even though their departure was mandated by the Lord. After all, Jacob would not have generated such feelings on his own. They must have come from his family environment.[21]

Yes, the extended family had learned from Lehi just before his death that the prophetic warning about the fall of the city had come to dreadful fulfillment, thus sparing the lives of family members as the Lord had promised.[22] And yes, they all must have been grateful that they had not been ground down in the inevitable and terrible retributions leveled against citizens by the fierce Babylonian warriors.[23] But home was home.

In this light, the following will set out for us the reasons for, and dimensions of, family feelings about abandoning home. Significantly, most of them have to do with their journey through the desert which, with finality, separated them from Jerusalem.

First, Jacob speaks of "our lives" passing away "as it were unto us a dream," an expression that sounds tones of disappointment. When one combines this sort of language with his term "wanderers" for his people, who were "cast out from Jerusalem" (Jacob 7:26), one senses a mass of chafed, tender emotions lying barely below the surface. In an attempt to grapple with this passage, John Tanner has observed that "one feels the cost that the wilderness exacted on Jacob." He then attributes Jacob's words to "the accumulated sorrows of a nomadic life."[24] Yet there must be more. One must see that Jacob's sentiments also expressed those of others in the family, illuminating the strong cords that bound all of them to their former lives in Jerusalem. Moreover, one understands that a nomad, speaking realistically, would not be unhappy with life in the desert. Jacob, who had really known no other kind of existence in his youth, would not have expressed dissatisfaction about this kind of life if he had not been exposed to the misgivings and sorrows of others around him.

Second, from a review of other passages it becomes clear that the time in the desert had left a bitter taste in the mouths of family members[25]—nothing but bad memories.[26] For instance, Lehi called the eight-year desert crossing "the wilderness of mine afflictions; . . . the days of my greatest sorrow" (2 Ne. 3:1). In addition, at the end of the desert trek Lehi's sons complained—and it is important to note that, on one level, Nephi entered the complaints into his record because they told of unspeakable suffering—that "we have wandered in the wilderness for these many years; and our women have toiled, . . . and suffered all things, save it were death."[27] So severe were the desert sufferings, they cried, that "it would have been better that [the women] had died before they came out of Jerusalem" (1 Ne. 17:20).[28] Further, generations later Alma would look back to the desert era and, hinting at specific experiences known to him and his hearers, say that the Lord had "delivered our fathers out of the hands of their enemies" and had "saved [them] from famine, and from sickness, and all manner of diseases" (Alma 9:10, 22), underscoring the ferocity of the challenges faced by Lehi's family. Hence, Jacob's choice of terms points to plainly painful events in the desert.[29]

Third, moving from Jerusalem had torn the family to the point that family members split more than once about whether to return to their family estates, this in direct disobedience to the Lord's directives to flee (1 Ne. 2:11–14; 7:6–7).[30] Additionally, complaints about having to leave the city continued to surface throughout the desert journey, as illustrated first by the grieving of the daughters of Ishmael, vocalized *before* trudging into the heart of the Arabian peninsula, and later by the gripes of Lehi's older sons, articulated *after* emerging from the desert. As Nephi records, in a burst of emotion Ishmael's daughters murmured that Lehi had wronged them by bringing "them out of the land of Jerusalem" only to "perish in the wilderness with hunger" (16:35). On the subsequent occasion, Lehi's older sons whined that their father, "led away by the foolish imaginations of his heart," had "led [them] out of the land of Jerusalem," with the result that "we have wandered in the wilderness for these many years" and could not enjoy "our possessions and the land of our inheritance" (17:20–21). By any standard, they desperately missed home.

Fourth, the memory of days in Jerusalem had evidently been cultivated at least in story, if not in song and verse, in such a way that the next generation was imbued with a nostalgia for a place that they had not seen. One thinks of Jews, at Passover, when they say as part of their celebration, "Next year in Jerusalem." Something like this must have become a part of family tradition, naturally turning hearts back to their original home.[31]

Fifth, Jacob's words betray a feeling that even though the hand of the Lord had brought the families of Lehi and Ishmael to the promised land, it was not the same as possessing an inheritance in the land promised to Abraham.[32] One need only notice that Jacob called his extended family "a lonesome and a solemn people," hardly a happy description (Jacob 7:26). To be sure, Jacob does not strictly contradict Lehi, and would have been horrified to be thought of as espousing a different view of the status of their people.[33] But his father spoke more warmly of obtaining "a land of promise, a land which is choice above all other lands," which "the Lord God hath covenanted with me should be a land for the inheritance of my seed" (2 Ne. 1:5).[34] Even so, some fifty or so years later Jacob mournfully portrayed the self-image of his people as "wanderers," outcasts "from Jerusalem" (Jacob 7:26).

Sixth, Nephi reveals the need for comforting his people when bringing forward the chapters that he cites in the middle of his second book. To recall his words quoted above, "I write some of the words of Isaiah, that whoso of my people shall see these words may lift up their hearts and rejoice" (2 Ne. 11:8). As background, one must recollect that by the time Nephi copied these chapters, family members had already split geographically because of a bitter quarrel over leadership in the clan, those loyal to Nephi having fled their original place of residence (5:1–7). In this light, the fact that Nephi seeks to lift the spirits of his followers, now separated from other family members, reveals an underlying, unspoken despondency. This despondency, in my view, had to do with the fact that even after arriving in the land of promise, Nephi's part of the family had been forced to move from its original settlement, thus compounding the feeling of estrangement from home in this distant place. Even the observation that the flight came at the urging of the Lord (5:5) does not seem to have eased the loss of homes and property and family associations.[35]

Seventh, prophecies about the Messiah held believers' focus on Jerusalem. Circumstantial evidence exists, for instance, that the prophecies of Zenos spoke of the Messiah dying there (1 Ne. 19:10, 13).[36] Further, by vision Nephi—and before him Lehi—had evidently learned the place of the Messiah's death and resurrection. For in one scene out of their parallel visions "the great city of Jerusalem" appeared, followed shortly afterward by the following vista: "And I [Nephi] . . . beheld the Lamb of God, that he was taken by the people; yea, . . . was judged of the world; and . . . was lifted up upon the cross and slain for the sins of the world" (1 Ne. 11:13, 32–33). It stands to reason that if Nephi saw in his vision "the city of Nazareth,"[37] the place of Jesus' youth, he would have noticed the place of his death, even though he does not record it directly.[38] It is Jacob who clinches the case, providing the proof that Jerusalem was known to the founding generation as the place of Jesus' death. Speaking to those in the colony of Nephi, he says, "Ye know that . . . he [Jesus] shall show himself unto those at Jerusalem, . . . for it is expedient that it should be among them; for . . . he suffereth himself to . . . die for all men" (2 Ne. 9:5). Naturally, the Messiah's tie to the city kept both memory and anticipation alive among Book of Mormon peoples.

Eighth, one gauge of the intensity of impressions from the wilderness lies in the names of the two sons born there to Lehi and Sariah—Jacob and Joseph. There is no doubt in my mind that these two boys were named after Jacob, the father of the twelve tribes,[39] and Joseph, his son, who was sold into Egypt.[40] One naturally asks what these two personalities from the Bible had in common, besides sharing the same tent for the years of Joseph's youth. The answer, of course, has to do with the fact that they both spent long periods of time away from home. In the case of Jacob, he was forced to flee after receiving the blessing that his brother Esau claimed for himself, living several hundred miles away for two decades in the home of his father-in-law. In addition, Jacob spent the last years of his life in Egypt because of the severe famine in the land of Canaan. In the case of Joseph, his brothers sold him to caravanners who in turn took him to Egypt where he lived out his days, dying with only one wish: to be buried at home, in the land of his ancestors.

Ninth, a further indicator concerns place names. It was Lamanites, joined by dissident Nephites, who founded a city named Jerusalem more than five hundred years after Lehi's family departed from Jerusalem, creating an administrative territory of the same name, "after [the name of] the land of their fathers' nativity" (Alma 21:1). Evidently, in their tradition Lamanites had perpetuated a deep tie to their distant homeland.[41] Of course, the name Jerusalem also comes into play in discussions of the New Jerusalem. Even though the expectations were millennial, the risen Jesus felt the need to explain that the New Jerusalem would be "in this land," in the New World (3 Ne. 20:22), a point that Moroni repeats almost four hundred years later, tying its existence to that of the ancient city (Ether 13:3–10).[42] Thus, the memory of the Jerusalem from which both the founding family and the scriptures had come continued to live on in Book of Mormon society.

Tenth, the eight-year crossing indicates serious troubles in the wilderness (1 Ne. 17:4). It suggests that the family spent considerable time in at least one location, possibly at an oasis or a grazing area, and probably dependent on desert tribesmen. Eight years is far too long even for a cautious crossing of the Arabian desert. To make the point, the time required in antiquity for a loaded caravan to travel from the coast of the Indian Ocean to the Mediterranean Sea—approximately the assumed route traveled by Lehi and his family, though in reverse—was a matter of sixteen weeks, not eight years.[43]

Isaiah Connections

The deep, at times terrible, impact that the desert trek made in the soul and memory of Nephi, I believe, can be seen in his choice of Isaiah passages that follow the narrative of his family's trip to the land of promise. Understanding that Nephi saw Isaiah as one who had been shown matters "concerning us" (1 Ne. 19:21), a number of possible allusions to the family's journey stand in chapters 48 and 49. We turn first to those that have to do with flight, next with difficulties in a desert clime, and then to passages which bring assurance of the Lord's aid.[44]

Passages in Isaiah 48 and 49 spoke to the circumstance of Lehi's departure from Jerusalem, directed by the Lord and forced by public pressure.[45] One must understand that less than a year earlier the Babylonians had forced the city to surrender and had installed Zedekiah as a puppet king (2 Kgs. 24:10–19). In this connection, one notices expressions in Isaiah that make reference to Babylonians. For instance, in an affirmation that the Lord is in charge, Isaiah says that the Lord "will do his pleasure on Babylon, and his arm shall be on the Chaldeans" (Isa. 48:14 = 1 Ne. 20:14).[46]

In addition, for those who find themselves captive to the Babylonians, the Lord will exercise his right to seek the release of his people who are enslaved abroad,[47] saying to them, "Go ye forth of Babylon, flee ye from the Chaldeans, with a voice of singing declare ye, . . . The Lord hath redeemed his servant Jacob" (Isa. 48:20 = 1 Ne. 20:20).[48] In addition, one finds reference to the corruption and iniquity in the city that met Lehi when he began his preaching. Isaiah holds that the citizens of Jerusalem will "swear by the name of the Lord, and make mention of the God of Israel, yet they swear not in truth nor in righteousness. Nevertheless, they call themselves of the holy city, but they do not stay themselves upon the God of Israel" (1 Ne. 20:1–2 = Isa. 48:1–2).[49]

However, in addressing scattered Israel, Isaiah's condemnation is even more scathing. In a passage that does not appear in the received Hebrew text of Isaiah, the prophet admonishes, "Hearken, O ye house of Israel, all ye that are broken off and are driven out because of the wickedness of the pastors of my people" (1 Ne. 21:1).[50] Here Isaiah had anticipated a day in which corrupt officials would rule people in the city, a situation that Lehi suffered in his day. And, it seems, Nephi had seen the relevance of this passage to the family's situation.

The strongest statement on difficulties in the desert arises from the refining process in "the furnace of affliction," which of course can also allude to the heat that one experiences in the desert, or a place of trial.[51] "I do this," the Lord says, because "I will not suffer my name to be polluted" (1 Ne. 20:10–11 = Isa. 48:10–11).[52] Many examples can be found in these chapters of Isaiah which give assurances of the Lord's assistance to those who may struggle. For instance, Nephi, if not others, must have taken courage from the Lord's assurance that he "leadeth thee by the way thou shouldst go" and that those who trust in him "thirsted not" because "he led them through the deserts" and "caused the waters to flow out of the rock for them" (1 Ne. 20:17, 21 = Isa. 48:17, 21). Moreover—continuing the desert imagery—"They shall not hunger nor thirst; neither shall the heat nor the sun smite them: for he that hath mercy on them shall lead them, even by the springs of water shall he guide them" (Isa. 49:10 = 1 Ne. 21:10). Plainly, one can identify a number of passages that naturally would have spoken to the situation of the family while traveling through Arabia.[53]

This situation becomes evident in words of Isaiah about a river and the sea, recalling both that Lehi named a river after his son Laman and that the Red Sea, into which the river flowed, was one of the major geographical features near the first camp (1 Ne. 2:5, 8–9). In addition, on the far side of the Arabian desert the sea formed both a barrier as well as a highway of sorts to the promised land (17:5–6; 18:8, 23). Isaiah wrote, "O that thou hadst hearkened to my commandments! then had thy peace been as a river, and thy righteousness as the waves of the sea" (Isa. 48:18 = 1 Ne. 20:18). Lehi spoke similar words to Laman at the time he named the river after him: "O that thou mightest be like unto this river, continually running into the fountain of all righteousness!" (1 Ne. 2:9). The tie between Isaiah's words and those of Lehi stands in plain relief. A dozen or more years later Lehi pleads with Laman and his siblings that they not be "carried away . . . down to the eternal gulf of misery" (2 Ne. 1:13), evoking a combined image of river and sea. In sum, Nephi's record of Lehi's words to his wayward sons, both at the departure from Jerusalem and in the New World, brims with allusions to words from Isaiah 48–49.[54]

Conclusion

What have we learned? First, we have seen that Nephi balances two kinds of reasons throughout his story as to why he appeals to Isaiah, one public and the other personal. He holds to the former while he allows the voices of others to express the latter. In both cases, the ultimate reason for bringing the Isaiah passages into 1 Nephi was to bring comfort and joy to his people by directing their attention to the Holy One of Israel and his covenants with his people. Nephi's secondary purpose radiates through the perceptible connections between Isaiah's prophecies of the future scattering and gathering of the house of Israel and the experiences of Nephi's family during their exodus from Jerusalem to the land of promise. Thus, Nephi found calming solace as well as proof of prophetic fulfillment in the words of Isaiah, words which he knew and loved.

Notes

1. One can see that the desert formed a watershed in the family by the way that Lehi addressed his son Jacob at the time of his blessing, "my first-born in the wilderness" (2 Ne. 2:2, 11), clearly distinguishing him from his sons born in Jerusalem.

2. Nephi employs far more quotations from Isaiah in his second book, including a number to which his younger brother Jacob appeals. A handy list appears in the article by LeGrande Davies, "Isaiah: Texts in the Book of Mormon," in *Encyclopedia of Mormonism*, ed. Daniel H. Ludlow (New York: Macmillan, 1992), 700. For the most part, these passages have to do with the second exodus of God's people in the latter days or with the future Messiah and his work.

3. Even Blake T. Ostler, who has sought to identify "anachronisms" in the Book of Mormon ("The Book of Mormon as a Modern Expansion of an Ancient Source," *Dialogue: A Journal of Mormon Thought* 20, no. 1 [spring 1987]: 66–115), admits that the Isaiah chapters quoted in the text had "appeared in the Nephite record in some form" although without qualification he maintains that "Joseph Smith clearly used the KJV translation," copying from it wholesale (77). What he fails to appreciate in the first instance is that in passages where the Book of Mormon text of Isaiah differs from the King James translation, the Book of Mormon reading agrees at least 9 percent of the time with the Septuagint version. This significant percentage stands firmly against the notion that Joseph Smith slavishly copied the KJV of Isaiah into the Book of Mormon. In addition, he has not taken into account the overwhelming evidence that the Book of Mormon was dictated—not copied—from beginning to end. See Davies, "Isaiah: Texts in the Book of Mormon," 700–701; and Royal Skousen, "Translating the Book of Mormon: Evidence from the Original Manuscript," in *Book of Mormon Authorship Revisited*, ed. Noel B. Reynolds (Provo, Utah: F.A.R.M.S., 1997), 61–93.

4. For Nephi, the future survival of the posterity of his older and younger brothers was beyond question (1 Ne. 12:19–20; 2 Ne. 3:3, 23). Even though Nephi knew—and this knowledge brought him deep pain (1 Ne. 15:5; 2 Ne. 26:7, 10)—that his own descendants would eventually be destroyed, there are indisputable hints that a remnant would survive along with descendants from the other members of the family. See 1 Ne. 13:30; 15:13–14, 18; 22:7–8; 2 Ne. 10:2. Cf. 2 Ne. 3:3, 23; 4:7; 9:53; 25:8, 21; 3 Ne. 21:7; Ether 13:7.

5. See, for example, an allusion to both the scattering and gathering in the Lord's words to his Servant, "to restore the preserved of Israel" (1 Ne. 21:6 = Isa. 49:6).

6. The passage quoted here stands neither in the Hebrew nor in the Greek text of Isa. 49:1.

7. See also "They shall not hunger nor thirst, neither shall the heat nor the sun smite them; for he that hath mercy on them shall lead them, even by the springs of water shall he guide them" (1 Ne. 21:10 = Isa. 49:10).

8. Nephi says that the Lord "did show unto many [prophets] *concerning us*" (1 Ne. 19:21, emphasis added)—which must also have included Zenock, Neum, and Zenos, whose words he had just quoted (19:10–17). Nephi then immediately introduces Isaiah 48–49 by instructing his people not only to "hear . . . the words of the prophet [Isaiah]" but also to "liken [these words] unto yourselves" (2 Ne. 19:24; cf. Jacob's observation in 2 Ne. 6:5).

9. The depreciating claims of Jerald and Sandra Tanner in *Covering up the Black Hole in the Book of Mormon* (Salt Lake City: Lighthouse, 1990) that the Book of Mormon plagiarizes sections of Isaiah rather than Nephi copying them or being influenced thereby have been answered by Matthew Roper in his review of their work, *Review of Books on the Book of Mormon* 3 (1991): 170–87. A number of examples that follow match Roper's observations.

10. Notice Nephi's personal responses: "my soul delighteth in the words of Isaiah" (2 Ne. 25:5) and "my soul delighteth in [Isaiah's] words . . . for he verily saw my Redeemer, even as I have seen him" (11:2).

11. In his second book, of course, Nephi discusses chapter 29 of Isaiah at length in a prophetic vein (2 Nephi 26–27), introducing the issues by citing Isa. 29:14 (2 Ne. 25:17).

12. On "Holy One of Israel," see 1 Ne. 19:14; etc. (from Isa. 48:17 = 1 Ne. 20:17; Isa. 49:7 = 1 Ne. 21:7, although the Nephite text omits the last phrases of this verse, including the title Holy One of Israel). On "Savior," see 1 Ne. 10:4; 13:40; Isa. 43:3, 11; 45:15, 21; 49:26; 60:16; 63:8. Cf. "Lamb of God" (1 Ne. 10:10 from Lehi; 11:21, 27, 31–32; etc.), which may recall the Servant of Isa. 53:6–7 who is "brought as a lamb to the slaughter" (this last was suggested by Roper, 178).

13. 2 Ne. 28:7; Isa. 22:13; cf. 2 Ne. 28:8; see Martin S. Tanner, *Review of Books on the Book of Mormon* 6 (1994): 426. Tanner also points to Nephi's reference to the cynical view of God beating sinners only "with a few stripes" (2 Ne. 28:8) as an echo of Isaiah's more serious words about God's Servant who receives stripes so that we can be healed of sin (Isa. 53:5).

14. 1 Ne. 19:16; cf. "the four corners of the earth" in Isa. 11:12 (= 2 Ne. 21:2).

15. Isa. 7:14; the common terms in 1 Ne. 11:7 are the verb *to give* and the noun *sign*.

16. One must also recall that the prophecies cited by Nephi in 1 Nephi 19 from the prophets Zenock, Neum, and especially Zenos correlate with Isaiah's words about the Messiah (19:10–12). The point of quoting these three prophets was so that he "might persuade [his people] that they would remember the Lord" (19:18). In a sense, Nephi is specifying that Isaiah stands

as another witness of the coming Messiah, side by side with these three earlier prophets. See also 2 Ne. 11:2–3.

17. This passage constitutes one of the four so-called Servant Songs of Isaiah (42:1–4; 49:1–6; 50:4–9; 52:13–53:12). For further discussion, see Otto Eissfeldt, *The Old Testament: An Introduction* (New York: Harper and Row, 1965), 340–41; also Bernard W. Anderson, *Understanding the Old Testament*, 4th ed. (Englewood Cliffs, N.J.: Prentice-Hall, 1986), 488. In the version embedded in 1 Nephi, one finds not only the Servant Song, in which the Servant speaks following a long introduction not found in the Hebrew text (1 Ne. 21:1b–6), but also other expressions that point to the Messiah, such as "him whom man despiseth" and "him whom the nations abhorreth" (Isa. 53:3, part of the fourth Servant Song) in whose presence "kings shall see and arise, princes also shall worship" (1 Ne. 21:7 = Isa. 49:7). In addition, one reads that the Lord will give "my servant for a covenant of the people, to establish the earth, to cause [them] to inherit the desolate heritages" (1 Ne. 21:8 = Isa. 49:8). Further, Isaiah speaks of the one who will bring freedom and be able to "say to the prisoners: Go forth; to them that sit in darkness: Show yourselves [in the light]" (1 Ne. 21:9 = Isa. 49:9). In another possible reference to the Messiah, Isaiah mentions him "that hath mercy on them [and] shall lead them, even by the springs of water shall he guide them" (1 Ne. 21:10 = Isa. 49:10).

18. 1 Ne. 20:15 (= Isa. 48:15) also contains a possible reference to the work of the Messiah.

19. Actually, Nephi's introduction to Isaiah is addressed directly to his hearers: "Ye who are a remnant of the house of Israel, a branch who have been broken off" (1 Ne. 19:24). This kind of address conveys the reassurance that points to the need for rejuvenation.

20. Nephi, stalwart that he was, seems to soften the severity of the problems that faced family members by speaking simply of "much affliction" (1 Ne. 17:1) and "many afflictions and much difficulty" (17:6). But he does reveal the existence of personal difficulties when he expressed gratitude to the Lord, in his poetic lament, for guiding him "through mine afflictions in the wilderness" (2 Ne. 4:20; cf. 4:26).

21. Notice that even though Jacob has never visited the city, in behalf of the family he speaks of "Jerusalem, from whence *we* came" (2 Ne. 9:5, emphasis added).

22. 2 Ne. 1:3–4; cf. also 1 Ne. 5:4; 7:15; 19:20. The situation within the city of Jerusalem was to be so terrible that Jeremiah was forbidden to marry because of the certainty of death and suffering to family members (Jer. 16:1–4).

23. 2 Kgs. 25:1–4, 8–10, 18–21; 2 Chr. 36:17–20.

24. John S. Tanner, "Literary Reflections on Jacob and His Descendants," in *Jacob through the Words of Mormon, To Learn with Joy*, ed. Monte S. Nyman and

Charles D. Tate Jr. (Provo, Utah: Religious Studies Center, Brigham Young University, 1990), 251–69; the quotations are from p. 267.

25. To be sure, Nephi remained positive by saying that "the blessings of the Lord upon us" were "great" during "our journey in the wilderness" (1 Ne. 17:1–2). But his later use of the term *sojourn* (17:3–4), which often carries the sense of servility, points to a knot of difficulties, which Nephi rather blandly styles "much affliction" (17:1), and "many afflictions and much difficulty" (17:6). For the possible connections of his expression *sojourn* to servility, see my study in this volume, chapter 4, "Sojourn, Dwell, and Stay: Terms of Servitude."

26. For other depictions of the period in the desert of Arabia, as well as some general details about experiences there, see 1 Ne. 17:1–2, 12; 2 Ne. 1:24; 2:2; 3:3; Alma 18:37–38; 36:29.

27. For women as a measure of suffering or severe difficulty in a situation, see Matt. 24:19 (JS–M 1:16); Morm. 4:14, 21; Moro. 9:8.

28. Before turning "nearly eastward" across the southern end of the Arabian peninsula (1 Ne. 17:1), the daughters of Ishmael responded in part to Ishmael's death, which came only months after beginning the journey, by complaining that they had already "suffered much affliction, hunger, thirst, and fatigue" after wandering "much in the wilderness" (16:35). The most difficult part of the journey still lay ahead of them.

29. Isaiah prophesied of troubles in the desert, speaking of "destroyers" who make "thee [a] waste" (1 Ne. 21:17 = Isa. 49:17). One thus victimized will become "desolate, a captive" (1 Ne. 21:21 = Isa. 49:21). But such "captives of the mighty . . . shall be delivered" by the Lord (1 Ne. 21:25 = Isa. 49:25), with the result that "they that swallowed thee up shall be far away," because the captive has been released (1 Ne. 21:19 = Isa. 49:19). The "children" of the captives, multiplying in their lands of inheritance, shall say, "the place [of inheritance] is too strait [small] for me" (1 Ne. 21:19–21 = Isa. 49:19–21).

30. In the latter instance, Nephi indicated to his older brothers that they had a "choice" whether to return, but that they would surely perish in the coming conflagration (1 Ne. 7:15). The effect of Nephi's warning was to persuade the older brothers to remain with the family, thus assuring that the future would be fraught with family antagonisms. Isaiah could be understood as anticipating such a situation when he wrote that there would be "no peace . . . unto the wicked," mirroring the Lord's warning to Nephi and his posterity that the descendants of his brothers would be "a scourge unto [Nephi's] seed" whenever "they rebel against me" (1 Ne. 2:24; cf. 2 Ne. 5:25).

31. Although descendants continued to thank God for delivering their ancestors from Jerusalem (e.g., Mosiah 2:4), interest in Jerusalem permeated society until the final generation, as one can see in Moroni's quotation of expressions about the city from Isa. 52:1–2 and 54:2 (Moro. 10:31).

32. One notes the prominent mention of Abraham and his seed, the latter to bless "all the kindreds of the earth" (1 Ne. 22:9). Centuries later, the resurrected Jesus seems to have felt the need to address this issue during his visit by reassuring his hearers that "the Father hath commanded me that I should give unto you this land, for your inheritance," and "this people will I establish in this land, unto the fulfilling of the covenant which I made with your father Jacob" (3 Ne. 20:14, 22). Isaiah's prophecies in chapters 48–49 also allude to the promise made to Abraham, speaking of "thy seed" which is "as the sand," never to be "cut off nor destroyed from before [the Lord]" (1 Ne. 20:19 = Isa. 48:19).

33. In other passages, Jacob speaks much more positively about the situation of the clan in their new land, the recorded occasions falling during the lifetime of his older brother Nephi. See 2 Ne. 9:1–4, 53; 10:2, 18–23. But even the passage in 2 Ne. 9:1–4 reveals a despondency that Jacob seeks to address. One guesses that his accompanying discussion of the resurrection was occasioned by the death of several persons, perhaps prominent, in the colony.

34. Cf. also Lehi's characterization of "this land, which is a most precious land" (2 Ne. 3:2).

35. In preparing for flight, Nephi took "all those who would go with me" (2 Ne. 5:6). One can imagine the trauma that this necessity caused among family members who were close to one another but found themselves on different sides on the question of leadership in the clan. In addition, those fleeing took "tents and whatsoever things were possible" (5:7), evidently leaving behind property that they had acquired since their arrival but could not carry, an action that would have chafed feelings even more.

36. In Zenos' prophecy, events following the crucifixion are tied to Jerusalem, a circumstance which most certainly points to Jerusalem as the place of the Messiah's death (1 Ne. 19:13); compare Alma's words that summarize prophecies from Zenos and Zenock, implicitly pointing to Jerusalem as the place of Jesus' death (Alma 33:22).

37. It is a bit puzzling that Nephi recognized Nazareth (1 Ne. 11:13). Archeological remains date no earlier than the third century B.C. and indicate only a very small settlement, not a "city." One has to assume help from his angelic guide.

38. The same is hinted in Nephi's summary of his father's words about his own vision (1 Ne. 10:4); so Nephi's expectation, "[the Messiah] cometh . . . six hundred years from the time my father left Jerusalem" (19:8). Comes where? To earth? The only place mentioned in the passage is Jerusalem. Cf. Nephi's later words which also imply that Jerusalem would be the place of the Messiah's death, in 2 Ne. 25:10–14; also Abinadi's quotation of Isa. 52:9 at Mosiah 12:23 and 15:30.

39. First suggested by Hugh Nibley in *Lehi in the Desert, The World of the Jaredites, There Were Jaredites* (Salt Lake City: Deseret Book and F.A.R.M.S.,

1988), 42. See also Robert J. Matthews, "Jacob: Prophet, Theologian, Historian," in *Jacob through the Words of Mormon,* ed. Nyman and Tate, 33–53; the idea is expressed on 35–36.

40. Lehi all but says that his son Joseph was named after the Joseph who was sold into Egypt (2 Ne. 3:3–5), tying the Lord's promise about the endurance of the posterity of Joseph in Egypt (3:5) to a similar promise to his son Joseph (3:3, 23).

41. Cf. Alma 22:9. In reviews of the "traditions" of the Lamanites, this sort of element has not yet come in for discussion; see, for example, Noel B. Reynolds, "Nephi's Political Testament," in *Rediscovering the Book of Mormon,* ed. John L. Sorenson and Melvin J. Thorne (Salt Lake City: Deseret Book and F.A.R.M.S., 1991), 223; and the comments on Mosiah 10:12 by Joseph F. McConkie and Robert L. Millet, *Doctrinal Commentary on the Book of Mormon* (Salt Lake City: Bookcraft, 1988), 2:198.

42. See also 3 Ne. 21:23–24.

43. According to Nigel Groom, the maximum time for a caravan to travel from Zufar (or Dhofar) on the Indian Ocean to Gaza on the Mediterranean coast was 120 days, a distance of about 2,100 miles; *Frankincense and Myrrh: A Study of the Arabian Incense Trade* (London: Longman, 1981), chart on 213. Lynn and Hope Hilton also reckon the distance as 2,100 miles, offering a different beginning point; *Discovering Lehi* (Springville, Utah: CFI, 1996), 16. Naturally, caravans did not include flocks, something which Lehi's family seems to have eschewed (see 1 Ne. 2:4; 16:11–12). A handy summary of travel to and through the "empty quarter" of the Arabian Peninsula is found in Eugene England's work, "Through the Arabian Desert to a Bountiful Land: Could Joseph Smith Have Known the Way?" in *Book of Mormon Authorship,* ed. Noel B. Reynolds (Provo, Utah: Religious Studies Center, Brigham Young University, 1982), 143–56.

44. If passages in Isaiah 48–49 can be seen to anticipate, even outline, the family's trip through the desert, then one is justified in understanding Isaiah's words about releasing captives to describe, in a somewhat roundabout way, circumstances that the family faced in the wilderness (e.g., 1 Ne. 20:20; 21:21, 24–26 = Isa. 48:20; 49:21, 24–26). Simply stated, they appear to have spent time as indentured servants, as I have argued in the article in this volume, chapter 4, entitled "Sojourn, Dwell, and Stay: Terms of Servitude." It is also possible to understand Lehi's phraseology about the latter-day release from "captivity unto freedom" (2 Ne. 3:5) as a prophetic insight sharpened by personal experience.

45. See 1 Ne. 2:1–2 ("the Lord commanded my father . . . that he should . . . depart"); 7:14 ("they have driven him [Lehi] out of the land").

46. These verses (Isa. 48:14 and 1 Ne. 20:14) are not the same. The Book of Mormon text adds an entire sentence in the middle of the verse that concerns

the fulfillment of prophecy and does not appear in the Hebrew or Greek texts of Isaiah.

47. This legal right undergirds the entire exodus saga of the Hebrew slaves. See David Daube, *The Exodus Pattern in the Bible* (London: Faber and Faber, 1963), 39–41. In addition, I have set out the meaning of this legal right for the visit of the risen Jesus to Nephites and Lamanites in "Moses and Jesus: The Old Adorns the New," chapter 10, and in "The Exodus Pattern in the Book of Mormon," chapter 5, both in this volume.

48. Compare Lehi's interest in freedom and captivity (2 Ne. 2:26–29; 3:5) and the words of Isaiah on the same subject (Isa. 49:21–26 = 1 Ne. 21:21–26); and see my "Sojourn, Dwell, and Stay: Terms of Servitude," chapter 4.

49. The Book of Mormon text, which I follow here, differs in important ways from the underlying Hebrew text of Isa. 48:1–2.

50. Referring to the wickedness in Jerusalem, Nephi will later say that "their works were works of darkness, and their doings were doings of abominations" (2 Ne. 25:2).

51. As in the portrayal of Egypt in Deut. 4:20; 1 Kgs. 8:51; Jer. 11:4.

52. I follow the reading of 1 Nephi, not that of the King James Version.

53. Assuming a period of servitude suffered by the family, one can also include reference to those whom the Lord looses from prison and darkness, whom he "shall feed in the ways, and their pastures shall be in all high places" because the Lord "will . . . not forget thee" since "I have graven thee upon the palms of my hands" (Isa. 49:9, 15–16 = 1 Ne. 22:9, 15–16). In addition, it is the Lord "who leadeth thee by the way thou shouldst go" (1 Ne. 20:17 = Isa. 48:17). On darkness and prison, see Lehi's appeal to his older sons to "awake from a deep sleep" in order to "shake off the awful chains by which ye are bound" that make them "captive" (2 Ne. 1:13; see also 1:21, 23). On feeding and pasturing "in all high places," as well as the Lord's promise to "make all my mountains a way" (1 Ne. 21:9–11 = Isa. 49:9–11), compare the function of the brass ball that "led us in the more fertile parts of the wilderness" (1 Ne. 16:16). See my "A Case for Lehi's Bondage in Arabia," *Journal of Book of Mormon Studies* 6, no. 2 (fall 1997): 205–17.

54. Without multiplying examples, we note that other allusions to the family's situation appear in Isaiah 48–49. For instance, the reference to "children" born while one is "a captive" (1 Ne. 21:21 = Isa. 49:21) could be understood as allusions to Jacob and Joseph. In addition, the expression "those who are in the east" (1 Ne. 21:13 = Isa. 49:13) could be seen as referring not only to the extended family who traveled east through Arabia to reach the shore of the sea, but possibly to the direction that they traveled by sea in order to reach the Americas. Moreover, the remark about the one who "wouldst deal very treacherously" but from whom the Lord "will . . . defer mine anger . . . that I cut thee not off" (1 Ne. 20:8–9 = Isa. 48:8–9) could be understood to apply

to Nephi's older brothers, for whom the Lord showed abundant patience during the journey and whose posterity was to survive.

3

Recovering the Missing Record of Lehi

Clues in the Book of Mormon beam a light on the missing record of Lehi. Martin Harris lost the original 116-page translation of the Book of Lehi in 1828, and subsequently Joseph Smith received a commandment not to retranslate it. Hence the scope and nature of this text has remained unknown. But through examining quotations and paraphrases found chiefly in Nephi's recollections of his father's life, we can identify Lehi's prophetic call, his visions and dreams, and his prophecies to his children as central pieces of the missing manuscript. Lehi's vision of the tree of life and his final admonition to his children appear in Nephi's account as large quotations from this record. Lehi's teachings also featured other fundamental doctrines, such as opposition in all things and the relationship between the Fall and the Atonement.

The Book of Mormon teems with references to works known by its compilers and authors but not included in its final collection of texts. Documents comprising the plates of brass, for instance, are mentioned merely in passing.[1] Further, Mormon alludes to a substantial collection from which he distilled the nearly thousand-year history of his people.[2] These countless unnamed texts, moreover, do not include the so-called "sealed plates" which formed part of what was entrusted to Joseph Smith but remained untranslated.[3] Among these accounts, the record of Lehi is singled out by name. It constituted, I propose, both a major source behind and an important influence on the writings of Lehi's two literary sons, Nephi and Jacob.[4] In fact, a hint exists that Lehi's record-keeping served as a model for scribes in later centuries.[5] Furthermore, a surprising amount of information exists that allows us to determine substantially the content and compass of Lehi's record.[6]

As he opens his own story, Nephi announces that he is writing "a record of my proceedings in my days" (1 Ne. 1:1). But a few lines later, after reporting the divine calling of his father to be a prophet (1:5–15), he adds this important notation: "I, Nephi, do not make a full account of the things which my father hath written, for he hath written many things which he saw in visions and in dreams; and . . . many things which he prophesied and spake unto his children. . . . But I shall make an account of my proceedings in my days. Behold, I make an abridgment of the record of my father . . . ; wherefore, after I have abridged the record of my father then will I make an account of mine own life" (1:16–17). Thus, even though he intended to "make a record of [his] proceedings," Nephi introduces his own account with the news of his father's calling (1:5–15), adding a note that he is abridging his father's record. According to verse 16—and this sets our agenda—this record includes (a) the notice of Lehi's prophetic call, (b) "things which he saw in visions and in dreams," and (c) "things which he prophesied and spake unto his children."[7]

Lehi's Record in the Large and Small Plates

It is important to notice that Nephi inscribed two records on metal plates: the first on the large plates of Nephi[8] and the second on his small plates,[9] each making use of his father's journal.[10] Concerning the large plates, Nephi recounts: "And upon the plates . . . I did engraven the record of my father, and also our journeyings in the wilderness, and the prophecies of my father" (1 Ne. 19:1). Notably, this verse outlines the material found in 1 Nephi and in the first three chapters of 2 Nephi. To illustrate: (a) "the record of my father" corresponds roughly to 1 Nephi 1–10; (b) the "journeyings in the wilderness" appear in 1 Nephi 16–18, beginning with the discovery of the Liahona compass; and (c) the "prophecies of my father" would include 2 Nephi 1–3 and, possibly, 1 Nephi 10. This overall scheme is interrupted only by Nephi's dream (1 Nephi 11–15) and his discourse to the extended family (1 Nephi 19–22), both of which digress from the main story that focuses primarily on Lehi.

It was evidently after Lehi's death that Nephi began his second account—the small plates—which came to include the first six records of the Book of Mormon.[11] Nephi himself states: "I, Nephi, had kept the records upon my [large] plates . . . thus far. And it came to pass that the Lord God said unto me: Make other plates; and thou shalt engraven many things upon them which are good in my sight, for the profit of thy people. Wherefore, I, Nephi . . . went and made these [small] plates upon which I have engraven these things. And I engraved that which is pleasing unto God. . . . And if my people desire to know . . . the history of my people they must search mine other [large] plates" (2 Ne. 5:29–33). According to this view, the books of 1 and 2 Nephi comprise Nephi's second record. In the case of this narrative, too, Nephi acknowledges that his father's work underlays its foundation; for only "after I have abridged the record of my father," Nephi affirms, "will I make an account of mine own life" (1 Ne. 1:17). Plainly it was Nephi's avowed purpose to incorporate parts of his father's work into this second composition.[12]

The structure of the early verses of 1 Nephi 1 shows Nephi's dependence on his father's account, preserving the opening of Lehi's record itself. As a matter of custom, ancient prophets introduced an account of their divine callings near the beginning of their record, coupling it with a colophon about the year of the reign of the local king[13]—precisely what we find in 1 Ne. 1:4–15. Directly after Nephi's opening remark about himself (1:1–3) there is a notation that the story began during the first year of king Zedekiah's reign (1:4). Next, as expected, we read of God commissioning the prophet (1:5–15). But it is not the call of Nephi; it is Lehi's call.[14] In this light, I believe that Nephi inserted the opening of his father's book into 1 Ne. 1:4–15.[15]

When and on What Did Lehi Write?

Lehi must have completed much of his record by the time Nephi began to write his first narrative: "Upon the [large] plates which I made I did engraven the record of my father" (1 Ne. 19:1). If so, when and how did Lehi's book come into existence? Clearly Lehi's account was already extant when Nephi inscribed it on the large plates. Further, someone apparently kept a journal, possibly on perishable material, during the years that Lehi's family lived in the desert (17:4). We turn now to evidence for these observations.

The report of the voyage of Lehi's family to the promised land appears in 1 Nephi 18, followed by Nephi's comment that he then manufactured plates for writing by smelting ore (19:1–2).[16] By Nephi's account, he already possessed (a) the record of Lehi, (b) the genealogy of Lehi's fathers, and (c) an itinerary of the family's travels in the desert. Nephi, of course, could have obtained the genealogy from the brass plates (5:16). But Lehi's narrative, including the desert wanderings, must have come from another source. It seems, then, that Lehi's account, basically complete when Nephi began his first record, served as one of Nephi's sources. Thus Lehi evidently was already composing his narrative while traveling in the desert and crossing the sea.

Another indicator of a running log of the family's travel experiences is that after relating Lehi's discovery of the compass in 1 Ne. 16:10, Nephi begins to narrate the family's trek by a series of "we" passages.[17] These passages, narrated in first person plural, bear the marks of a summary of a diary-like record. That Nephi was evidently summarizing such an account appears in 1 Ne. 17:4 where, after mentioning the physical well-being that the family enjoyed in the desert (17:2–3), he compresses his long story into a few words: "We did sojourn for the space of many years, yea, even eight years in the wilderness."[18]

We have no way of knowing what material Lehi originally used for record keeping. However, Lehi's fifth son, Jacob, makes an incidental remark which may shed light on this question as well as on the reason the Lord commanded Nephi to keep records on metal plates. After acknowledging the difficulty of inscribing on metal, Jacob says: "We know that the things which we write upon plates must remain; but whatsoever things we write upon anything save it be upon plates must perish and vanish away" (Jacob 4:1–2). In this connection, it is worth noting that Nephi had obtained the brass plates before Jacob was born.[19] And Jacob must have noticed their durability since he could read and teach from them after he had become a grown man. Consequently, his remark that writing "remains" when engraved on metal tablets no doubt derived from his own experience, as did his assertion that other types of material for writing "must perish and vanish away." How had Jacob observed this latter? The most natural answer is that someone in his father's family had written on nonmetallic substances. Compared to the durability of the brass plates, these materials had evidently proven unsatisfactory for permanent records.[20]

Other hints, or the lack of them, suggest that initially Lehi kept his record neither on metallic plates nor on empty leaves (if any) of the brass plates. First, no reason appears for Lehi to carry engraving tools into the desert. It was only after he had left Jerusalem, in fact, that the Lord instructed him to seek custody of the brass plates (1 Ne. 3:2–4). Furthermore, the only item that Nephi seems to have brought later to his father from Jerusalem, along with the brass plates, was the sword of Laban (2 Ne. 5:14; Jacob 1:10). No tools are mentioned.[21] Finally, no account even hints that anyone in Lehi's family smelted ore either for plates or for tools while living in the desert. On the contrary, they avoided kindling fires even for cooking (1 Ne. 17:2, 12). To be sure, Nephi possessed the skill to refine ore for metal plates, since after crossing the desert he crafted metal tools for constructing his ship (17:16).[22] These observations, then, when coupled with Jacob's note about nonmetallic writing substances, lead one to postulate that records kept in the desert were written on something other than metal, although we cannot be certain of the material.[23]

What can we distill from our discussion thus far? In the first place, Lehi's record both served as a source for each of Nephi's accounts, those on the large and small plates, and specifically underlay most of the opening of 1 Nephi, a text from the small plates. Second, Lehi's record was essentially complete by the time he and his family reached the land of promise, since Nephi employed it as a source for his annals on the large plates soon after arriving. Third, we surmise that Lehi initially wrote his narrative on a substance less durable than metal, and that it was Nephi who first inscribed it on metallic leaves when he recopied it onto his large plates.

The Scope of Lehi's Book on the Small Plates

Our next task is to determine how extensively Lehi's account underlies 1 and 2 Nephi as well as Jacob's book. We shall first explore direct quotations and, afterwards, passages that Jacob and Nephi appear to paraphrase from the account of their father. In this connection, two of the most important and lengthy quotations from Lehi are his portrayal of the vision of the tree of life (1 Ne. 8:2–28) and the report of his last instructions and blessings to his family (2 Ne. 1:4–3:25; 4:3–7, 9, 11).

The Quotations

The vision of the tree certainly comes from Lehi's own record. The piece in 1 Ne. 8:2–28 stands in the first person singular, an important criterion. By the way Nephi introduces the story, he is obviously quoting from his father: "He [Lehi] spake unto us, saying: Behold, I have dreamed a dream" (8:2). Additionally, Nephi leaves no doubt as to when he ceases quoting Lehi and begins to paraphrase: "And now I, Nephi, do not speak all the words of my father. But, to be short in writing, behold, he saw other multitudes pressing forward; and they came and caught hold of the end of the rod of iron" (8:29–30).

Concerning Lehi's last blessings and instructions to his family, there is some question whether they formed part of his record.[24] We cannot be entirely certain, chiefly because the scenes occurred close to Lehi's death. Of course, it is probable that not many years had passed between Lehi's arrival in the promised land (1 Ne. 18:23) and his death (2 Ne. 4:12).[25] During this period, Nephi had been keeping a record of his people on the large plates "thus far" (2 Ne. 5:29). Had Lehi also continued to write? If he had, we would expect him to include his last blessings and instructions; for, as Nephi tells us, "he [Lehi] also hath written many things which he prophesied and spake unto his children" (1 Ne. 1:16), observations which fit Lehi's last blessings. Perhaps most significantly, the section of 2 Nephi comprising Lehi's last instructions exhibits the expected first person singular narrative. This characteristic, especially in such a long section, impels us toward the view that Lehi himself was responsible for the report. Of course, someone may have written Lehi's words as he spoke and, afterwards, Nephi inserted them into the large plates.[26] Whichever the case, we should view Lehi's last words to his family as a continuation of what he had written simply because they match, according to Nephi's description, what Lehi had already recorded.

One other long quotation, preserved by Jacob, also came from Lehi's record. It lies in Jacob 2:23–33, a discussion of fidelity in marriage. After chastising his people for their pride (2:12–22) and then for their "grosser crimes," Jacob declares: "For behold, thus saith the Lord: This people begin to wax in iniquity; . . . for they seek to excuse themselves in committing whoredoms, because of the things which were written concerning David, and Solomon his son" (2:23). A quotation from the Lord opens this verse, which runs through verse 33. But who received these instructions? At first glance it appears that Jacob was repeating what he himself had received, since a few lines earlier he had written: "As I inquired of the Lord, thus came the word unto me, saying: Jacob, get thou up into the temple on the morrow, and declare the word which I shall give thee unto this people" (2:11). Was not Jacob carrying out the Lord's instructions by retelling what he had been told? Not really.[27] A more careful look at chapter 2 reveals that the counsel concerning one wife indeed came from the Lord but that Jacob was not the first to receive it. In fact, the recipient of these directions was Lehi. After the long quotation from the Lord (2:23–33), including Jacob's short comment (2:27a), we find this statement: "And now behold, my brethren, ye know that these commandments [concerning fidelity to one's wife] were given to our father, Lehi; wherefore, ye have known them before" (2:34). Therefore, as Jacob insists, it was Lehi who previously received "these commandments."

An equally compelling passage occurs a few lines later in which Jacob accusingly announces: "Behold, the Lamanites your brethren . . . are more righteous than you; for they have not forgotten the commandments of the Lord, which was given unto our father—that they should have save it were one wife, and concubines they should have none, and there should not be whoredoms committed among them" (3:5). Except for punctuation, this verse stood thus in the Printer's Manuscript.[28] Every printed edition of the Book of Mormon has changed the word *commandments* in this passage to the singular, and except in the 1981 edition, the word *father* has appeared as plural. Significantly, the Printer's Manuscript demonstrates unequivocally that these "commandments" were delivered to Jacob's "father," Lehi. Consequently, we conclude that in Jacob 2:23–33 we find instructions that the Lord entrusted to Lehi. Jacob, in his sermon, quotes them to his hearers from Lehi's record, which "ye have known" (2:34).

Other quotations likely from Lehi's record are shorter, and all occur in 1 Nephi.[29] We must use caution, however, in attributing these extractions to Lehi's record, since, because of their brevity, they may be based on the memory of one or another family member.

The Paraphrases

As one might expect, the paraphrases from Lehi outnumber the quotations. With two exceptions (2 Ne. 1:1b–3; Jacob 3:5b), all of the restatements which may go back to Lehi's record turn up in 1 Nephi. The two visions associated with Lehi's call must of course be included since Nephi has apparently recast the account from first person to third person (1 Ne. 1:4–12, 13b–14a, 15). This report, as already noted, is sprinkled with direct quotations, presumably from Lehi's original narration (1:13a, 14b). Then follows Nephi's summary, which indicates that he is restating his father's chronicle: "And now I, Nephi, do not make a full account of the things which my father hath written, for he hath written many things which he saw in visions and in dreams" (1:16).

Much of chapter 2 may also depend on Lehi's narrative.[30] Mixed with these lines are Lehi's own words[31] as well as Nephi's observations both about his brothers' attitudes at having to leave Jerusalem (2:11–13) and about a revelation that he himself received (2:16–24). At the end of the summary from Lehi, Nephi concludes by saying, "And my father dwelt in a tent" (2:15).

A third important paraphrase occurs in chapter 8, summarizing the remainder of Lehi's dream and his consequent exhortation to Laman and Lemuel (8:30–33; 8:35–9:1). Nephi introduces this restatement by conceding that he cannot repeat "all the words of [his] father" (8:29) and closes it thus: "And all these things did my father see, and hear, and speak, as he dwelt in a tent, . . . and also a great many more things, which cannot be written upon these [small] plates" (9:1). Nothing in this verse states specifically that Lehi had written down what Nephi had just recapitulated. But Lehi's dream and the accompanying exhortations to his family fit so well with Nephi's description of his father's written work (1:16) that I feel confident that all of chapter 8, except Nephi's inserted remarks, goes back to Lehi's record.

Another very important summary from Lehi's record stands in 1 Ne. 10:1–16, which Nephi prefaces in an unusual way: "And now I, Nephi, proceed to give an account . . . of my proceedings, and my reign and ministry; wherefore, to proceed with mine account, *I must speak somewhat of the things of my father*" (10:1, emphasis added). After a synopsis of Lehi's prophecies to his sons about the coming Messiah and the scattering and gathering of the Nephites and Lamanites, Nephi concludes: "And after this manner of language did my father prophesy and speak unto my brethren, and also many more things which I do not write in this book; for I have written as many of them as were expedient for me in mine other book. And all these things . . . were done as my father dwelt in a tent" (10:15–16).[32] Although Nephi here does not claim that he is paraphrasing Lehi's prophetic words from a written source, he does acknowledge that he had already included them in his "other book" (i.e., the large plates) from which he likely took the material for 1 Ne. 10:1–16. Remembering that his father's record contained "many things which he prophesied and spake unto his children" (1:16), it would be surprising indeed if Nephi were not ultimately dependent in this instance upon Lehi's own written account.

In his original record, this segment (10:1–16), which sets out Lehi's teachings on the coming Messiah and the scattering and gathering of Israel, may well have continued the earlier account of his vision and exhortation to his sons (8:2–9:1). Two observations are relevant. First, just a few lines separate these two longer sections (9:2–6). Apparently Nephi's attention to "these [small] plates" in 1 Ne. 9:1 presented an opportunity to discuss them briefly in verses 2–6 before resuming his father's account in chapter 10. Second, when we compare the content of these two units with the content of Nephi's own analogous dream of the tree of life (1 Nephi 11–14), it seems obvious that the two pieces belong together. Although it is not apparent from the narrative of Lehi's dream of the tree that the prophecies regarding Israel's destiny and the Messiah (10:1–16) are parts of a whole, their connection becomes clear from Nephi's parallel dream. Hence we conclude that the discussion in 1 Ne. 9:2–6 stands between two sections which likely formed a unit in Lehi's narrative.

The last paraphrase requiring review is the desert itinerary (16:11–17, 33; 17:1–6). To be sure, Nephi himself could have kept the log in the desert. One observation, however, inclines me toward the view that the itinerary was Lehi's. Nephi mentions the desert journal twice in 1 Ne. 19:1–2. In verse 1, when itemizing sources for the large plates, Nephi lists "the record of my father, and also [the record of] our journeyings in the wilderness, and the prophecies of my father." It is worth noting that Nephi mentions the desert journal *between* items from Lehi. Only after naming the sources from his father does Nephi say, "And also many of mine own prophecies have I engraven upon [the large plates]" (19:1). Verse 2 paints a similar picture. Here too Nephi itemizes the sources that he drew on when composing his record on the large plates: "the record of my father, and the genealogy of his fathers, and the more part of all our proceedings in the wilderness." Again Nephi has associated the "proceedings" of the desert period with his father's work. Consequently, the itinerary almost certainly came from Lehi's pen.

In sum, the following segments of 1 Nephi paraphrase Lehi's record: Lehi's two visions at the time of his call (1:4–12, 13b–14a, 15), his departure into the desert (2:1a, 2–9a, 10a, 14–15), parts of Lehi's vision of the tree of life (8:30–33; 8:35–9:1), his prophecies concerning Israel and the Messiah (10:1–16), and the desert itinerary (16:11–17, 33; 17:1–6). There are others shorter in length which almost all appear in 1 Nephi: Lehi's prophecies and subsequent rejection in Jerusalem (1:18–20a), his prophecies regarding the brass plates (5:17–19),[33] Lehi sending for Ishmael and his family (7:1–2), Nephi's interpretation of Lehi's words concerning Israel's destiny (15:17–18),[34] the Lord's command to Lehi to move on and the accompanying discovery of the compass (16:9–10),[35] and the revelation to Lehi by means of the compass (16:25–27).[36]

Character of the Record

To portray the content of Lehi's record is a formidable task, since we possess only fragments and summarized accounts. Consequently, we run the risk of overstatement or underestimation. But we can discern a tentative outline. So far, three ingredients have appeared: prophecies, visions, and teachings.

The Prophecies

Concerning prophecies, Nephi informs us that his father included many among his writings (1 Ne. 1:16; 19:1). Although Lehi prophesied on several occasions about his family (1 Ne. 7:1; 2 Ne. 29:2), a unique opportunity presented itself when he blessed and instructed them before his death, assuring them that their posterity would survive to the last days (2 Ne. 1:1–4:12). With an eye to the future, Lehi mentions first the promised land "which the Lord God hath covenanted with me should be a land for the inheritance of . . . my children forever" (1:5). Of course, dwelling in the land is conditional upon obedience to the Lord and his principles (1:7). Sadly, Lehi prophesies of a time when his posterity will turn their backs on their "Redeemer and their God" (1:10). In that day, he foresees, the Lord "will bring other nations . . . and he will give unto them power, and he will take away from [Lehi's descendants] the lands of their possessions, and he will cause them to be scattered and smitten" (1:11). Although this prospect grieves Lehi deeply, he acknowledges that the Lord's "ways are righteousness forever" (1:19).

Even in the face of such gloomy prospects, Lehi beams a light on the divine pledge that the family's progeny will survive these most vexing times (4:7, 9), agreeing with a vow made to Joseph of Egypt that God would preserve Joseph's offspring (3:16), a promise recorded on the brass plates (4:2). In fact, much of the prophetic radiance that Lehi draws from this Joseph (3:6–21) shines on a special seer (3:7, 11) who in the last days will carry the word of the Lord both to Joseph's seed through Lehi (3:7) and to the house of Israel (3:13).[37] Then Lehi prophesies to his own son Joseph that this seer will be "an instrument in the hands of God . . . and do that thing which is great in the sight of God, unto the bringing to pass much restoration unto the house of Israel, and unto the seed of thy brethren" (3:24).

One aspect of Lehi's prophecies about his descendants holds out the promise that their records will come forth to the world (29:2). A similar assurance had come to Joseph of Egypt, to whom the Lord declared regarding the seer: "I will give unto him that he shall write the writing of the fruit of thy loins, unto the fruit of thy loins. . . . And it shall be as if the fruit of thy loins had cried unto them from the dust" (3:18–19). Lehi simply obtained the same divine commitment awarded to Joseph: that his posterity's writings would cry out as if "from the dust" to others of his descendants (3:19).

Because he knows the destiny of his progeny, Lehi compares his family to an olive tree whose branches have been broken off (1 Ne. 10:12–14; 15:12–13), a comparison tied to the prophet Zenos's allegory of the olive tree, also found in the brass plates.[38] In this allegory, the house of Israel is likened to an olive tree whose branches are removed and grafted elsewhere but eventually restored to the main trunk of the tree. Such a prophetic image had a deep influence on Lehi, for Nephi relates that his father spoke "concerning the house of Israel, that they should be compared like unto an olive-tree, whose branches should be broken off and . . . scattered upon all the face of the earth. Wherefore, he said it must needs be that we should be led . . . into the land of promise, unto the fulfilling of the word of the Lord, that we should be scattered upon all the face of the earth" (10:12–13). That these words were prophetic is evident in Nephi's summarizing remark a few lines later: "After this manner of language did my father prophesy" (10:15).[39]

The coming Messiah also enlivens Lehi's prophecies. Almost predictably, in his last blessings to his family, Lehi turns to the Messiah, illuminating his mission as redeemer from the Fall, as guarantor of human freedom, and as mediator of eternal life (2 Ne. 2:26–28). An earlier prophecy about the Messiah played a role in Lehi's preaching in Jerusalem (1 Ne. 1:19), the inspiration coming from his vision of a book (1:8–14). In that vision, Lehi at first seemed not to recognize the "One descending out of the midst of heaven" whose brightness "was above that of the sun at noonday" (1:9), even though Lehi had been rather certain that he saw God "sitting upon his throne" earlier in the vision (1:8). But this second figure who descended, followed by "twelve others," apparently remained unknown to Lehi until he began to read in the book brought to him: "The things which [Lehi] read in the book, manifested plainly of the coming of a Messiah" (1:10, 19). At the same time, Lehi learned of the threatening destruction of Jerusalem because of the inhabitants' wickedness (1:13).[40] This mournful outlook, along with the prediction of the Messiah's coming, formed the core of his prophesying to the people in the city (1:19).

Lehi also accentuates the Messiah when he recounts his vision of the tree of life (10:4–11), much of his prophecy evidently growing out of this later vision. This vision of the tree, and of the Messiah and his forerunner, appears to considerably expand Lehi's knowledge of the Messiah's ministry in Palestine. In the earlier vision (1:8–13), Lehi had learned of his coming for "the redemption of the world" (1:19). But whether this prior occasion had taught Lehi more remains uncertain, since Nephi offers only a sketchy summary (1:14, 19). In contrast, Lehi relates many more specific details about the Redeemer in the later prophecy (10:4–11) than we find in chapter 1.

It is worth making a point here concerning Lehi's expressions for the Messiah. Whether his words are paraphrased or quoted directly, Lehi never used the Greek title *Christ* when speaking of the *Messiah,*[41] nor did he ever call him *Son of God* or the like.[42] Only Lehi's sons Nephi and Jacob employed titles of this sort.[43] To be sure, Lehi would have known the designation *Son* from the works of Zenos and Zenock, whose works appeared on the brass plates.[44] But in the few quotations from these latter two prophets, whose works Alma also cited when speaking of the coming Messiah (Alma 33:11, 13, 16), nowhere do Zenos and Zenock expand the title to *Son of God* or something related.[45]

Can we say whether Lehi knew expressions such as *Son of God* and *Christ*? Concerning both the title *Christ* and the name *Jesus,* the answer is a definite no. According to 2 Ne. 10:3, an angel revealed the title *Christ* to Jacob only after Lehi's death, and Nephi makes use of this term only after narrating Jacob's experience (11:4). In addition, Nephi writes the name *Jesus* for the first time only near the end of his second book (26:12), and Jacob records it but once in the latter half of his work (Jacob 4:6). Therefore, we can safely conclude that Lehi did not know these expressions. In the case of *Son of God* and related titles, we cannot be sure that Lehi did not know them, but at least he did not use them.[46]

Visions and Dreams

Besides Lehi's prophecies, we know of seven of his visions and inspired dreams if we include the instructions given to him by means of the compass (1 Ne. 16:26–27). Nephi recounts that Lehi had included such in his record: "[Lehi] hath written many things which he saw in visions and in dreams" (1:16). In this connection, Lehi himself admits that he was "a visionary man" (5:4). Incidentally, Lehi saw little difference between the terms *dream* and *vision*.[47]

Lehi's earliest vision likely stood at the beginning of his own record. Nephi recounts that "as [Lehi] prayed unto the Lord, there came a pillar of fire and dwelt upon a rock before him; and he saw and heard much; . . . And it came to pass that he returned to his own house at Jerusalem; and he cast himself upon his bed, being overcome with the Spirit and the things which he had seen" (1:6–7). That Lehi's experience constituted a vision grows out of the emphasis on what he saw. Remarkably, while Nephi repeats nothing of the vision's content, it certainly must have included Lehi's calling as a prophet. And it is reasonable that some of the content of this vision coincided with what Lehi saw immediately thereafter in the vision of the book. Nephi possibly thought that juxtaposing the two visions would indicate corresponding content.[48] We come to this view when we realize that Nephi must have abbreviated as much as possible, owing to the difficulty of inscribing on metal plates.

Nephi opens his summary of Lehi's second vision, the vision of the book, by picturing what Lehi saw when he was caught away by the Spirit: "And being thus overcome with the Spirit, he was carried away in a vision, even that he saw the heavens open, and he thought he saw God sitting upon his throne, surrounded with numberless concourses of angels" (1:8).[49] Lehi then saw "One descending out of the midst of heaven" and "twelve others following him" (1:9–10). Nephi continues: "The first came and stood before my father, and gave unto him a book, and bade him that he should read. . . . And he read, saying: Wo, wo, unto Jerusalem, for I have seen thine abominations! Yea, and many things did my father read concerning Jerusalem—that it should be destroyed, and the inhabitants thereof; . . . and many should be carried away captive into Babylon" (1:11, 13). This passage captures the warning of Lehi's vision: Jerusalem had become iniquitous and was to be ravaged. This warning, of course, formed the core of the messages of contemporary prophets at Jerusalem.[50] Although Nephi does not allude to it here, at some point Lehi had also learned about the approaching redemption through the Messiah, for Nephi's tight summary of Lehi's later preaching reads: "And

[Lehi] testified that the things which he saw and heard, and also the things which he read in the book, manifested plainly of the coming of a Messiah, and also the redemption of the world" (1:19).

In narrating his father's third vision, Nephi includes words of divine assurance as well as forewarning: "The Lord spake unto my father, yea, even in a dream, and said unto him: Blessed art thou Lehi, because of the things which thou hast done; and because thou hast been faithful and declared unto this people the things which I commanded thee, behold, they seek to take away thy life" (2:1). In this same vision the Lord also charged Lehi to leave Jerusalem, the first step in a very long journey that would take him halfway around the world: "The Lord commanded my father, even in a dream, that he should take his family and depart into the wilderness" (2:2). Lehi's response to this command eventually led him and his family to a distant land of promise, the Americas.

Lehi's fourth vision directs the return of his sons to Jerusalem for the record on the plates of brass (3:2–6). Nephi quotes the very words of Lehi: "[Lehi] spake unto me [Nephi], saying: Behold I have dreamed a dream, in the which the Lord hath commanded me that thou and thy brethren shall return to Jerusalem. For behold, Laban hath the record of the Jews and also a genealogy of my forefathers, and they are engraven upon plates of brass" (3:2–3). Nephi and his brothers were to go to Laban and "seek the records, and bring them down hither" (3:4). Notably, Lehi received this vision only after he and his family had established a base camp near the Red Sea (2:5–9).

The fifth vision has to do with the tree of life and the Messiah (8:2–28). As we have seen, this section preserves a long excerpt from Lehi's record. There were elements of the vision, however, that Lehi apparently left out.[51] The most notable illumines the time of the Messiah's coming. Oddly, neither Lehi nor Nephi relates this detail in the accounts of their visions—at least not in the small plates. It is only afterward that Nephi brings up this particular while recollecting his vision (19:7–10). Nephi speaks thus: "And behold [the Messiah] cometh, according to the words of the angel, in six hundred years from the time my father left Jerusalem" (19:8). If "the angel" in this passage (see 11:14) is the same as the "man . . . dressed in a white robe" of Lehi's vision (8:5)—and this seems apparent—then we can reasonably assume that Lehi had learned what Nephi learned concerning when the Messiah would come.

In my reckoning, the revelation written on the compass constitutes Lehi's sixth vision (16:26).[52] On this occasion, Lehi had prayed to know where Nephi should go to find food. In his response, the Lord chastised Lehi and his family for complaining because of their hardships (16:24–25). Nephi then writes that "when my father beheld the things which were written upon the ball, he did fear and tremble exceedingly, and also my brethren and the sons of Ishmael and our wives" (16:27). Like the Urim and Thummim among the ancient Israelites, the compass-ball thus served as an important means of revelation.[53]

The last recorded vision is noted briefly in 2 Ne. 1:4: "For, behold, said [Lehi], I have seen a vision, in which I know that Jerusalem is destroyed; and had we remained in Jerusalem we should also have perished." That Lehi was granted a vision of the destruction of Jerusalem should not surprise us. Other prophets beheld the same.[54] For example, Lehi's son Jacob recounts seeing "that those who were at Jerusalem . . . have been slain and carried away captive" (2 Ne. 6:8). And Ezekiel was transported in vision from Babylon to Jerusalem where he witnessed the abominable practices of the priests and the consequent withdrawal of the Lord from the temple before the city fell (Ezek. 8:3–10:19).

The Doctrines

Among the important doctrines taught by Lehi, in addition to those already noted, three stand out: fidelity in marriage, "opposition in all things," and Adam's role. Concerning fidelity to one's spouse, Lehi linked this principle to the question of plurality of wives. Jacob, we recall, quotes at some length the relevant words of Lehi (Jacob 2:23b–26, 27b–33). While the occasion when Lehi received this divine injunction remains unknown, according to Jacob the Lord had told Lehi that "this people[55] begin to wax in iniquity . . . for they seek to excuse themselves in committing whoredoms" (2:23). More to the point, people had sought "to excuse themselves" on scriptural grounds, "because of the things . . . written concerning David, and Solomon his son." God, through Lehi, was very emphatic that no "man among you [shall] have save it be one wife" (2:27) unless God himself reverses this commandment: "For if I will, saith the Lord of Hosts, raise up seed unto me, I will command my people" (2:30). What had angered the Lord in Jacob's day was having "seen the sorrow, and heard the mourning of the daughters of my people . . . because of the wickedness and abominations of their husbands" (2:31). In Lehi's account of it, fidelity to one's marriage partner was so crucial to his family's presence in the promised land that, if not observed, God would soundly curse "the land for their sakes" (2:29).

A second significant teaching of Lehi elucidates the doctrine of "opposition in all things." As part of his last instructions to his son Jacob (2 Ne. 2:11–13), Lehi testifies that God's final judgment leads either to "punishment which is affixed" or to "happiness which is affixed" (2:10). He then reasons: "It must needs be, that there is an opposition in all things. If not so . . . righteousness could not be brought to pass, neither wickedness, neither holiness nor misery" (2:11). Lehi further maintains that without opposition we have no power to be righteous or unrighteous. We note the dramatic result that Lehi says would ensue: "And if these things are not there is no God. And if there is no God we are not, neither the earth; for there could have been no creation" (2:13). According to Lehi, then, the totality of existence would cease if opposition disappeared. He repeats this perception in different terms: "All things must needs be a compound in one; wherefore, if it should be one body it must needs remain as dead, having no life neither death, nor corruption nor incorruption, happiness nor misery, neither sense nor insensibility. Wherefore, it must needs have been created for . . . naught; wherefore there would have been no purpose in the end of its creation" (2:11–12). The stance that all existence would be utterly wasted if no antithetical relationships existed leads Lehi to say: "Wherefore, this thing [no opposition] must needs destroy the wisdom of God and his eternal purposes, and also the power, and the mercy, and the justice of God" (2:12). Since Lehi has just previously been dealing with the coming redemption through the Messiah (2:6–10), we should probably understand this doctrine in terms of the Redeemer's work. That is, if no opposition exists, there is no reason for a Redeemer who can bring about God's mercy *and* justice.

A third element of Lehi's teaching ties into his concerns about the role of the Redeemer and about opposition in all things: the role of Adam in the drama of salvation (2:15–27). Lehi insists that two ingredients were joined together in Adam's situation—a choice along with the freedom to make that choice: "It must needs be that there was an opposition; even the forbidden fruit in opposition to the tree of life. . . . Wherefore, the Lord God gave unto man that he should act for himself" (2:15–16). For Lehi, the opposition facing Adam was necessary so that the choice could be made—the forbidden fruit versus the tree of life. In fact, had not Adam been enticed to make the choice that brought both mortality and the capability of parenthood, the earth would never have been peopled, thus frustrating God's plan: "And now, behold, if Adam had not transgressed he would not have fallen, but he would have remained in the garden of Eden. . . . And [Adam and Eve] would have had no children. . . . Adam fell that men might be" (2:22–23, 25). The whole point is that if Adam had not fallen, the human race would never have existed. But since he did fall, "the Messiah cometh . . . that he may redeem the children of men from the fall. And because that they are redeemed from the fall they have become free forever . . . to choose liberty and eternal life, through the great Mediator of all men, or to choose captivity and death, according to the captivity and power of the devil" (2:26–27). The reasons for opposition, then, are (a) to perpetuate existence—and Adam's fall led to this—and (b) to bring about God's plan, which is to save us through the Messiah's redemption.[56]

Conclusion

In summary, a strong case exists for the argument that Lehi's written record underlay much in the writings of Nephi and Jacob. The most persistent problem, of course, is whether a particular quotation or paraphrase indeed goes back to Lehi's written source. Naturally, Nephi's brief characterizations of his father's writings (1 Ne. 1:16; 19:1–2) enable us to grasp important clues regarding the nature of Lehi's work. Yet in the final analysis we can be certain about only a portion; the rest remains merely suggestive. Far from being a futile exercise, however, our review has made it abundantly clear that Lehi's writings and teachings deeply impressed his sons Nephi and Jacob, a fact which allows us to assess with increased accuracy the positive influences of Lehi, the man and the prophet.

This article, now revised, originally appeared as "Lehi's Personal Record: Quest for a Missing Source," BYU STUDIES 24, no. 1 (winter 1984): 9–42.

NOTES

1. These included, for instance, the books of Moses and Jeremiah's prophecies (1 Ne. 5:11–14; Alma 18:36).

2. See, for example, W of M 1:3–11; Morm. 4:23; 6:6.

3. Ether 4:1–7; 5:1; see also 2 Ne. 27:6–10.

4. In an article entitled "Nephi's Outline," *BYU Studies* 20, no. 2 (winter 1980): 131–49, Noel B. Reynolds argues that a literary framework undergirding the first book of Nephi takes the form of a chiastic balancing of themes throughout. While it may be possible that Nephi indeed succeeded in doing what Reynolds says he did, I believe it possible to demonstrate (a) that Nephi utilized Lehi's record as the basis for his own, and (b) that Nephi included a brief outline—a virtual "table of contents"—of his historical narrative in 1 Ne. 19:16.

5. About five hundred years after Lehi left Jerusalem, during a transfer of sacred records from king Mosiah to Alma, Mosiah charged Alma to "keep a record of the people, handing them down . . . even as they had been handed down from the time that Lehi left Jerusalem" (Mosiah 28:20), revealing a tie between the tradition of keeping records and the name of Lehi.

6. As with any study of literary sources, difficulties persist. The major problem is how to distinguish written reports from oral communications, an issue not easily solved in every instance affecting Lehi. On the one hand, we can be certain that Nephi and Jacob appealed to a written source (a) when they say they have done so and (b) when they quote their father at some length, cases which clearly point to an extant document. On the other hand, we may in fact be dealing with oral reports when a written source is neither mentioned nor apparently quoted extensively. While bearing this in mind, I shall deal with the Lehi materials as if they were largely derived from his written record unless reasons exist for understanding them otherwise.

7. As observed in 1 Ne. 1:16, Lehi's record apparently did not include much, if anything, from Lehi's brief ministry in Jerusalem (see 1:18–20). Concerning prophecies, as Nephi details them, Lehi's writings contained primarily those which were directed to his family, "his children."

8. The relationship between (a) the large plates of Nephi, (b) the book of Lehi which was translated by Joseph Smith and then lost (see the first edition of the Book of Mormon published by E. B. Grandin of Palmyra, N.Y., 1830, p. 1),

e remainder of the Book of Mormon has been graphically worked recently by Grant R. Hardy and Robert E. Parsons, "Book of Plates and Records," in *Encyclopedia of Mormonism*, ed. Daniel H. ew York: Macmillan, 1992), 195–201. The book of Lehi, translated Smith, consisted of an abridgment by Mormon of the record begun by Lehi's son Nephi (ca. 590 B.C.) and continued by succeeding scribes virtually down to the era of king Mosiah (ca. 130 B.C.). Aside from employing his name honorifically, this work apparently was not written in any part by Lehi and thus does not come within the purview of this study.

9. See 1 Ne. 19:1–2. Discussions appear in George Reynolds and Janne M. Sjodahl, *Commentary on the Book of Mormon*, 4th ed. (Salt Lake City: Deseret News Press, 1962), 1:194; Sidney B. Sperry, *Book of Mormon Compendium* (Salt Lake City: Bookcraft, 1968), 16, 43, 282; and Eldin Ricks, *Book of Mormon Commentary*, 2d ed. (Salt Lake City: Deseret News, 1953), 226.

10. Others have also noticed that Nephi employed Lehi's written account when compiling his own. For instance, Sidney B. Sperry suggests that the nine opening chapters of 1 Nephi were based upon Lehi's record, Nephi's personal work beginning only with chapter 10 (*Compendium*, 94). Although the commentary compiled from the work of George Reynolds and Janne M. Sjodahl expresses a similar view regarding the early chapters of 1 Nephi, it indicates that the division between the works of Lehi and Nephi occurs at the end of chapter 8 rather than chapter 9 (*Commentary*, 1:10; it may be important to note that Reynolds and Sjodahl did not collaborate to produce this commentary). In a discussion of the early segments of the Book of Mormon, Eldin Ricks basically adopts the position of Reynolds and Sjodahl (*Commentary*, 110). A close inspection of these and later chapters, however, indicates that these suggestions must be modified considerably since (a) Nephi includes important material in his opening chapters about himself and (b) both he and Jacob quote and paraphrase their father's words in later chapters.

11. Lehi's death is recorded in 2 Ne. 4:12, just before Nephi wrote that the Lord directed him to make the second, smaller set of plates (5:30).

12. There remains the question why the "table of contents" for the large plates (1 Ne. 19:1) seems to correspond so accurately to the content of 1 Nephi and 2 Nephi 1–3, which derive from the small plates. It is clear thus far that Lehi's record underpins both works of Nephi. If only because Lehi's record is reported to underlie both accounts (1 Ne. 19:1; 2 Ne. 5:29–33), the "table of contents" for the large plates would, in my view, approximate the content of the small plates. Furthermore, since 1 Ne. 19:1 describes so plainly what we find in 1 Nephi and 2 Nephi 1–3, it seems thoroughly safe to maintain that the two records of Nephi roughly paralleled one another (see again 1 Ne. 1:16–17).

13. Jeremiah, for example, opens his book by mentioning the kings whose reigns his ministry spanned (Jer. 1:2–3) just before the account of his call

(1:4–10). Similar juxtapositions occur in Isa. 6:1; Ezek. 1:1; Zeph. 1:1; and Zech. 1:1.

14. In fact, Lehi's call consisted of two visions which came in rapid succession. In the first, he had a surprising manifestation of a pillar of fire resting on a nearby rock, accompanied by a voice (1 Ne. 1:6). In the second, after returning home bewildered and fatigued by his first vision, Lehi saw the divine council as well as the coming Messiah, who brought him a book containing a prophecy of Jerusalem's fate (1:8–15).

15. In addition, Nephi probably altered the opening account of Lehi's visions from first to third person. Nephi's narrative exhibits clear evidences of summarizing his father's report in at least two passages: (a) after a direct quotation in verse 13a, Nephi outlines in verses 13b and 14a what his father had seen in the second vision; (b) verse 15 also forms a summary of what Lehi said (and sang) in response to his visions.

16. It may be argued that Nephi made the plates while still traveling in the Arabian wilderness, before coming to the ocean. In my opinion, however, the phrase "and it came to pass," found at the beginning of 1 Ne. 19:1, indicates that these events followed those recounted in chapter 18, since this expression in Hebrew serves to continue the story. Had Nephi smelted and fashioned this set of plates while still in the desert, he would doubtlessly have said so.

17. 1 Ne. 16:11–19, 33; 17:1–6. Sandwiched between these "we" passages are the accounts of how Nephi was able to find food after breaking his bow (16:20–32) and of what occurred when Nephi's father-in-law, Ishmael, died (16:34–39), incidents constituting digressions in the travel narrative.

18. The question naturally arises as to why I view the itinerary as the work of Lehi, not of Nephi. The matter cannot be decisively settled, for it remains possible that Nephi himself was largely responsible for the chronicle of "our journeyings in the wilderness" (1 Ne. 19:1). However, a review of the possibilities suggests that Lehi was responsible for the desert itinerary. These are the options: (a) Lehi himself wrote the whole record (in this instance, the question would be solved); (b) Lehi dictated the record to a member of his family who served as scribe (in this case as well, the record would be ascribed to Lehi); (c) Lehi directed Nephi or another family member to keep a desert diary (in this event, it is most probable that the record would reflect the name of the person who commissioned the work, that is, Lehi); (d) Nephi, with permission of and input from his father, wrote the wilderness record (to my mind, there is serious question whether the account would have been ascribed to Nephi even in this instance, since it was a record of the desert wanderings of the family of Lehi, he being the patriarch); and (e) Nephi kept a diary in the desert without the knowledge of Lehi (a highly dubious proposition).

19. Nephi mentions only three other brothers when Lehi moved his family into the desert (1 Ne. 2:5). Later, in 2 Ne. 2:1, Lehi calls Jacob his firstborn "in

the wilderness," clarifying that Jacob was born after the departure from Jerusalem.

20. The use of impermanent writing materials for certain purposes seems to have continued in Nephite society because some 450 years later king Mosiah hypothetically describes the actions of a wicked king who "*teareth up* the laws of . . . righteousness" (Mosiah 29:22, emphasis added). In addition, the observation that a name can be "blotted out" (5:11) may point to a use of ink, besides engraving tools for metals.

21. Whether Nephi or Lehi would have mentioned engraving tools, even if Nephi had brought them back from Jerusalem along with the brass plates, is certainly open to question. As illustration, the sword of Laban is not mentioned with the annotated list of the content of the brass plates (1 Ne. 5:11–16)—even though Nephi brought it. Rather, it is noted in contexts widely removed from concerns for records and record keeping (2 Ne. 5:14; Jacob 1:10). It is also possible, though unlikely, that one of Lehi's family may have acquired engraving tools along the way.

22. The problem for Nephi was not how to refine ore but where he should go to find it (1 Ne. 17:9–10). An intriguing though unprovable suggestion is that if Lehi's family traveled through the Aqaba region (at the northern tip of the east arm of the Red Sea), where ore has been refined for millennia, Nephi may have learned his smelting skills there. See Lynn M. and Hope Hilton, *In Search of Lehi's Trail* (Salt Lake City: Deseret Book, 1976), 107, 110.

23. Ricks (*Commentary*, 227) suggests that "Nephi copied his father's record in its entirety from manuscript or scroll form to the durability of metal sheets." But he does not adduce any evidence.

24. It would be interesting to compare Lehi's last words to his family with the multiplying testamental literature which claims to record, in rather standardized ways, the last instructions of ancient patriarchs and prophets to their children. For recent studies on Lehi's last instructions, see Monte S. Nyman and Charles D. Tate Jr., eds., *The Book of Mormon: Second Nephi, The Doctrinal Structure* (Provo, Utah: Religious Studies Center, Brigham Young University, 1989).

25. Sperry (*Compendium*, 151–52) observes that "we are told neither how old Lehi was at the time of his death nor how many years had elapsed from the time the party had left Jerusalem before he passed away. This we do know—that less than thirty years had passed away after the Nephites left Jerusalem before his death" (see 2 Ne. 5:28).

26. In 1 Ne. 2:9–10, Nephi relates that "when my father saw that the waters of the river emptied into the fountain of the Red Sea, he spake unto Laman, saying: O that thou mightest be like unto this river, continually running into the fountain of all righteousness! And he also spake unto Lemuel: O that thou mightest be like unto this valley, firm and steadfast, and immovable in keeping the commandments of the Lord!" Hugh W. Nibley, in *An Approach*

to the Book of Mormon, 3d ed. (Salt Lake City: Deseret Book and F.A.R.M.S., 1988), 268, maintains that "Nephi seems to have been standing by, for he takes most careful note of the circumstance. . . . The common practice was for the inspired words of the leader to be taken down in writing immediately."

27. On this occasion, in Jacob's discussion of pride, the other major topic (Jacob 2:13–22), it does not once appear that he quotes directly what the Lord told him the night before (2:11). Instead, he paraphrases the Lord's words and intermingles his own observations with them. Only in verses 23–33 does he repeat directly the Lord's words, those pertaining to having one wife.

28. See Stanley R. Larson, "A Study of Some Textual Variations in the Book of Mormon Comparing the Original and Printer's Manuscripts and the 1830, the 1837, and the 1840 Editions" (master's thesis, Brigham Young University, 1974), 95–96. The Printer's Manuscript of the Book of Mormon was copied by Oliver Cowdery from the one originally dictated by Joseph Smith. The copy made by Oliver Cowdery was taken to the printer, E. B. Grandin, and became the basis for the first printed edition of the Book of Mormon. The Original Manuscript, written at Joseph Smith's dictation, is no longer extant for the passage in question (Jacob 3:5).

29. They consist of an extract that Lehi read from the book brought to him in the second vision of his call (1 Ne. 1:13), his exclamation at having read this book (1:14b), words of the Lord spoken to Lehi in a dream (2:1b), Lehi's remark to his son Laman (2:9b) and the following comment to his son Lemuel (2:10b), his instructions to Nephi to return to Jerusalem for the brass plates (3:2b–6), Sariah's complaint against her husband Lehi (5:2b) and his conciliatory conversation with her (5:4b–5), a further extract from Lehi's vision of the tree of life (8:34), and what the Messiah's forerunner would say about the Messiah (10:8).

30. 1 Ne. 2:1a, 2–9a, 10a, and 14–15 all speak directly of Lehi.

31. 1 Ne. 2:1b, 9b, 10b.

32. This is the third time Nephi mentions that his father "dwelt in a tent." The earlier occurrences are in 1 Ne. 2:15; 9:1. One is tempted to suggest that since these three instances all mark conclusions to sections wherein Nephi has summarized Lehi's record, Nephi may be using the phrase "dwelt in a tent" as a literary device to indicate a return to the narrative about himself. In support of this observation, I note that Nephi speaks of his father's tent twice more in 1 Nephi, the second instance underscoring my point. In the first case, Nephi merely relates that he returned there after his own vision of the tree of life (15:1). But in the second instance, Nephi's mention of the tent forms part of a clear literary transition between two segments of his narrative (16:6). Compare Ps. 78:55, 60; also compare Mitchell Dahood, *Psalms III*, Anchor Bible 17A (Garden City, N.Y.: Doubleday, 1970), 445.

33. It may well be that the "table of contents" of the brass plates (1 Ne. 5:11–16) also derives from Lehi's work.

34. In 1 Nephi 15, we find several references to Lehi's dream as Nephi relates how he interpreted it for his brothers (see 15:12–18, 21, 23, 26–30).

35. The commands to Lehi to move his camp may have derived from the itinerary (see 1 Ne. 2:2; 16:9; 17:44; 18:5).

36. The number of allusions to what Lehi did and said are too many to list and discuss. In most, it is impossible to determine whether we are dealing with matters from Lehi's annals. Many such references doubtless came from the memories of Nephi and Jacob.

37. The prophecy of Joseph came from the brass plates (2 Ne. 4:2). Lehi knew of other prophecies by Joseph since he speaks of "the prophecies which he [Joseph] wrote."

38. This allegory is quoted at length in Jacob 5. For studies on this important chapter, see Stephen D. Ricks and John W. Welch, eds., *The Allegory of the Olive Tree* (Salt Lake City: Deseret Book and F.A.R.M.S., 1994); Kent P. Jackson, "Nourished by the Good Word of God," in *Studies in Scripture, Vol. 7: 1 Nephi to Alma 29*, ed. Kent P. Jackson (Salt Lake City: Deseret Book, 1987), 185–95; and L. Gary Lambert, "Allegory of Zenos," in *Encyclopedia of Mormonism*, ed. Daniel H. Ludlow (New York: Macmillan, 1992), 31–32.

39. A similar point is made in 1 Ne. 15:12 as Nephi attempts to explain what Lehi meant. His brothers had not understood Lehi's comparison of themselves with the olive tree (10:12–14). So Nephi declares to them "that the house of Israel was compared unto an olive-tree, by the Spirit of the Lord which was in our father; and behold are we not broken off from the house of Israel, and are we not a branch of the house of Israel?" This is the reading of 1 Ne. 15:12 in the original manuscript, after adding punctuation. Beginning with the printer's manuscript and continuing through the printed editions of the Book of Mormon, an *s* had been added to the word *father*. The reading of the original manuscript clarifies that it was Lehi who was moved by the Spirit to apply the olive tree comparison to his family and posterity, and this sense is recognized in the 1981 edition of the Book of Mormon, where the singular spelling has been restored (see Larson, "Some Textual Variations," 59).

40. On the family learning of the fulfillment of this prophecy, refer to 2 Ne. 1:4 and 6:8.

41. The titles *Christ* (Greek) and *Messiah* (Hebrew) mean the same thing: "anointed." It is possible, of course, that Joseph Smith—while translating—used the title *Christ* in contexts which dealt with the word *Messiah*, but see notes 43 and 44.

42. The terms by which Lehi designates the Messiah are *Lamb of God* (1 Ne. 10:10); *Holy One of Israel* (2 Ne. 1:10; 3:2); *God* (2 Ne. 1:10, 22, 24, 26–27; 2:2–3,

10); *Lord God* (2 Ne. 1:17); *Holy Messiah* (2 Ne. 2:6, 8); *Messiah* (1 Ne. 1:19; 10:4–5, 7, 9–11, 14, 17; 2 Ne. 1:10; 2:26; 3:5); *Lord* (1 Ne. 10:8, 14; 2 Ne. 1:15, 19, 27); *Prophet* (1 Ne. 10:4); *Savior* (1 Ne. 10:4); *Redeemer* (1 Ne. 10:5–6, 14; 2 Ne. 1:10; 2:3); *One* (1 Ne. 1:9); *first fruits* (2 Ne. 2:9); *Holy One* (2 Ne. 2:10); *Mediator* (2 Ne. 2:28).

43. Nephi and Jacob use several titles which apparently go beyond what they could have found in the brass plates, assuming the brass plates included the full Pentateuch and many of the prophets' writings (see 1 Ne. 5:11–13; 19:21–23). 1 Ne. 19:23 presents an interesting problem. In all the printed editions, except the most recent, we find the reference "the book of Moses." The Original Manuscript has it "the books of Moses." When Oliver Cowdery copied down the manuscript for the printer, he accidentally made *books* singular. This misreading persisted until the edition of 1981 (see Larson, "Some Textual Variations," 67–68). The following titles and names used by Nephi seem more at home in a later era such as that of the New Testament or early Christianity: *Beloved Son* (2 Ne. 31:11); *Beloved* (2 Ne. 31:15); *Son of the living God* (2 Ne. 31:16); *Son of righteousness* (2 Ne. 26:9 [should this be *Sun of righteousness? Sun* is the word used in Mal. 4:2]); *Son of the most high God* (1 Ne. 11:6); *Son of God* (1 Ne. 10:17; 11:7, 24; 2 Ne. 25:16, 19); *Only Begotten of the Father* (2 Ne. 25:12); *Jesus* (2 Ne. 26:12; 31:10; 33:4, 6); *Jesus Christ* (2 Ne. 25:19–20; 30:5); *Christ* (2 Ne. 11:4, 6–7; 25:16, 23–29; 26:1, 8, 12; 28:14; 30:7; 31:2, 13, 19–21; 32:3, 6, 9; 33:7, 9–12); *true vine* (1 Ne. 15:15); *light* (1 Ne. 17:13). The following names from Jacob fit the same situation: *Only Begotten Son* (Jacob 4:11); *Christ* (2 Ne. 10:3, 7; Jacob 1:4, 6–8; 2:19; 4:4–5, 11–12; 6:8–9; 7:2–3, 6, 9, 11, 14, 17, 19); *Jesus* (Jacob 4:6).

44. In 1 Ne. 19:10–17, Nephi summarizes points from the writings of Zenock, Neum, and particularly Zenos. In verse 21 of that chapter he indicates that these teachings were on the brass plates (see also Alma 33:12).

45. It may be urged that in the Book of Mormon we have mere hints and glimpses from the writings of Zenock and Zenos and that, consequently, it is not possible to draw very firm conclusions. In my view, however, Alma brought together the passages from the writings of these two men which proved a point about the Son of God (Alma 33:11, 13, 16). Zenos and Zenock called the Messiah *Son* whereas Alma called him *Son of God* (33:14, 17, 18, 22). Had Alma known of a passage in which either Zenock or Zenos mentioned the *Son of God,* he surely would have cited it to make his point to the Zoramites.

46. The first to adopt such a title was Nephi in his narration of how he had sought to receive the vision which his father had seen of both the tree of life and the Messiah (1 Ne. 10:17). Curiously, as soon as Nephi inscribes the title *Son of God,* he adds the parenthetical explanation, "And the Son of God was the Messiah who should come." When did Nephi initially learn this title, especially since Lehi apparently did not use it? The only clear hint occurs at the beginning of his own parallel vision of the tree of life which he begins narrating a few lines later, starting in chapter 11. On that occasion, he was

told by the Spirit that after he had seen "a man descending out of heaven," he was to "bear record that it is the Son of God" (11:7). In Nephi's account on the small plates, this is the first recorded notice of Nephi's having heard the title *Son of God* (he had apparently learned from the Spirit the expanded form—*Son of the most high God*—just before this [11:6]). It might be argued that Nephi knew such titles but had not utilized them in 1 Nephi until now. Against this, I should point out that thus far, when speaking of the Messiah, Nephi had consistently employed the language of his father. Then in 1 Ne. 10:17, when he introduces the term *Son of God,* he even adds a note of explanation. Since evidently the first person ever to mention that title to Nephi was the Spirit in the vision (11:6–7), we are left to presume that before this experience Nephi did not know the term.

47. The term *dream* is clearly to be understood in the inspired sense. Of the seven dreams and visions of Lehi, three are called dreams (1 Ne. 2:1–2; 3:2; 8:2). In the final instance, Lehi himself equates dream with vision: "Behold, I have dreamed a dream; or, in other words, I have seen a vision" (8:2).

48. Nephi's employment of the phrase "saw and heard" (1 Ne. 1:19) may be intended to recall what Lehi "saw and heard" in the very first vision (written twice in 1:6). If so, it becomes very likely that Lehi had learned about the coming Messiah in this first experience. It is impossible, however, to recover exactly how much was revealed to him concerning the Messiah on this occasion, since Nephi does not elaborate.

49. This type of vision forms the standard motif of the prophet or seer being introduced into the council of the Lord. Isaiah, for example, experienced this when he received his call (Isa. 6:1, 8; see also Jer. 23:18, 22; Rev. 4:2–4).

50. In 1 Ne. 1:4 we read that "many prophets" had come to Jerusalem "prophesying unto the people that they must repent, or the great city Jerusalem must be destroyed." Among those prophets would have been Jeremiah, who had already been saying this for twenty-five years, and Habakkuk, who was prophesying and writing between 608 and 598 B.C. See also Zephaniah 1.

51. One item has to do with the condition of the stream of water, which Lehi had overlooked when he saw the vision. It was Nephi who, after recounting his experience with the corroborating vision, adds this curious note: "The water which my father saw was filthiness; and so much was his mind swallowed up in other things that he beheld not the filthiness of the water" (1 Ne. 15:27). When one examines Lehi's narration, what Nephi says proves true. Lehi describes the water simply as "a river of water" (8:13), not indicating whether it appeared muddy or clear. In contrast, Nephi is very explicit about its appearance, calling it "the fountain of filthy water . . . and the depths thereof are the depths of hell" (12:16).

52. Incidentally, Nephi explains that "from time to time" writing would appear on the compass to give directions to Lehi's family while still in the desert (1 Ne. 16:29).

53. In regard to the Urim and Thummim in Old Testament usage, see Ex. 28:30; Lev. 8:8; Num. 27:21; Deut. 33:8; 1 Sam. 28:6; Ezra 2:63; and Neh. 7:65. See also Paul Y. Hoskisson, "Urim and Thummim," in *Encyclopedia of Mormonism*, 1499–1500.

54. Nahum saw a similar vision of Nineveh under siege and finally falling (Nahum 2:1–3:3, 10–15).

55. The revelation may have concerned people at Jerusalem or it may have concerned Lehi's extended family. If the latter, Benjamin's assertion that members of the traveling party "were unfaithful" takes on a more focused meaning (Mosiah 1:17).

56. These three major elements of Lehi's instruction—fidelity to spouse, opposition as an essential ingredient of existence, and the Adam–Redeemer relationship in the plan of salvation—are supplemented by other less-emphasized themes which, when noted, exhibit a rich variety: Lehi's teachings on the tree of life (1 Ne. 8:2–35), the fall of Jerusalem (e.g., 1 Ne. 1:13, 19), the coming of the Messiah (e.g., 1 Ne. 1:19b; 10:4–11; 2 Ne. 2:6–9), the scattering and gathering of Israel (e.g., 1 Ne. 9:3; 10:3, 12–14), and the important ministry of the seer of the latter days who is to take God's message to Lehi's descendants (2 Ne. 3:6–21).

4

Sojourn, Dwell, and Stay: Terms of Servitude

Two accounts employ terms whose Hebrew roots point to service relationships. The first consists of the desert crossing of Lehi's party, hinting that its members were obliged to sell themselves for protection or for food. The second, the service of Ammon in King Lamoni's court, also uses expressions of servitude when describing the interaction of these two princes. Notably, such terms adhere to established biblical custom.

The terms *to sojourn, to dwell,* and *to stay* often describe servile relationships in the Bible,[1] a feature mirrored in the Book of Mormon. The scene that makes the case for the verb *to sojourn* is that of Lehi's trip through the Arabian desert. For the expressions *to dwell* and *to stay,* the account of the service of Ammon, son of Mosiah, to the Lamanite king Lamoni illustrates servility most clearly. Naturally, to proceed with a study of this sort, one has to assume—correctly, in my view—that the English text of the Book of Mormon represents an accurate translation which in turn can serve as the basis for studies of terms, whether individual words or phrases. According to Moroni, the last Nephite writer, the language of discourse and therefore of the text was an "altered" Hebrew (Morm. 9:33). Hence, the proper window to gaze through is that of ancient Hebrew.

Nephi's claim that his family sojourned for "eight years" in the desert of Arabia (1 Ne. 17:4) predictably brings a reader face to face with the possibility, even likelihood, that family members had to come under the domination of desert tribesmen either for protection or for food.[2] How so? Before taking up this issue, we should explore the ties between servanthood and the terms *to sojourn, to dwell,* and *to stay.*

In English, of course, we perceive connections between the expressions *to sojourn, to dwell,* and *to stay,* for they all mean something like *to sit* or *to reside.* It is ancient Hebrew that illuminates the threads which securely link these English terms in the Bible to one another. At base, all of these verbs in Hebrew, and their derivative nouns, are related to the notion of sitting. The verb *yšb*—whose chief meanings are *to sit, to dwell,* and *to stay*—is the root of the noun *tôšāb,* which signifies "resident alien" or "sojourner." The other Hebrew term for "sojourner" or "alien," *gēr,* often connotes the same sense of living as a subject. Hence, whether one lives as a stranger in a foreign society or dwells as a subject, either "resident alien, hireling, slave or inferior wife," the verb *yšb,* whose meanings stem "from legal institutions," often describes a person's legal status.[3]

On the broader stage, the set of issues before us plucks at strings which tie the Book of Mormon to the world of the Bible and, beyond it, to the ancient Near East. While we possess mostly fragmentary bits of information, occasionally a piece draws us inside the world of the Book of Mormon to an unusual depth, guiding a beam of light onto one more cord that stretches between the Book of Mormon and the biblical world. Simply stated, there is more than meets the eye.

"We Did Sojourn"

Only two references to sojourning appear in the Book of Mormon, both in a part of Nephi's record that must go back to the account of his father Lehi.[4] Writing in the style of a diary-like travel narrative that is framed on a series of "we" passages (1 Ne. 16:11–19, 33; 17:1–6), Nephi recorded that turning "nearly eastward" into the desert, "we did again take our journey in the wilderness; and we did . . . wade through much affliction. . . . [God] did provide means for us while we did *sojourn* in the wilderness. And we did *sojourn* for the space of . . . eight years in the wilderness" (17:1, 3–4, emphasis added).[5] In my view, Nephi's use of the verb *to sojourn* points to one or more periods of servility. Scattered clues hint that family members lived in a dependent or servile relationship to desert peoples—whom they could not avoid[6]—suffering difficulty and conflict.[7]

We notice that the verbal phrase "did sojourn" appears in Nephi's restrained retelling of the extended trip deep into the southern Arabian desert, through an environment whose harsh character has become well known to the West only relatively recently.[8] Moreover, one observes that the expression *to sojourn* often means "to live as a resident alien" in territory where one owns no property and has no family roots. Further, "in not a few passages throughout the Old Testament the verb definitely has the connotation 'to live as a subject'—be it as resident alien, hireling, slave or inferior wife."[9]

In this light, the question naturally follows whether Nephi's parents and siblings, traveling as resident aliens, experienced subjugation to, or dependence on, desert dwellers. As far as I am aware, no one has suggested such a possibility.[10] Instead, interpreters have focused only on what Nephi recorded in his typically understated way about the severe difficulties encountered by the family.[11] Commentators have left matters vague because the language of Nephi's account is vague and clipped.

Nephi wrote about the desert crossing in a tight summary fashion, stressing the dependence of the family on the Lord for well-being.[12] Not surprisingly, it is the complaint of Laman and Lemuel, which Nephi allows to stand in his record, that may unveil the first piece of evidence concerning their experience in the desert. At the end of the trip, Laman and Lemuel bemoaned that "our women have toiled, . . . and suffered all things" so terribly that "it would have been better that they had died" (1 Ne. 17:20).[13] Does the grievance "our women have toiled" possibly refer to the labor of subjects dependent on people in the desert? By holding up this piece alone we cannot be certain. But any answer must embrace this prospect, however tentative. Again the complaint of the brothers: "These many years *we* have suffered" (17:21, emphasis added). What had occurred? This misery was so deep that others also wrote of it.[14]

The first to refer backward to this period was Lehi. When he blessed his younger sons Jacob and Joseph, he called the years of his family's sojourn in the wilderness not merely "the days of my tribulation" (2 Ne. 2:1) but "the wilderness of mine afflictions" and "the days of my greatest sorrow" (3:1). For Lehi, it was the worst of times.[15] How so? Evidently Lehi was well equipped for desert living, and thus long before he and his family fled Jerusalem he must have known the rigors that one encounters in such a clime.[16] If Lehi, then, was apparently equipped and experienced, there must have been an event—or series of events—which had soured him so that he termed the desert trek "the days of my greatest sorrow" (3:1). What had happened to cause Lehi to speak thus? For rays of illumination, we turn to Alma the Younger.

In a telling passage, Alma rehearsed for his son Helaman the kindnesses of God to the founding generation—Lehi and his family—by recalling that "[God] has also brought our fathers out of the land of Jerusalem; and he has also . . . delivered them out of bondage and captivity" (Alma 36:29). The quotation points plainly to at least one divinely assisted deliverance from "bondage and captivity" suffered by the family of Lehi and Sariah.

In an earlier address to people in Ammonihah, making reference to past events known to himself and his audience, Alma recounted that "our father, Lehi, was brought out of Jerusalem by the hand of God. . . . And have ye forgotten so soon how many times he delivered our fathers[17] out of the hands of their enemies, and preserved them from being destroyed?" (9:9–10). In this same address, Alma also recalled that these very ancestors had been led "out of the land of Jerusalem, . . . having been saved from famine, and from sickness, and all manner of diseases, . . . they having waxed strong in battle, that they might not be destroyed" (9:22). In these two passages, the references to physical difficulties such as "sickness" and "diseases,"[18] as well as to "enemies" and to "battle," point to the expected hardships found in a harsh desert environment, and perhaps more, considering their lack of food, water, and fuel, and the presence of unfriendly tribesmen.

Another detail points in the same direction. The eight-year duration of the wilderness experience suggests that besides the time at the first camp (1 Ne. 2:6–16:12), the family must have spent a considerable period in at least one location, possibly at an oasis or an area of pasture land, dependent on the household of a desert tribesman. The period is far too long even for a cautious crossing of the Arabian desert. As an example, the time required in antiquity for a loaded caravan of several hundred camels to travel from the coast of the Indian Ocean to the Mediterranean Sea—approximately the assumed route traveled by Lehi and his family, though in reverse—was a matter of weeks, not years.[19]

One further consideration is both relevant and illuminating. It concerns the principle that the Lord orchestrates experiences for prophets so that they come to see matters as the Lord sees them, thus adding intensity and acuity to their messages. Abraham Heschel noted this aspect of prophetic experience, selecting the marriage of Hosea as proof.[20] In this light, we turn to Lehi's prophetic messages *after* he had emerged from the desert.

As he speaks to his children and grandchildren just before his death, Lehi lifts to view the clashing concepts of captivity and rejuvenating freedom. For instance, in language that recalls slavery, he pleads with his sons that they "shake off the awful chains" by which they "are carried away captive," being "led according to the . . . captivity of the devil" with no control over their own destinies (2 Ne. 1:13, 18). He then urges them to "shake off the chains . . . and arise from the dust" (1:23).[21] As a second example, Lehi's whole concern with "redemption . . . through the Holy Messiah" borrows language from the freeing of slaves (2:6). Thus, he declares that the Messiah is to "redeem the children of men," making them "free forever," terminology associated with ending servility (2:26).[22] One naturally asks, does not the force of these concepts arise partially from the experiences shared with his children? In light of what we have been able so far to determine, the answer has to be yes.[23]

In sum, it seems reasonable that the years spent by Lehi and his family in crossing the desert were characterized by the not uncommon practice "in times of scarcity" of "the bargaining away of freedom—or part of it—in return for food."[24] Whether the "enemies" (Alma 9:10), the escape from destruction "in battle" (9:22), and the "bondage and captivity" (36:29) had to do with a single experience with desert dwellers is impossible to determine. Whatever the case, Nephi's choice of the term *to sojourn*—commonly denoting servanthood in the Old Testament—when combined with Lehi's touching remarks and the brothers' bitter complaints about the heavy labor of their wives, likely points to a period of servility and conflict during the desert journey.[25]

"I Desire to Dwell among This People"

The verb translated *to dwell* in the Book of Mormon, as in the Old Testament, occasionally means to reside in a domicile. For example, Nephi said of his father that he "dwelt in a tent" in the desert (1 Ne. 2:15).[26] Similarly, though on a celestial plane, "the heavens is a place where God dwells" (Alma 18:30). But more to our point, the term *to dwell* can also carry the connotation of living in a condition of dependency, even subjugation or slavery, consistent with Old Testament usage. In this latter sense, one "dwells" in the house of another, under circumstances that one does not fully control, and effort is required—legal or otherwise—to bring the person out free, as God did for the enslaved Israelites.[27]

The most interesting case in the Book of Mormon consists of the introductory meeting between the Nephite prince Ammon and the Lamanite regent-king Lamoni (Alma 17:21–25). Of course, other occurrences of the verb *to dwell* set out some of the legal and social dimensions of this term.[28] But it is the story of Ammon and Lamoni that catches our attention. The key passage reads: "And the king inquired of Ammon if it were his desire *to dwell* in the land among the Lamanites, or among his people. And Ammon said unto him: Yea, I desire *to dwell* among this people for a time; yea, and perhaps until the day I die. And it came to pass that king Lamoni was much pleased with Ammon, . . . and he would that Ammon should take one of his daughters to wife. But Ammon said unto him: Nay, but I will be thy servant" (17:22–25, emphasis added).

Before attempting to elucidate this passage, we should set out the Mosaic law that governs the relationship between Israelite masters and servants. According to the so-called Covenant Code, which follows directly after the Ten Commandments,[29] the following regulation governs an Israelite overlord: "If thou buy an Hebrew servant, six years he shall serve: and in the seventh he shall go out free for nothing. If he came in by himself, he shall go out by himself: if he were married, then his wife shall go out with him. . . . And if the servant shall plainly say, . . . I will not go out free: Then his master . . . shall bore his ear through with an aul; and he shall serve him for ever" (Ex. 21:2–3, 5–6). This law is repeated in the Deuteronomic code, which adjusts and adds the following significant instructions for the master: "And when thou sendest him out free from thee, thou shalt not let him go away empty: Thou shalt furnish him liberally out of thy flock, and out of thy floor, and out of thy winepress. . . . And thou shalt remember that thou wast a bondman in the land of Egypt, and the Lord thy God redeemed thee" (Deut. 15:13–15). This restatement in Deuteronomy appends two important elements. First, a master is not to dismiss a servant without presenting gifts to the latter. Second, the stated reason for offering gifts to a departing servant goes back to the exodus from Egypt wherein the Israelite slaves received the divine gift of redemption, in addition to taking gifts—willingly offered—from the Egyptians.[30]

Now to the story. To begin, two important features emerge. First, Ammon's quoted words reflect the dual time element spelled out in the Covenant Code for one Israelite serving another: for a limited time, to a maximum of six years ("for a time," Ammon said), and for one's life ("until the day I die"). Second, Ammon's response to Lamoni's offer of marriage to his daughter properly interprets the negotiation and tells us how the conversation between them was understood: "I will be thy servant."[31] Thus, their conversation had to do with Ammon's social and legal status in Lamoni's kingdom, a status that potentially bore not only liabilities but also benefits because Ammon was a Nephite prince, one of four sons of king Mosiah.[32] Hence, a marriage between a Lamanite princess and a Nephite of similar rank could have been a political coup of sorts for both the Nephite and, under the circumstance, especially the Lamanite royal families. But the issues went well beyond the obvious political dimensions. In fact, as Ammon specifically articulated, they involved the status and treatment of a servant.[33]

Ammon had traveled by himself into the land of Ishmael, Lamoni's domain. He was captured and brought before the king to determine his fate, whether "to slay [him], or to retain [him] in captivity, or to cast [him] into prison, or to cast [him] out of [the king's] land" (Alma 17:20; see also 19, 21).[34] At some early point, evidently the king learned Ammon's royal identity. Then initiating the conversation, as he should, the king asked Ammon whether he wished "*to dwell* in the land among the Lamanites."[35] As is manifest from the direction that the discussion finally took, Ammon understood Lamoni's question—about dwelling among the Lamanites—to mean doing so in a relationship of dependency.

Not surprisingly, the legal right of the king to set the status of an encroacher seems to be one of the points of Alma 17:20. Lamanite "custom" left it "to the pleasure of the king [whether] to slay [Nephite intruders], or to retain them in captivity, or to cast them into prison, or to cast them out of his land." Because the text differentiates between "captivity" and "prison," the former term likely refers to a servile condition, possibly tied only to the royal house. If so, this Lamanite "custom" illumines the negotiation between Ammon and the king.

Whether one thinks that Ammon, in light of his royal station, should or should not have accepted the king's offer "to dwell" in the land as a dependent vassal, he did. Significantly, his acceptance conformed to that of an Israelite who seeks to become a servant in the house of an Israelite master, indicating that he wanted "to dwell" there "for a time; yea, and perhaps until the day I die." After all, Ammon was probably out of food, out of money, and certainly far away from home. Wherever he might go, he would surely be shunned because he was among Lamanites, the avowed enemies of his own people.

In his acceptance, Ammon links his decision to two important statutes of law. In raising the first, Ammon repeated the verb "dwell" that Lamoni had uttered. By so doing, he signified that he understood the general thrust of Lamoni's question and indicated that he had accepted the implicit offer of protection that a master is to guarantee to a dependent, whether servant or otherwise.[36] Second, Ammon signaled that he would reserve judgment for a later time whether to remain "until the day I die," conforming to the explicit option that according to the Covenant Code lies with the servant, not the master: "If the servant shall plainly say, I love my master, . . . I will not go out free: . . . he shall serve him for ever" (Ex. 21:5–6). As far as Lamoni was concerned, Ammon was simply keeping his options open—"perhaps"—until he could decide whether he liked his master and his situation well enough "to dwell" under his protection for the rest of his life (Alma 17:23).

Lamoni's offer of his daughter brings up at least five matters. All bear directly on Ammon's status. First, presenting the woman seems to be a natural overture to the prince when it became evident that he might stay on permanently. But the other four points brighten with interest.

The second concerns the regulation in the Deuteronomic code quoted above—that of a master supplying a departing servant with gifts. To be sure, gifts were to be bestowed at the end of the servant's employ and, what is more, they were to come from the flock, the threshing floor, and the winepress (Deut. 15:14). So what was going on with Lamoni and Ammon? On one level, as we noticed, one has to see the obvious political ingredient in the offer, a marriage between a Nephite prince and a Lamanite princess. On another level, however, one discovers an offer of a gift, a payment of sorts, that comes at the beginning of an underling's period of service. Two questions naturally arise, both pointing in one direction: Why was the gift not simply of produce or of the flock? And what was the precedent to offer a wife in exchange for service? In response, the report that comes readily to mind is that of Jacob receiving his two wives, Leah and Rachel, from their father Laban. As David Daube has pointed out, Jacob undertook "service for a reward," even though he was a member of the family and should have served "for nothing as any junior member of the family has to."[37] In the case of Ammon, he was not a member of Lamoni's family and hence his service could be performed for pay. Certainly this is the thrust of the provision in the Deuteronomic code that called for a master to furnish gifts to an outgoing servant. Further, the episode involving Lamoni appears to be the only example in the Book of Mormon text of willing conformity to this requirement.[38]

This set of considerations brings up the third point. According to the Covenant Code, if a servant "came in by himself, he shall go out by himself." Further, "if his master have given him a wife, and she have born him sons or daughters; the wife and her children shall be her master's, and he shall go out by himself" (Ex. 21:3–4). In this light, if the king were treating Ammon in accord with custom established by ancient Israelite law, as I believe he was, there was reason for Ammon to wonder whether Lamoni might keep his daughter when Ammon's period of service ended, not allowing her to leave. Certainly a falling-out between the two men could lead to this consequence. Under the terms of the Covenant Code, if a servant received a wife during his period of service to a master, the woman remained the property of the master when the servant finished his service. One must keep in mind that according to the sequence of the story, the conversation *before* Lamoni's offer of his daughter had concerned Ammon's status as a servant, not as a prince.

We now come to the fourth point: the servant was to go away happy, satisfied that the master had been generous. In this connection, the Bible required that the master "furnish [the servant] liberally" (Deut. 15:14). Stinginess on the part of the master would only lead to unhappiness on the part of the outgoing servant. It is this ingredient of the law, in fact, that is linked closely with actions of the Lord, for "to be generous to a departing slave, is not enforceable by secular authority."[39] Speaking to the Israelite master, the Lord required that "of that wherewith the Lord thy God hath blessed thee thou shalt give unto [the departing servant]" (15:14). Further, the law promised to the master, "It shall not seem hard unto thee, when thou sendest him away free from thee; . . . the Lord thy God shall bless thee" (15:18). Ultimately, it was to secure divine blessings that a person was generous in dismissing a servant with gifts in abundance.

Fifth and finally, even though he would become a servant of the king, Ammon could not appear unadorned—that is, without a suitable gift. This was because before the negotiation over his status had concluded, he was still a visiting member of a royal family. There was precedent that a visiting dignitary receive a gift from the hosting king, even though it could bring Ammon under an obligation to the throne[40] and even though he was apparently not in a position to reciprocate.[41] Importantly, this point connects closely to that of "furnishing" a servant generously, discussed just above. In Old Testament society there was a strong cultural "feeling against sending a person away 'empty.'"[42] To thus treat a prince of a neighboring, even if hostile, kingdom would constitute a colossal cultural breach.[43] In the case of Lamoni, the king offered a gift that he evidently thought would bring happiness to Ammon, as well as satisfaction to himself that he had been more than fair.

But Ammon declined. Obviously the offer from Lamoni could have elevated Ammon, raising him from one who would dwell in a dependent station to one who would dwell in regal splendor. But, in a measure, Ammon would still be dependent on the king, in this instance because of his wife. In response, Ammon concluded the negotiation by agreeing to the original offer, to "dwell" in the country as a "servant" of the king. To be sure, it was important that he keep his options open in terms of his long-term relationship with the royal house of Lamoni, as custom allowed. But Ammon carried a hidden purpose in steering the negotiation in this direction: he also wanted ultimately to bring the message of the gospel to the Lamanite people (Mosiah 28:1–9; Alma 17:9–11). The negotiation with the king also allowed him to control in a measure what might happen to himself. In the end, being a servant opened more opportunities to Ammon—as subsequent events bore out—than he might have enjoyed as a son-in-law of the king, with its attendant family ties and points whereby Ammon could be pressured. For his part, Lamoni had perhaps conceived an agenda, that of joining his kingdom politically to that of the Nephites. For this reason, instead of dismissing Ammon, or worse, Lamoni entered into the time-honored process of negotiating the status of this visitor to his kingdom, as Lamanite custom apparently allowed,[44] keeping the matter securely within accepted legal and social traditions which exhibit firm ties to the world of the Old Testament.

"Rabbanah, the King Desireth Thee to Stay"

The final term to investigate is *to stay*.[45] Let us deal first with the meanings of this term in the Book of Mormon that go beyond the connotations of residing or living in a place.[46] In at least two passages, the verb carries the sense of relying upon another person for support. One thinks, for instance, of Nephi's quotation from the book of Isaiah: "They call themselves of the holy city, but they do not *stay* themselves upon the God of Israel" (1 Ne. 20:2, emphasis added).[47] With a different slant, in one verse quoted from Isaiah, the verb signifies "to linger" or "to come to a stop": "All ye that doeth iniquity, *stay* yourselves and wonder" (2 Ne. 27:4, emphasis added).[48] In a contrasting vein, other passages employ *to stay* with the meaning "to withhold" or "to hold back." For example, in king Benjamin's speech, in an imagined disdainful retort to the pleas of impoverished people, the king hypothesized what one might say about a poor person: "The man has brought upon himself his misery; therefore I will *stay* my hand, and will not give unto him . . . of my substance" (Mosiah 4:17, emphasis added).[49]

We now turn to four cases wherein connotations of the verb *to stay* lie closer to those of *to sojourn* and *to dwell* already noted; all denote more than the sense of residing in a place. The first involved the prophet Nephi, son of Helaman, who had just returned from an extended preaching tour among inhabitants of the "land northward," having preached the "word of God" and prophesied "many things." These people had rejected "all his words, insomuch that he could not stay among them" (Hel. 7:2–3). In my view, here the verbal phrase "could not stay" means in the context that Nephi could not make spiritual headway among the people of the north because of their spiritual depravity.[50]

The second instance appears in a letter from the illegally deposed chief judge Pahoran to his military commander Moroni. In discussing defensive warfare, Pahoran wrote, "We would not shed the blood of the Lamanites if they would stay in their own land" (Alma 61:10). To my mind, "to stay in their own land" means more than simply to reside "in their own land." It carries the additional sense not to make war.[51] Thus, the rich connotations of the verb here embrace both peacefully residing in one's homeland and not going off to war.

The third and fourth examples are more interesting in a legal sense and come up in passages that deal with some sort of subjugation. One is in the book of Mosiah, in the incident wherein male subjects of a Nephite colony were encouraged by king Noah to abandon family members in the face of an invading Lamanite army. While some men fled without family members, setting up a legal snarl for those whom they had abandoned,[52] "there were many that would not leave them, but had rather *stay* and perish with them" (Mosiah 19:12, emphasis added). Although the expression is a bit awkward, the sense seems plain. By deciding to stay, the men were deciding to die at the hands of captors. As events turned out—and the narrator of course knew the result—they became "captives" and were obliged to "pay tribute to the king of the Lamanites" (19:15).[53] In the end, then, staying really meant captivity for the colonists.[54]

In the fourth case, the context brims with servility. The story again concerns the Nephite prince Ammon and the regent Lamoni. The scene follows Lamoni's offer of his daughter in marriage to Ammon and Ammon's subsequent nonacceptance, making of the latter a palace servant. Three days later, in the company of others, Ammon was taking care of the king's flocks. When Ammon and his fellow servants attempted to water the flocks, "a certain number of the Lamanites" scattered the king's flocks in order to steal them and to cause trouble for the king's servants (Alma 17:27–35; 18:7). But Ammon turned the tables on those would-be thieves, defeating them in hand-to-hand combat and bringing the flocks safely back to the king's "pasture" (17:36–39). When the king heard the news, he was struck by "the faithfulness of Ammon" (18:2, 10)—a phrase that carries servile overtones.[55] But he appeared to be most deeply impressed by the seemingly indestructible nature of Ammon, leading him to believe that Ammon was "more than a man. Behold, is not this the Great Spirit?" (18:2, 11). A short time later, when Ammon came to see the king, "he saw that the countenance of the king was changed" (18:12). In apparent deference, the Nephite prince turned to leave. But one of Lamoni's attendants said to Ammon, "Rabbanah,[56] the king desireth thee *to stay*" (18:13, emphasis added).

The attendant and the king evidently intended that Ammon remain because everyone was impressed with what he had done. For Ammon's part, even though he saw that the tables had been turned so that he was momentarily regarded as more than the king, he cleverly and appropriately—after all, it was Lamoni's palace—responded to the request as a servant. At least he answered thus. For, after trying without success to coax a response out of the king, he said in reassuring terms, "I am a man, and am *thy servant*; therefore, whatsoever thou desirest which is right,[57] that will I do" (18:17, emphasis added). Hence, the request that Ammon stay in the king's presence was understood, at least as Ammon explained it, as the request of master to servant. Thus, the use of the verb *to stay* in this context points to the servile status of Ammon, though that status was changing as Ammon spoke. This conclusion brings us back to the opening observations of this study. For in becoming a servant, he and Lamoni had negotiated as two Israelites who followed procedures whose closest parallels lie in Old Testament law and custom.

NOTES

1. David Daube sets out such inferences for the biblical text in *The Exodus Pattern in the Bible* (London: Faber and Faber, 1963), 24–26, pointing out that these terms go back to a common root. One verb (Hebrew *yšb*) has the basic sense "to sit." In the Book of Mormon, as in the Bible, the verb "to sit" and its noun derivative, "seat," usually carry a sense of sitting in a special place, often because of divine action. The other verb form (Hebrew *gwr*) frequently takes the word "stranger" as its subject (Ex. 12:48–49; Lev. 16:29; 17:8; etc.). See also John R. Spencer, "Sojourner," in *The Anchor Bible Dictionary*, ed. David Noel Freedman (New York: Doubleday, 1992), 6:103–4.

2. For the possibilities, see S. Kent Brown, "A Case for Lehi's Bondage in Arabia," *Journal of Book of Mormon Studies* 6, no. 2 (fall 1997): 206–17.

3. Daube, *Exodus Pattern*, 24–26.

4. See chapter 3 in this volume, "Recovering the Missing Record of Lehi."

5. To my knowledge, no one has explained *why* the family spent this extended stay in the desert, other than suggesting that they stopped to raise crops, as do Lynn M. and Hope A. Hilton in *In Search of Lehi's Trail* (Salt Lake City: Deseret Book, 1976), 50, 77, 92, and Warren P. and Michaela K. Aston in *In the Footsteps of Lehi* (Salt Lake City: Deseret Book, 1994), 5, 21, 31. Typically, commentators have attempted only to outline *how* Lehi and his family coped in the desert, including the Lord's requirement that they not "make much fire" (1 Ne. 17:12). For example, George Reynolds and Janne M. Sjodahl portray the family as successfully avoiding contact with desert peoples because of the aid of the Liahona: *Commentary on the Book of Mormon* (Salt Lake City: Deseret News Press, 1955), 1:166–67, 173. Hugh Nibley similarly observes that the desert was a dangerous place and that Lehi's family did their best to avoid contact with its inhabitants: *Lehi in the Desert, The World of the Jaredites, There Were Jaredites* (Salt Lake City: Deseret Book, 1988), 5:47–49, 63–67.

6. Among LDS authors, both the Hiltons (*In Search of Lehi's Trail*, 28) and the Astons (*In the Footsteps of Lehi*, 10) rightly emphasize that, on the basis of what has come to light about early Arabian governments, settlements, and economy, the family would have met many people during the journey.

7. Dependency should not surprise us in light of the need for protection in the desert. Even along the "incense trail" that ran inland from the Red Sea, as Nigel Groom points out, caravaneers "moved through harsh tribal areas inhabited by nomads, where unpredictable squabbles could put both their profits and, perhaps, their lives at risk." Away from major centers of civilization, he writes, "in the absence of strong rule, law and order must have been precarious"; *Frankincense and Myrrh: A Study of the Arabian Incense Trade* (London: Longman Group, 1981), 197–98. Pliny the Elder (A.D. 23–79), in his

Natural History, observed that "of these innumerable tribes an equal part are engaged in trade or live by brigandage" (6.32 [§ 162]).

8. For example, Bertram Thomas, *Arabia Felix* (New York: Charles Scribner's Sons, 1932). A first-rate study on the incense trade through the Arabian desert is that of Nigel Groom, *Frankincense and Myrrh.* See also the discussion by Eugene England, "Through the Arabian Desert to a Bountiful Land: Could Joseph Smith Have Known the Way?" in *Book of Mormon Authorship,* ed. Noel B. Reynolds (Provo, Utah: Religious Studies Center, Brigham Young University, 1982), 143–56.

9. Daube, *Exodus Pattern,* 24.

10. The hint that Nephi preached while "in the wilderness" (D&C 33:8) does not alter this possibility.

11. See Reynolds and Sjodahl, *Commentary,* 1:173–74; Nibley, *Lehi in the Desert,* 63–65; Robert L. Millet and Joseph F. McConkie, *Doctrinal Commentary on the Book of Mormon* (Salt Lake City: Bookcraft, 1987), 1:131–32. Nephi summarizes rather blandly the severity of the problems that faced family members by speaking generally of "much affliction" (1 Ne. 17:1) and "many afflictions and much difficulty" (17:6).

12. This dependence arises especially in discussions of the Liahona (e.g., Mosiah 1:16–17; Alma 37:38–42). In linking the family's well-being with the gracious actions of the Lord, Nephi tied the story of his family's exodus from Jerusalem to that of the exodus of the ancient Israelites from Egypt. See Ps. 105:37: "He brought them forth also with silver and gold: and there was not one feeble person among their tribes." In the case of the extended family of Lehi and Sariah, evidently all survived the trip, including newborns, with the exception of Ishmael (1 Ne. 17:1–2).

13. Raising the prospect of dying in the wilderness clearly echoes similar complaints by the Israelites in the desert; see Terrence L. Szink, "Nephi and the Exodus," in *Rediscovering the Book of Mormon,* ed. John L. Sorenson and Melvin J. Thorne (Salt Lake City: Deseret Book, 1991), 38–51.

14. Nephi wrote in a guarded way, including only hints of the intensity of suffering, that "we had suffered many afflictions and much difficulty, yea, even *so much that we cannot write them all*" (1 Ne. 17:6, emphasis added).

15. As one gauge of the severe impact of the desert experience, Jacob, who had been born in the desert to Lehi and Sariah, seems to have remained a sober, serious person all of his life (see Jacob 7:26).

16. Lehi was equipped with "tents" and other means for desert living and was apparently able to leave his home without delay (e.g., 1 Ne. 2:4; 3:9; 16:12). See Nibley's discussion, *Lehi in the Desert,* 46–49. John Tvedtnes takes a dim view of Lehi's possible involvement with desert trade: "Was Lehi a Caravaneer?" *F.A.R.M.S. Preliminary Report* (Provo, Utah: F.A.R.M.S., 1984).

17. One may argue that the phrase "our fathers" points to an intermediate generation, nearer Alma's time, who had suffered difficulties with "their enemies." But the notation that immediately follows—"even by the hands of their own brethren" (Alma 9:10)—clarifies that the reference is to Lehi and his children, since the older sons sought at least once to kill Lehi (1 Ne. 16:37; 17:44) and three times to kill the younger son Nephi (1 Ne. 7:16; 16:37; 2 Ne. 5:3–4; cf. 2 Ne. 1:24).

18. Writing of an unsuccessful military foray into western Arabia in 25–24 B.C., the Roman geographer Strabo noted that soldiers died from "hunger and fatigue and diseases" (*Geography*, 16.4.24). It is possible, of course, that by Lehi's day some wells and water sources had been polluted by camel dung and urine left behind by caravans, as nowadays.

19. According to Groom, the maximum time for a caravan to travel from Zufar (or Dhofar) on the Indian Ocean to Gaza on the Mediterranean coast was 118 days, a distance of about 2,100 miles (*Frankincense*, chart on 213). The Hiltons also reckon the distance as just over 2,100 miles, though using a different beginning point ("In Search of Lehi's Trail, Part 2," *Ensign*, October 1976, 39; cf. *In Search of Lehi's Trail*, 32). Naturally, caravans did not include flocks, something Lehi's family seems to have eschewed (see 1 Ne. 2:4; 16:11–12).

20. Heschel wrote that Hosea's strange marriage "was a lesson" instead of "a symbol." Further, its "purpose was not to demonstrate divine attitudes to the people, but to educate Hosea himself in the understanding of divine sensibility" (*The Prophets* [Philadelphia: Jewish Publication Society, 1962], 56).

21. Dust is also tied to the notion of servanthood or low social status in the speech of king Benjamin (Mosiah 2:25–26; cf. 4:2).

22. It is also important to note how he speaks of the promised land, calling it "a land of liberty" whose inhabitants "shall never be brought down into captivity" and "shall dwell safely forever," except for the cause "of iniquity" (2 Ne. 1:7, 9).

23. For the relevance of certain passages in Isaiah 48–49, quoted in 1 Nephi 20–21, see Brown, "A Case for Lehi's Bondage in Arabia," 213–16.

24. Daube, *Exodus Pattern*, 25. For the fleeing family of Lehi, food ("provisions" [1 Ne. 2:4; 16:11] and "seed" [16:11]) was crucial. Nephi notes two occasions when the family faced starvation, both occurring before the party turned to the east (1 Ne. 16:21, 39).

25. An additional hardship was the family's infrequent use of fire. Whether it was to save fuel, along with the efforts that one expends to find fuel, or whether it was to avoid drawing attention to themselves that the Lord "suffered [not] that we should make much fire, as we journeyed in the wilderness," or both, is not clear from the account (1 Ne. 17:12). Reynolds

and Sjodahl (*Commentary*, 1:173) and Nibley (*Lehi in the Desert*, 63–67) opt for the second explanation.

26. The case is richer than one might think at first, for Lehi dwells in his tent because he is a servant of God and has been obedient to him, thus standing in a relationship of servanthood.

27. Daube, *Exodus Pattern*, 24–26; the verb, we presume, is Hebrew *yšb*. See above for discussion.

28. In the following passages (emphasis added), God brings about special circumstances, putting humans in a dependent relationship, a situation that matches the Old Testament. First, God leads people to a land and imposes obligations on that people: "It is a choice land, saith God . . . wherefore I will have all men that *dwell* thereon that they shall worship me" (2 Ne. 10:19). See also 1 Ne. 21:20 (= Isa. 49:20); 2 Ne. 1:9, 31; 8:6 (= Isa. 51:6); 16:5 (= Isa. 6:5); 19:2 (= Isa. 9:2); 20:24 (= Isa. 10:24); Mosiah 1:10; Alma 31:26; 3 Ne. 10:5, 7; cf. Ether 13:2. Compare the expectations that Israelites worship the Lord after he has led them to the promised land (e.g., Ex. 3:12, 17–18; 6:4–8; 8:1; 9:1; 15:17; also Lev. 20:22; Deut. 11:31–32; 12:10–14). The Canaanites "shall not *dwell*" in the promised land because they will "make thee sin against [the Lord]" (Ex. 23:33).

Second, God and an individual enjoy a relationship, for good or ill: "The Lord hath said he *dwelleth* not in unholy temples, but in the hearts of the righteous doth he *dwell*," and "the righteous shall *sit down* in his kingdom, to go no more out" (Alma 34:36). Sitting down lies at the base of the Hebrew verb *to dwell*. On the need for righteousness, see also 1 Ne. 10:21; 2 Ne. 2:8; Mosiah 2:37; 3:6; Alma 7:21; 18:35; Hel. 4:24; and 4 Ne. 1:15. Compare the requirement that Israelites be holy "unto me [God]" in Ex. 19:6; 22:31; also Ex. 9:27; 31:14–15; Lev. 11:44–45; cf. 1 Sam. 4:4; 2 Sam. 6:2; 2 Kgs. 19:15; Solomon's dedicatory prayer espouses an opposite view (1 Kgs. 8:27; 2 Chr. 6:18).

Third, those dwelling with God enjoy a special status: "Those that keep the commandments . . . may *dwell* with God in a state of never-ending happiness" (Mosiah 2:41; see also 3 Ne. 28:9). The reverse may be true, dwelling eternally as a subject to the devil. See also 1 Ne. 15:33, 35; 22:26, 28; Mosiah 15:23; Alma 24:22; 28:12; 36:28; 3 Ne. 28:40; Morm. 7:7; 9:3–4; Ether 4:19 (words of Moroni); and Moro. 8:26. The Old Testament rarely expresses the concept of dwelling with God, only in song; see Ps. 23:6; usually dwelling with God refers to being in the temple: Ps. 27:4; 84:4; 101:7.

Finally, dwelling on earth in a circumstance linked to the purposes and timing of the Lord entails a divinely offered privilege: "Blessed are they who *dwell*" in the New Jerusalem (Ether 13:10). In the days of the Messiah the "wolf also shall *dwell* with the lamb" (2 Ne. 21:6 [= Isa. 11:6]; see also 2 Ne. 30:12). At the other extreme is the fate of Babylon, where "wild beasts of the desert shall lie" and "owls shall *dwell*" (2 Ne. 23:21 [= Isa. 13:21]). Note that at the end of time, the Lord will "cast the lot" for the wasted land of his people and, after improvements, "from generation to generation shall they *dwell* therein" (Isa. 34:17; also 65:9).

29. Ex. 20:22–23:33. Some call it the Book of the Covenant. See Daube, *Exodus Pattern*, 5.

30. Ex. 12:36; cf. 3:22; 15:9; Gen. 15:14. There is an entire complex of legal and social issues associated with property, such as flocks and jewelry, as one observes in the escape of the people of Limhi (Mosiah 22:12). See Daube, *Exodus Pattern*, 47–61.

31. This point is made firm because Lamoni later reversed Ammon's status: "King Lamoni would not suffer that Ammon should serve him, or be his servant" (Alma 21:19).

32. Greg W. Stephens suggests that Lamoni's hospitality and offer of his daughter to Ammon arose from "the law of hospitality or asylum" ("Elements of Israelite Tribal Law in the Book of Mormon," Ancient Legal Systems Seminar, J. Reuben Clark Law School, 1981, 8). Mark Davis and Brent Israelson explain Ammon's warm reception by Lamoni as conforming to customary "alien's rights" in a foreign environment ("International Relations and Treaties in the Book of Mormon," *F.A.R.M.S. Preliminary Report* [Provo, Utah: F.A.R.M.S., 1982], 5). But the legal and social elements of the scene are more complex than these positions imply.

33. Servility cannot have been foreign to Lamanite society. To be sure, the entire issue of forced labor in the Book of Mormon has yet to be studied carefully. But Ammon labored among "other servants" of the king (Alma 17:25–29; 18:1, 5). Further, Ammon's brother Aaron "with his brethren" proposed that they be accepted as servants in the palace of Lamoni's father, a proposal that the father refused (Alma 22:2–3).

34. The text says "his land," apparently meaning land of the king. It is not clear whether in a legal sense the king was thought of as owner of the land or as its steward.

35. Emphasis added. One of the little-explored issues in the Book of Mormon that arises here is that of acquiring land—that is, of acquiring an inheritance. The matter teems with legal questions. Roger R. Keller has explored the way that land was thought of geographically and theologically in his *Book of Mormon Authors: Their Words and Messages* (Provo, Utah: Religious Studies Center, Brigham Young University, 1996), 103–50.

36. According to Spencer, "Sojourner," 104, this assurance in the ancient Near East is extended even to "sojourners."

37. Daube, *Exodus Pattern*, 63; also 64: "The two women were to be Jacob's wages and, strictly, he was paid when he wedded them."

38. One can think of examples in which persons took gifts that were not offered. For instance, Limhi's people took their "flocks" and "herds" as well

as "all their gold, and silver, and their precious things," even though by treaty half of these goods belonged to the Lamanites (Mosiah 22:11–12; also 19:15, 26).

39. Daube, *Exodus Pattern,* 51; also 52–53, 86–87. Of course, the case of Ammon is measurably different from the cases of the escaping Nephite colonists under Limhi and Alma the Elder from their respective Lamanite overlords. It was the Lord, not the Lamanites, who was generous in their release from captivity, freeing them all, guiding them to safety, and frustrating their pursuers (Mosiah 22:11–16; 24:16–25). As the Psalmist sang of the Exodus, "There was not one feeble person among their tribes" (Ps. 105:37), the stress resting "on the triumphant, miraculous, protective guidance of God" (Daube, *Exodus Pattern,* 55).

40. Few such incidents are recorded in the Bible. One thinks of the exchange of gifts between the queen of Sheba and Solomon (1 Kgs. 10:10, 13; 2 Chr. 9:9, 12), the land grant of Achish, the Philistine king, to David (1 Sam. 27:6), and Pharaoh's gifts to Abraham, who was a commoner (Gen. 12:20–13:2; *Genesis Apocryphon* 20.31–34).

41. Ammon's intended gift, of course, was to bring "salvation" to Lamanite converts (Alma 17:11).

42. See Daube, *Exodus Pattern,* 60–61.

43. In this context, one has to explain the very different treatment that Ammon's companions experienced in other parts of the extended Lamanite kingdom (Alma 21:13–14). The most natural response is that Ammon and Lamoni apparently liked one another. Camille Fronk suggests something similar ("Show Forth Good Examples in Me," in *Studies in Scripture, Vol. 7, 1 Nephi to Alma 29,* ed. Kent P. Jackson [Salt Lake City: Deseret Book, 1987], 323). Further, Ammon did not come preaching, as his companions did in other parts of the country. Thus, concern about the message that Ammon carried did not become an immediate issue, as it did in the other cases.

44. It is also evident that a generation earlier Amulon, the leader of the renegade priests of Noah, negotiated a favorable position for himself and his associates when the Lamanite king appointed him governor over Alma's colony in Helam (Mosiah 23:39) and his associates as "teachers" (24:4).

45. There are fifteen occurrences of the word "stay" in the Book of Mormon, mostly verbs. *The Oxford English Dictionary* notes each of the meanings for the verbal and nominal forms that are discussed in this section.

46. As with the other verbs of sitting, the usual Hebrew verb is *yšb.*

47. Isa. 48:2 (Hebrew niphal of *smk*), with the addition "they do not" in the Book of Mormon text; similarly, 2 Ne. 20:20 (= Isa. 10:20; Hebrew niphal of *š'n*; with the sense of "save," see 2 Kgs. 16:7). The nominal form "stay" refers to a support, as in 2 Ne. 13:1 (= Isa. 3:1; Hebrew *maš'ēn*): "the *stay* and the staff, . . . the whole *stay* of water" (emphasis added).

48. Isa. 29:9 (Hebrew hithpalpel of *mhh*). The New English Bible renders the verb "loiter." The RSV—and similarly the Jerusalem Bible—renders the first line of the Isaiah verse thus: "Stupefy yourselves and be in a stupor." Importantly, Nephi's text adds an address to the wicked: "For behold, all ye that doeth iniquity. . . ."

49. See also Alma 10:23; 3 Ne. 3:8; Morm. 8:26; Moro. 9:14.

50. It is possible, of course, that Nephi had suffered debilitating persecution or that he could not penetrate the social and political corruption in that part of the country (as in Hel. 7:4–5), or a combination of these factors.

51. The term here means more than residing, for when Lamanites depart home—at least in Pahoran's view—they come to make war.

52. As in most ancient cultures, there must have been laws that governed the standing of a wife who was abandoned, possibly allowing her to divorce the man who had left her and their children, and not to be responsible for his debts. One thinks of the laws governing cases of abandonment in the Code of Hammurabi (135–36).

53. According to Mosiah 19:15, the agreement held that the lives of the colonists would be spared and they would be allowed to "possess the land" again. Then, in Mosiah 19:25–26, the Lamanite king pledged "that his people should not slay" the Nephites while, on his part, the Nephite king Limhi promised that "his people should pay tribute . . . [of] one half of all they possessed." This level of payment had been established in an earlier accord (7:22).

54. Here *stay* does not denote servility, but the context is saturated with the sense of vassalhood.

55. While a master may be called "faithful," it is usually the master who applies this label, not the servant. Though the servants hailed Ammon as "a friend to the king" (Alma 18:3), evidently a title of some stature, both Ammon and Lamoni knew his real status at court, based on their prior negotiation (17:22–25).

56. This honorific term, as interpreted in the text, meant "powerful or great king" (Alma 18:13).

57. The phrase "which is right" may show that by this moment Ammon sensed he was in a position to exercise some control over what followed.

The Exodus Pattern in the Book of Mormon 5

The Israelite deliverance from Egypt serves as a type for several Book of Mormon accounts of deliverance. Book of Mormon authors and teachers such as Nephi, Alma, and Limhi allude to the Exodus and draw parallels with their own experiences. One perceives similarities not only with groups, such as Lehi's family leaving Jerusalem, but also with personal experiences, such as Alma's deliverance from the bondage of sin. The Atonement—an event surpassing the Exodus in the realm of God's miraculous works—also ties to the Exodus, and the Savior's three-day visit to the Americas brims with allusions as well. Connections between Moses and Jesus Christ as deliverers also appear. Noting these bridges, readers can take comfort from both the Exodus narrative and similar experiences that God fulfills his promises.

The memory of Israel's Exodus from Egypt runs so deep and clear in the Book of Mormon that it has naturally drawn the attention of modern students. The chief focus of recent studies has fallen on the departure of Lehi's family from Jerusalem as a replication, almost a mirror image—even in small details—of the flight of the Hebrews.[1] Such interest emerges naturally because Nephite teachers themselves drew comparisons between Lehi's colony and their Israelite forebears. For instance, in an important speech, king Limhi referred to the Israelites' escape from Egypt and, immediately thereafter, drew a parallel to Lehi's departure from Jerusalem (Mosiah 7:19–20). Additionally, in remarks addressed to his son Helaman, Alma consciously linked the Exodus from Egypt with Lehi's journey (Alma 36:28–29). But this does not exhaust the matter. More than once a prophet or teacher, who wanted to prove to others that divine assistance could be relied on, appealed to God's acts on behalf of the enslaved Hebrews. This was the very technique Nephi used, for example, in his attempt to convince his recalcitrant brothers that God was leading their father Lehi (1 Ne. 17:23–35). Furthermore, it was teachers in the Book of Mormon who first saw that the Exodus—the most wondrous of all God's acts on behalf of any people—was to be transcended by the grandeur of the Atonement.[2] In what follows I propose to sketch out some of the vivid colors of the variegated vista of the Exodus pattern that is portrayed in the Book of Mormon.

Lehi's Family Reenacts the Exodus

Although this topic may be the most inviting of all and, as noted above, has formed a chief focus among recent studies, it is also the one about which, I sense, more caution must be exercised. However, the payoff may well be more rewarding for the patient investigator. In my view, an examination of this issue requires care precisely because there is *no* unambiguous statement that the members of Lehi's immediate family understood their departure from Jerusalem as a reenactment of Israel's flight to freedom. Consequently, an investigator must sift the evidence piece by piece. Significantly, while the evidence must be seen as cumulative, the results are strikingly positive.

In one passage which points to a conscious reenactment of the Exodus (1 Ne. 4:1–3),[3] the comparisons are rather narrowly drawn. But this passage does not stand alone. Chapter 4 of 1 Nephi opens with Nephi's encouraging words to his brothers, who were understandably discouraged after a second unsuccessful attempt to obtain the plates of brass from Laban, having offered property as payment. Responding that the Lord could overcome the strength of Laban and any fifty of his associates, Nephi mentioned Moses and the miraculous crossing of the sea, which led to deliverance for the Israelites and to death for "the armies of Pharaoh" (4:2). Nephi then tried to shore up his brothers' resolve by pointing out that they had also been instructed by an angel, and adding that "the Lord is able to deliver us, even as our fathers, and to destroy Laban, even as the Egyptians" (4:3). By saying this, Nephi made clear his belief that the Lord would assist the efforts of his brothers and himself just as he had aided their Israelite forebears. But that was as far as he pursued the analogy.[4]

A second example points more directly to a connection, at least as Nephi grasped it. As he began his classic speech on the Exodus in response to his brothers' complaints about their father's "foolish imaginations" (17:20), Nephi recounted that "Moses was commanded of the Lord to do that great work" (17:26). Then, after reviewing the Lord's gracious actions on behalf of the Hebrew slaves and the eventual apostasy of their descendants who were then living in Jerusalem, he declared: "Wherefore, the Lord commanded my father that he should depart into the wilderness" (17:44), clearly tying a thread between Moses and Lehi. One could cite other possible links.[5]

In this connection, commentators from Hugh Nibley[6] to George S. Tate and Terrance L. Szink have drawn together an impressive array of evidence that points to Lehi's exodus as a replication of that of the Israelites. Those Nephite teachers who made the association very explicit were five hundred years downstream.[7] Of course, allusions plainly abound in the writings of Nephi and Jacob.[8] As a result, one can properly make a case for connections between the Hebrew Exodus and that of the family of Lehi.[9]

Nephite Bondage and the Exodus

The chapters which draw my attention here rehearse various fortunes of the Nephite colony which left Zarahemla under the leadership of a man named Zeniff (Mosiah 7–24). The avowed purpose of the colonists was to return to the land of Nephi, where Nephite civilization had grown up, in order "to go up to possess the land" (9:3).[10] Within these chapters, we read of the subsequent escape and return to Zarahemla of two different groups of these colonists. The one consisted of the people who followed Alma. In fact, they fled twice: first from the armies of king Noah[11] and later from Lamanite captors.[12] The second group was led by king Limhi, son of king Noah, who, with the aid of a squadron of sixteen warriors from Zarahemla, also eluded their Lamanite overlords.[13] In each case, it was not only the fact of the escape from bondage that was paramount but particularly the decisive role that the Lord's influence played in the outcome. In fact, it becomes clear from the text that it was the Lord who orchestrated events and maneuvered people in the period leading up to deliverance from bondage.[14] And this is precisely the way events in the book of Exodus are to be read.[15]

One concrete example will suffice. The Hebrew slaves in Egypt quickly learned that Pharaoh and his officers could not be trusted to maintain longstanding agreements, because as soon as the latter felt challenged, they changed the rules for the slaves.[16] That the Nephite colonists likewise saw themselves as victims of capricious overlords—as the Israelites did under the harsh rule of Pharaoh—can be seen in Limhi's impassioned speech at the temple in the city of Lehi–Nephi when he rehearsed what God had done for his two peoples in the past, referring first to the events of the Exodus from Egypt and then to the events of Lehi's departure from Jerusalem.[17] "Lift up your heads, and rejoice, and put your trust in . . . that God who brought the children of Israel out of the land of Egypt, and caused that they should walk through the Red Sea on dry ground, and fed them with manna that they might not perish in the wilderness. . . . And again, that same God has brought our fathers out of the land of Jerusalem, and has kept and preserved his people even until now" (7:19–20a). Turning next to the situation of his own people, Limhi declared that the Lamanite king had entered into an agreement with his own grandfather, Zeniff, "for the sole purpose of bringing this people into subjection or into bondage" (7:22). Whether anyone else in his society agreed, Limhi saw similarities between the difficulties faced by the people of his colony in their bondage, along with their accompanying desire for freedom, and those which both the earlier Israelites and the family of Lehi had faced. Of course Limhi knew the reason for the suffering of his people, and he laid it squarely at the feet of his father and the earlier generation's rejection of the word of the Lord brought by the prophet Abinadi.[18] Even so, king Limhi was determined to escape, his hope springing from the successes of his forebears (7:33).

At this point I should identify similarities between the Israelite Exodus and that of the two Nephite colonies: (a) In all instances the captives escaped into the wilderness with flocks and herds—no small matter,[19] for, according to David Daube, taking one's possessions was one of the rights of a slave when freed.[20] (b) According to Psalm 105:37, there was not a feeble person among the departing Hebrew slaves, a clear indication of God's care and protective guidance.[21] The same is plainly implied about the flight of everyone in the two Nephite groups. (c) The Lord softened the hearts of those who stood in the way of the departure of the captives. In the case of the Lamanite overseers and guards, their hearts were softened towards their captives, and they treated them in a kinder way.[22] But perhaps the most important ingredient to note is that (d) in each instance, the events prior to departure were all orchestrated by the Lord on his terms, a clear feature of the Exodus narrative. For instance, even with the arrival of the sixteen soldiers from Zarahemla in the midst of Limhi's people, Limhi was quick to recognize that the way out was not with the aid of swords or armor. As a matter of fact, he instructed his people to "lift up your heads, and rejoice, and put your trust in God, in that God who was the God of Abraham, and Isaac, and Jacob; and also, that God who brought the children of Israel out of the land of Egypt" (7:19).

One other possible similarity is found in the observation that it is possible to see Alma, the leader of the second group, as a type of Moses. While I do not wish to press this point too far, the parallels are intriguing. First of all, each was a member of a royal court who was forced to flee because of an injustice. Second, each led his people from the clutches of enslaving overlords. Third, each led his group through the wilderness to the land from which their ancestors had set out. Moreover, each gave the law to his people and placed them under covenant to obey the Lord.[23] In addition, because of his unusual spiritual gifts, Alma was commissioned by king Mosiah, whom he had never met prior to his arrival in Zarahemla, to lead and direct the affairs of the church there, even superceding in position and authority those priests who surrounded Mosiah and were obviously in positions to effect and make policy.[24] Moses too was placed by the Lord at the head of his people, who had been served by other priests.

To underscore further the connections with Moses, one of the most important passages consists of the Lord's assurances to a troubled Alma who was seeking to know what to do with members of the church who had gone astray and forsaken their covenants. Even though by this time Alma and his people had been delivered from physical bondage years before, and thus it was no longer a present concern, in his reply to Alma's prayers the Lord made certain kinds of promises for those who were willing to bear his name and remain faithful to their covenants. These promises were guaranteed in a particular way: by the Lord invoking his name "the Lord" as the ultimate assurance that he could be trusted (26:26).[25] Beginning in verse 17 of Mosiah 26 and continuing to the end of the Lord's revelation in verse 32, one reads through a consistent pattern of pronouns, "I" and "me" and "my" and "mine," which stand out in this part of the account. Important to my point is the above observation that a similar phenomenon occurred in the sixth chapter of Exodus, beginning with verse 1 and ending with verse 8. Here, too, a prophet—Moses—had come before the Lord with troubled heart. To be sure, the occasion of his appeal to God was different, for in this instance he was simply seeking to learn why Pharaoh had been successful not only in rejecting and rebuffing him but also in making life more difficult for the Hebrew slaves. From Moses' query (Ex. 5:22–23), it is evident that he had initially thought he would have an easier time overcoming Pharaoh's intransigence. Even so, in the Lord's answer to Moses there is a striking series of pronouns in the first person, a divine response richly clothed with references to "I" and "my." Perhaps most importantly, as a signal both to Moses and to Alma, the Lord identified himself by saying, "I am the Lord," the ultimate assurance to the hearer that God is to be trusted and relied upon.[26] It is his name, a name connoting trustworthiness and strength, which brings to the beleaguered believer the clearer view that in an ultimate sense God is in charge and that he will shape events to his own purposes. Anything less does an injustice to the passages in question.

One can summarize, then, by observing that a number of strands run through these chapters of Mosiah which not only chronicle the stories of a Nephite colony in the land of Nephi but also lead the reader to sense that the colonists' stories of escape and deliverance from bondage are to be understood as something of a reenactment—and thus a reassurance—of an earlier age, of an earlier people, of an earlier series of acts by a kind God toward a downtrodden people. Doubtless Mormon, the editor of these reports, saw an important purpose in narrating them. He himself may have taken comfort in their content. Standing where he could see his own people charging toward the abyss of extinction (Morm. 5:1–5; 6:17–22), he must have seen in these accounts a story of hope for those who stand in need of divine deliverance.

Exodus as Proof of God's Power

Reference above to Nephi's remarks of encouragement to his despairing brothers (1 Ne. 4:1–3) leads me to note another way in which the Exodus account was read by Nephite teachers and prophets. Plainly, they cited it as a proof of God's ability to fulfill his promises. Since I have already drawn attention to Nephi's citation of the miraculous crossing of the sea, let me bring forward other passages which exhibit a similar interest. For a second example I turn again to 1 Nephi 17, the chapter which chronicles the arrival of Lehi's family at the seashore of southeast Arabia, the Lord's command to Nephi to build a ship, and the brothers' belligerent reaction to this news. In Nephi's rather long response (17:23–51), his first and chief proof of "the power of God" (17:29) and the power of "his word" (17:31) consisted of the Exodus experience which Nephi recounted in some detail (17:23–31, 40b–42).

A third passage also comes to us from Nephi's hand (2 Ne. 25:20). Once again, elements of the Exodus experience—mentioned here between two oaths—stand as surety of God's unerring assurance, in this case that "there is none other name given under heaven save it be this Jesus Christ, of which I [Nephi] have spoken, whereby man can be saved." In this verse, only two incidents that occurred in the desert were specifically recalled as proofs: the healing of those bitten by the poisonous serpents that had invaded Israel's camp[27] and the miraculous flow of water from the rock struck by Moses.[28] Obviously, in Nephi's mind these events constituted sufficient proof for his point.

A fourth instance derives from words spoken by Nephi son of Helaman while he was upon the tower in his garden. His audience consisted largely of passersby (Hel. 7:11–12) and included "men who were judges, who also belonged to the secret band of Gadianton" (8:1). As is well known, after Nephi had warned his hearers that because of their sins they could expect destruction (7:22–28)—a fact which he knew by revelation (7:29)—he was rebutted by those who were offended at his words. The gist of their response appears as follows: "Behold, he [Nephi] doth condemn all this people, even unto destruction; yea, and also that these our great cities shall be taken from us, that we shall have no place in them. And now we know that this is impossible, for behold, we are powerful, and our cities great, therefore our enemies can have no power over us" (8:5b–6). It is Nephi's response to these notions which unfolds a series of proofs, all drawn from scripture, to the effect that God has power to fulfill his word. And as one might expect, his chief example consists of the Exodus account, specifically the miracle at the sea:[29] "Behold, my brethren, have ye not read that God gave power unto one man, even Moses, to smite upon the waters of the Red Sea, and they parted hither and thither, insomuch that the Israelites, who were our fathers, came through upon dry ground, and the waters closed upon the armies of the Egyptians and swallowed them up?" (8:11). Thus far, Nephi had drawn attention to this single incident to demonstrate God's marvelous power over nature and people. But for his immediate purposes he carried it one step further: "And now behold, if God gave unto this man such power, then why should ye dispute among yourselves, and say that he hath given unto me no power whereby I may know concerning the judgments that shall come upon you except ye repent?"(8:12). With this, Nephi made clear that the acceptance of God's power manifested at the Red Sea also leads to acceptance of his ability to reveal or make known "the judgments that shall come." In other words, it is the same divine power that brings about both the miraculous and the revelations of what is yet future. In a subsequent remark, Nephi could not pass up the opportunity to point out that another event associated with the Exodus, the raising of the "brazen serpent in the wilderness," also possessed a prophetic dimension which pointed forward to the coming Son of God (8:14–15). Most important for our discussion, once again, is the notion of the centrality of the Exodus as a proof.

The fifth and final passage that I shall review in this light appears in the instructions of Alma the Younger to his son Helaman (Alma 36).[30] This passage has been examined by others, though with a different set of questions.[31] Let me describe what I see in this chapter that has to do with the Exodus. Both verse 1 and verse 30, the first and last, restate the promise that "inasmuch as ye shall keep the commandments of God ye shall prosper in the land." The last verse alone adds these words: "And ye ought to know also, that inasmuch as ye will not keep the commandments of God ye shall be cut off from his presence" (36:30). These summarizing teachings of Alma concerning promises and penalties find a detailed counterpart in the book of Deuteronomy, which recounts Moses' last instructions to his people at the end of their wandering, just before they crossed the Jordan River into the land of Canaan. Significantly, the Israelites were about to take possession of a promised land, and Moses' words were not only full of promises to those who would obey the Lord but also bristling with penalties that would descend on those who might disobey.[32] Thus even the words which open and close Alma 36 are linked to the larger Exodus experience. Moreover, the second and third verses, along with three verses at the chapter's end (36:27–29), all speak of the Exodus as proof of God's marvelous power to deliver and support those in bondage and afflictions. The key terms are words such as "bondage," "captivity," and "afflictions" on the one hand, and "trust," "power," and "deliverance" on the other. At the heart of this chapter, of course, lies the remarkable story of Alma's dramatic conversion to the Lord, in which he was "born of God." And this story, as Alma recounted it, is inflected with reminiscences of the Exodus. For instance, he testified that trusting in the Lord leads to divine support and deliverance (36:3, 27).[33] Further, Alma's early life was characterized by rebellion, certainly a dimension of Israel's experience. In addition, the matter at issue in the Lord's intervention with Alma was not one of worthiness on his part. The same must be said of the Israelites. Lastly, the entire chapter consists of Alma's recitation of his own story; it resembles in a general sense the memorized recitations learned by Israelites of God's wondrous acts performed on their behalf during the Exodus.[34]

Exodus and the Atonement

A review of Alma 36 leads naturally to the observation that the Exodus was linked typologically to the effects of Jesus' atonement. And Alma's autobiographical recitation of his experience here, joined with the biographical account narrated in Mosiah 27, forms a transparent example.[35] As I have noted above, Alma's rehearsal of his remarkable experience of being born of God (Alma 36) is bracketed by both the mention of the Deuteronomic promise of prosperity (Alma 36:1, 30) and the appeal to his son Helaman to remember "the captivity of our fathers" (36:2, 28).[36] Between this pair of brackets, Alma recalled his experience in such a way that not only demonstrated how the Atonement was effective in his own case before Jesus worked it out but also linked his deliverance from the bonds of sin to Israel's deliverance from the bondage of slavery.[37]

One intriguing question concerns the one who first tied Exodus language to the Atonement. In my view, the earliest person to make this association was Jacob son of Lehi. Although any discussion is limited to the texts selected and edited for the Book of Mormon record, and although it is possible that someone else in Jacob's family—such as his father or older brother Nephi—saw the connection initially, the texts at hand point to Jacob. The threads between the two concepts are illumined in Jacob's long speech quoted in 2 Nephi 6–10.

In this address, Jacob quotes Isa. 50:1–52:2, a passage which speaks of Israel's new exodus or gathering when "the Messiah will set himself again the second time to recover" the house of Israel (2 Ne. 6:14). These particular verses of Isaiah brim with allusions to the Exodus even as they speak of the gathering. It is after quoting this extensive segment from Isaiah that Jacob turns to "things to come" (9:4). Interestingly, he first reviews the implications of the fall (9:6–9) before he turns to address the broader picture that includes the "power of resurrection" (9:6), and the "infinite Atonement" (9:7): "O how great the goodness of our God, who prepareth a way for *our escape* from the grasp of this awful monster; yea, that monster, death and hell, which *I call* the death of the body, and also the death of the spirit" (9:10, emphasis added).

Two features draw my attention. First, the notion of "our escape," while not mirroring specific vocabulary associated with the Exodus, certainly evinces the image of the Hebrews' flight from Egypt. Second, Jacob's use of the expression "I call" plainly points to the idea that this association of the second exodus—spoken of in the prior two chapters—with the Atonement was an interpretation that he had arrived at independently of others. And it is at this moment that Jacob chose to illustrate how closely these ideas are knit together: "And because of the way of *deliverance* of our God, the Holy One of Israel, this death, of which I have spoken, which is the temporal, shall deliver up its dead; which death is the grave. And this [other] death of which I have spoken, which is the spiritual death, shall *deliver* up its dead; which spiritual death is hell; wherefore, death and hell must *deliver* up their dead, and hell must *deliver* up its *captive* spirits, and the grave must *deliver* up its *captive* bodies, and the bodies and the spirits of men will be *restored* one to the other; and it is by the power of the resurrection of the Holy One of Israel" (9:11–12, emphasis added). The first word that catches one's eye in this passage is "deliverance," a term whose verbal root is fully at home—as I observed above—in the Exodus narrative. Further, an apparently related verbal form of "deliverance" appears four times as "deliver up" in the next few lines.[38] Moreover, the adjective "captive" obviously echoes Israel's bondage. Even though this term does not appear in the Exodus narrative *per se*, it occurs in Isaiah's prophecy concerning the new exodus of the last days (Isa. 51:14) which Jacob had just quoted to his hearers (2 Ne. 8:14). In addition, the notion of being "restored," while again not reflecting specific vocabulary associated with the Exodus, is certainly the central notion lying behind the concept of a new exodus or gathering back to former lands. Indeed, Jacob plainly understood the issue in this way because he observed that those "carried away captive" from Jerusalem "should return again" (6:8–9), and that "the Messiah will set himself again the second time to recover them" (6:14).

It is worth noting that the whole of Jacob's address is adorned with allusions to and echoes of the Exodus. At the outset, he stated that he would speak "concerning things which are, and which are to come" (6:4), as well as "concerning all the house of Israel" (6:5). It was to achieve the latter that he quoted a long segment from Isaiah.[39]

As I noted earlier, for believers among the Nephite and Lamanite peoples, the one event which transcended all others—including the Exodus—was the Atonement. And the surety of the Atonement, of course, was the risen Jesus' visit to the temple in the land of Bountiful. In this connection, one feature that has intrigued me and others in this report consists of the rich set of allusions to the Exodus.[40] Although one cannot explore all possibilities, I wish to focus attention on a few in order to illustrate the abundant series of ties that extends between the Exodus account and the report of Jesus' three-day visit.

One early, notable element consists of the prelude to Jesus' arrival in the Americas; namely, the tremendous destruction which must have harmed all life, whether human, plant, or animal. Even though Mormon does not include an evaluation of the devastation to food supplies for both humans and animals, the account can legitimately be read as pointing to such disruption.[41] On the side of the Exodus, the plagues resulted in the interruption of normal living in Egypt and, in some cases, destruction among all forms of life. One has only to recall the plague of hail which was especially ruinous, decimating "all that was in the field, both man and beast; and the hail smote every herb of the field, and brake every tree of the field" (Ex. 9:25). Moreover, the locusts which followed "did eat every herb of the land, and all the fruit of the trees *which the hail had left*," completing the devastation of crops that would sustain both human and animal life (10:15, emphasis added).

A second feature consists of Jesus' quotations from the Old Testament, particularly the work of Isaiah.[42] In 3 Nephi 16, which rehearses the Father's plans for both Gentiles and Israel, the ancient covenant people, the conclusion of Jesus' sayings—as well as those attributed to the Father (3 Ne. 16:7–15)—consists of a quotation of Isa. 52:8–10. Notably, this cited passage stands in a context in Isaiah which refers to the Exodus on the one hand (Isa. 52:2–4, 11–12) and on the other to the coming Servant of the Lord, the Messiah-king (52:13–53:12). General themes include the redemption of Zion "without money" (52:3) and the departure of God's people from the unclean to the clean (52:11). Besides mentioning Egypt as the place of Israel's sojourning (52:4), the Lord affirmed that he "will go before you [redeemed of Israel]; and the God of Israel will be your rereward" (52:12), a clear reference to the divine protection that the Israelite camp received during the Exodus. Moreover, in the new redemption there is to be a reversal of two features of the former Exodus: "For ye shall not go out with haste, nor go by flight" (52:12).

The third comparison that I have selected for discussion consists of Jesus' miraculous provision of bread and wine on the second day of his visit. While the analogy between Jesus' act and Jehovah's provision of water and manna to the children of Israel in the wilderness has already received some attention,[43] I propose to follow out additional dimensions of the account as it is narrated in 3 Nephi 20. One must note first that the gifts of water and manna in the desert brought life to the fleeing Hebrews. Although in the case of Jesus' gifts the bread and wine in a sense commemorate his death, they more importantly celebrate his life, with the accompanying promise that the partakers will "be filled" (20:8) and thus be nourished. My second point has to do with being filled. For the people at Bountiful, Jesus' actions constituted no mean miracle. The whole multitude ate and drank, an observation whose plain meaning indicates that the crowd's hunger and thirst had been satisfied, a condition also resulting from the first day's partaking of bread and wine.[44] It was in an effort to provide for Israel's physical needs that the Lord made the water and manna available, with obvious accompanying spiritual blessings. In this limited sense, the report in 3 Nephi echoes the earlier account. A third linkage comes in Jesus' miracle of producing the bread and wine (20:3–7) in recollection of the manna and water in the wilderness, an act more emphatically underscored when it is noted that on the first day of his visit he had asked for bread and wine to be brought (18:1–3). Indeed, the reader is left with the impression that bread would also have been available on day two—unless it were the Sabbath—and therefore Jesus went out of his way to make his point when miraculously providing the elements of the sacrament.

The final distinctive similarity I wish to feature arises from the legal customs[45] associated with recovering a person enslaved abroad.[46] In such cases, one or more envoys were sent by the protector at home to entreat with the captor and were supplied with credentials which they were to present as representatives of the one seeking recovery. Indeed, Moses returned to Egypt as one empowered to recover those enslaved. "That God, himself outside Egypt at the burning bush, should send Moses accords with the normal procedure in these affairs."[47] Further, it is significant that Jesus came to the gathering in the land of Bountiful as a Moses, an observation which Jesus emphatically underscored.[48]

In the Exodus account, Moses and Aaron were sent as envoys (Ex. 3:10; 4:14–15) and, in unusual fashion, presented to Pharaoh their "credentials" which demonstrated that they represented the Lord (7:8–12).[49] In a related vein, it was necessary on occasion to convince the prisoner himself of the representative's authority. In Moses' case, he had anticipated the need to win over the Hebrew slaves and consequently had been equipped by the Lord with tokens which the Israelites would recognize as coming from their God, namely, knowledge of his name and power to perform three signs.[50] When we turn to 3 Nephi, the need and the effort to recover those who were captives of sin becomes clear.[51] The principal differences, of course, were that (a) the risen Jesus, the one who sought the recovery, came in person rather than sending a messenger, and (b) there was no captor to whom he needed to present his credentials.[52] In this connection, important features of Jesus' visit grew out of the scene in which he presented his "credentials" and the tokens of his mission to those whom he sought to rescue. Note the following overtones in the wonderful moments just after his arrival: "Behold, I AM Jesus Christ whom the prophets testified shall come into the world. And behold, I AM the light and the life of the world" (3 Ne. 11:10–11, capitalization added). The similarities with Moses' situation cannot be missed. In the first instance, Jesus identified himself as the one whom the gathered crowd had been expecting. Moses, too, had to identify himself as the envoy of Israel's God (Ex. 4:29–31). Further, Jesus announced himself specifically by using the divine name I AM,[53] the same name which Moses carried from his interview on the holy mount (3:14). Additionally, as Moses had carried at least one token of his commission which had the form of a physical malady, namely, his arm which could be made leprous (4:6–8), so Jesus bore the tokens of his crucifixion in his person. Moreover, to demonstrate the validity of his wounds, Jesus asked the entire crowd of twenty-five hundred people (3 Ne. 17:25) to come forward so that "ye may thrust your hands into my side, and also that ye may feel the prints of the nails in my hands and in my feet" (11:14). My last point in this context is that as the children of Israel had "believed" Moses and had then "bowed their heads and worshipped" (Ex. 4:31), so the people in Bountiful, after "going forth one by one . . . did know of a surety and did bear record, that it was he, of whom it was written by the prophets, that should come" (3 Ne. 11:15). They too "did fall down at the feet of Jesus, and did worship him" (11:17). And like the scene in which worship was extended to Jesus who was present, the Israelite slaves worshiped the Lord who "had visited the children of Israel" (Ex. 4:31). Both the acceptance of the tokens and the response seem significant in each context.

Summary and Conclusion

Even though this study has not pushed into all of the corners and byways of the Book of Mormon text, I believe that I have explored enough to show that the theme of God's mighty acts in the Exodus, performed on behalf of an enslaved people, colors and tones many accounts in the Nephite record. The Hebrew Exodus was clearly seen as the paradigm which helped in understanding God's deliverance of Nephite peoples whenever they found themselves in bondage. Moreover, certain expressions and words appear throughout the narrative of the journey undertaken by the family of Lehi and Sariah which point to the conclusion that members of their family saw connections between their experiences and those of their ancient forebears. Further, the events of the Exodus were regularly appealed to by prophets and teachers as the proof *par excellence* that God is capable of seeing his own purposes to their divinely appointed ends. Lastly, the Exodus was surpassed only by the Atonement of Jesus as the most momentous event in the history of salvation. However, the descriptions of the Atonement and its significance—including the risen Jesus' visit to the temple in the land of Bountiful, which was the grand proof of the Atonement—were woven into tapestries of awe-inspiring hues by using threads and strands which also formed the warp and weft of the Exodus account.

While there is much to be done before the topic can be considered thoroughly examined, in my view the dominant colors of the landscape have now been largely revealed, and the faint and heavy lines have come into sharper focus. In addition, the results thus far invite the inquirer to further pursuit. In summary, the Book of Mormon can be seen as the repository of an extraordinarily rich tradition with deep, ancient roots. Taken as a whole, the work proves to be one of stunning complexity and nuanced subtlety—no small conclusion.

This article, now revised, was published as "The Exodus Pattern in the Book of Mormon," BYU Studies 30, no. 3 (summer 1990): 111–26.

NOTES

1. Notable are George S. Tate, "The Typology of the Exodus Pattern in the Book of Mormon," in *Literature of Belief: Sacred Scripture and Religious Experience,* ed. Neal E. Lambert (Provo, Utah: Religious Studies Center, Brigham Young University, 1981), 246–62; a summary of work by George S. Tate, John W. Welch, and Avraham Gileadi in "Research and Perspectives: Nephi and the Exodus," *Ensign,* April 1987, 64–65; Noel B. Reynolds, "The Political Dimension in Nephi's Small Plates," *BYU Studies* 27, no. 4 (fall 1987): 15–37, particularly the Moses–Nephi typology on 22, 24, 29, 33; Terrance L. Szink, "To a Land of Promise (1 Nephi 16–18)," in *Studies in Scripture, Vol. 7: 1 Nephi to Alma 29,* ed. Kent P. Jackson (Salt Lake City: Deseret Book, 1987), 60–72; and three essays in *Rediscovering the Book of Mormon,* ed. John L. Sorenson and Melvin J. Thorne (Salt Lake City: Deseret Book and F.A.R.M.S., 1991): Terrance L. Szink, "Nephi and the Exodus," 35–51; Alan Goff, "Mourning, Consolation, and Repentance at Nahom," 92–99; and David R. Seely, "The Image of the Hand of God in the Book of Mormon and the Old Testament," 140–50.

2. Tate, "Typology," 254–59, has drawn attention to a few aspects of this theme as it appears in the Book of Mormon.

3. Reynolds, "Political Dimension" (22, 24), has suggested that at this point "Nephi practically likens himself to Moses." Compare also Tate's observations: "Though the correspondences between the exodus of the Israelites and this exodus are compelling, Nephi's conscious sense of reenacting the pattern is even more striking [1 Ne. 4:2]. But at this point he cannot have known how apt the allusion [to the Red Sea incident] really is. . . . As his awareness grows, he alludes with increasing frequency to the Exodus" ("Typology," 250). In my view, this is difficult to maintain, since Nephi's principal interest here is to cite Moses' experience as proof that the Lord can and will aid him and his demoralized brothers. However, in other passages to which Reynolds has drawn attention, the possible comparisons—consciously noted by Nephi—between himself and Moses are stronger ("Political Dimension," 29, 33).

4. The issue turns additionally on the understanding of the word "also" in 1 Ne. 5:15, hardly a feature upon which to erect a thesis. If Nephi meant that the Israelite slaves had been led by God, as his family had, then it would be possible to conclude that the first generation or two plainly saw the family's departure to a promised land as a replication of the earlier Exodus. But the passage can readily be understood in other ways. Compare also 1 Ne. 17:13–14, 37.

5. One intriguing connection, that of the Lord providing light at night to both the Israelites (1 Ne. 17:30) and Lehi's family (17:13), not only ties the Exodus to the flight of the family but also provides an important detail in the family's travel, since the heat of the day in Arabia forced travelers to journey into the night. It is probably this necessity that elevated the moon god as the most

important among the civilizations which the family would encounter farther south in Arabia. See Adel Allouche, "Arabian Religions," in *The Encyclopedia of Religion*, ed. Mircea Eliade (New York: Macmillan, 1987), 1:364; and Gus W. Van Beek, "Marib," in *The Oxford Encyclopedia of Archaeology in the Near East*, ed. Eric M. Meyers (New York: Oxford, 1997), 3:417.

6. Hugh W. Nibley, *An Approach to the Book of Mormon* (Salt Lake City: Deseret Book and F.A.R.M.S., 1988), 135–44.

7. Mosiah 7:19–20, words of king Limhi; Alma 36:28–29, words of Alma the Younger.

8. Tate's chart and its column 3 mention twelve Exodus features which are touched on or replicated in 1 Nephi; of these, fully nine are linked more or less closely with chapter 17 alone ("Typology," 258–59).

9. It is possible to see an extended series of similarities, and even echoes, between the experiences of the Israelites and Lehi's family: (a) the call to the responsible leader through a revelation accompanied by fire (Ex. 2:–4; 1 Ne. 1:6); (b) despoiling the Egyptians and taking Laban's possessions (Ex. 12:35–36; 1 Ne. 4:38; 2 Ne. 5:12, 14); (c) deliverance on the other side of a water barrier (Ex. 14:22–30; 1 Ne. 17:8; 18:8–9, in which the driving wind surely is divinely directed); (d) an extended period of wandering (Ex. 16:35 and Num. 14:33; 1 Ne. 17:4); (e) complaints along the way (Ex. 15:24; 16:2–3; 17:2–3, etc.; 1 Ne. 2:11–12; 5:2–3; 16:20, 25, 35–38; 17:17–22); (f) outright rebellion (Num. 16:1–35; 25:1–9; 1 Ne. 7:6–16; 18:9–21); and (g) a new law which was to govern the Lord's people (Ex. 20:2–17; 1 Ne. 2:20–24). Szink's observation, for example, on the use of the verb "to murmur," is compelling ("To a Land of Promise," 64; "Nephi and the Exodus," 39–40). Of course, other similarities and allusions could be listed.

10. The first region settled by Lehi's family was called both the land of Nephi (2 Ne. 5:8; Omni 1:27) and the land of Lehi–Nephi (Mosiah 7:1; 9:6). Approximately four hundred years later, the Nephite inhabitants were forced to abandon this region because of military pressures (Omni 1:12–13).

11. This group of people numbered 450 and escaped soldiers sent by king Noah (Mosiah 18:31–35; 23:1–3), eventually settling in a land they called Helam (23:4–5, 19).

12. Mosiah 24:10–25. The vocabulary alone echoes that of the Israelite exodus: they *cried* to the Lord (Mosiah 24:10–11; cf. 23:28 and Ex. 3:7, 9) because of their *bondage* (Mosiah 24:13, 16, 17, 21; cf. Ex. 1:14; 2:23; 6:6); and he set about to *deliver* them (Mosiah 24:13, 16–17, 21; cf. 23:23–24, 27 and Ex. 3:8).

13. Mosiah 22:1–13; in this case too, certain key terms are sprinkled throughout these verses, terms which recall Israel's exodus: *bondage* (22:1–4), *cry* (21:14–15), and *deliver* (22:1–2; cf. 21:5, 14, 36).

14. For Limhi's situation, see Mosiah 21:5, 14–15; Alma 1:8; for that of Alma's group, see Mosiah 23:23–24; 24:13, 16–17; Alma 5:4–5. The difference in the

apparent relative strength of the Lord's involvement in the deliverance of the two peoples may be due to the fact that Alma's group was blessed with the presence of a prophet and Limhi's people were not. Note king Mosiah's views on the matter in his public letter (Mosiah 29:19–20).

15. J. Coert Rylaarsdam, "The Book of Exodus: Introduction and Exegesis," in *The Interpreter's Bible* (Nashville: Abingdon, 1952), 1:853–55; S. Kent Brown, "Trust in the Lord: Exodus and Faith," in *The Old Testament and the Latter-day Saints, Sperry Symposium 1986* (Salt Lake City: Randall Book, 1986), 85–94.

16. Ex. 5:6–19; see Rylaarsdam, "Exodus," 886–87.

17. The speech is recorded in Mosiah 7:18b–33; in Mosiah 8:1, Mormon noted that Limhi had said a good deal more on this occasion.

18. Mosiah 7:25–28; incidentally, Limhi immediately quoted in succession three sayings of the Lord which are not part of Abinadi's recorded preaching nor do they come from any known source (7:29–31). Furthermore, the three passages all share a concern for "my people," a term familiar from the Exodus narrative which also denotes a covenant relationship (see Ex. 6:7; 8:20–21, 23; 9:13; 10:3–4).

19. Ex. 12:32, 38; Mosiah 22:10–11 (Limhi's people); 23:1 (Alma's first escape); 24:18 (second flight).

20. David Daube, *The Exodus Pattern in the Bible* (London: Faber and Faber, 1963), 48–51; further, Deut. 15:16b makes it clear that the slave should have been happy under the master's rule. Because the Lamanites were harsh in the view of the Mosaic code, this aspect of the relationship was ruptured as well, justifying the Nephites' desertion.

21. See Daube, *Exodus Pattern,* 55.

22. Ex. 11:3; 12:36; Mosiah 21:15 (Limhi's group); 23:29 (Alma's people).

23. The terms of the covenant are rehearsed in Mosiah 18:8–10; the sign of the covenant consisted in baptism (18:12–16); the name of the covenant people was "the church of God, or the church of Christ" (18:17); and the terms of the new law, including the priesthood offices, are outlined in Mosiah 18:18–28.

24. See reference to such priests with whom Mosiah consulted regularly on sensitive religious matters in Mosiah 27:1.

25. The passage reads: "And then shall they *know that I am the Lord* their God, that I am their Redeemer." The parallel words to Moses in Ex. 6:7 are impressive: "And I will take you to me for a people, and I will be to you a God: and ye shall *know that I am the Lord* your God, which bringeth you out from under the burdens of the Egyptians" (emphasis added). In addition, this seems to be the principal objective in both the exodus of the Israelites and that of Lehi's family; compare 1 Ne. 17:14 with Ex. 7:5; 8:2; 9:2; 14:4, 18

(the Egyptians too were to know that the Lord is God); 16:12; 19:1–2; 29:45–46; Lev. 25:38; 26:13; Num. 15:41; Deut. 4:35.

26. In giving the law to Moses, following the covenant made at Sinai, the Lord consistently used the phrase "I am the Lord" as the ultimate authority for the various legal and religious requirements that his people, now recovered, were to follow in order to retain their favored status. See, for example, Lev. 18:1–6; 19:3–4.

27. Num. 21:6–9; see also mention of this in 1 Ne. 17:41. Although I cannot draw any firm conclusions, I find it interesting that it is not Nephi but Alma the Younger who, as far as I know, made the connection between (a) Moses' action of raising the serpent on the pole which, if looked upon, brought healing, and (b) the Messiah's mission "to redeem his people" and "atone for their sins" (Alma 33:19–22); see also Nephi son of Helaman's words in Hel. 8:14–15, as well as John 3:14–15, where remarks have a different focus.

28. According to the biblical text, Moses struck a rock and water flowed out on two occasions: once at the holy mount (Ex. 17:5–6) and once at Kadesh in the wilderness of Zin (Num. 20:1–11). It is obviously to one of these that Nephi refers also in 1 Ne. 17:29. Notably, the biblical sequence of the incident at the rock and of the report of the serpents is maintained only in 1 Nephi 17, whereas 2 Ne. 25:20 reverses them. It is clear, of course, that the context of 2 Ne. 25:20 is that of oath-making to prove a point, while Nephi's recital of God's acts in 1 Nephi 17 follows the main points of the story of the Exodus, as well as of the Conquest. In fact, this latter passage seems steeped in the (memorized) Israelite recitations which summarized God's actions on behalf of his people when he rescued them from slavery (see Deut. 6:21–24; 26:5–9; Josh. 24:2–8).

29. The order of the proofs is interesting, for the first and principal proof—the Exodus—is out of chronological order, underscoring its importance: (a) Moses and the Exodus, Hel. 8:11–15; (b) Abraham, 8:16–17; (c) those who preceded Abraham, 8:18; (d) those who followed Abraham, including Zenos, Zenock, and others, 8:19–20; (e) the forebear Mulek who escaped Jerusalem's destruction, a prophesied event, 8:21; and (f) Lehi, his son Nephi, and the Nephite prophets, 8:22. Except for Jeremiah, who prophesied of Jerusalem's fall (8:20) and was vindicated by the testimony of Mulek, son of Zedekiah (8:21), all of the persons mentioned in this passage are affirmed by Nephi to have known of the coming Messiah (so 8:23). One further note: the list of proofs, in this order, raises the question whether the Nephite believers had developed catalogues of such topics taken from scripture.

30. Alma's instructions to his sons (Alma 36–42), as well as Lehi's last words to his children (2 Ne. 1:1–4:11), all fit the genre known as testament literature, which consists of accounts of various patriarchs giving their last instructions and blessings to their children. These passages all invite the student to examine them carefully in light of what is now known about this literary genre. For a study of Lehi's last words from a legal viewpoint, see John W.

Welch, "Lehi's Last Will and Testament: A Legal Approach," in *Second Nephi, The Doctrinal Structure*, ed. Monte S. Nyman and Charles D. Tate Jr. (Provo, Utah: Religious Studies Center, Brigham Young University, 1989), 61–82.

31. See, for example, John W. Welch, "Chiasmus in the Book of Mormon," in *Book of Mormon Authorship: New Light on Ancient Origins*, ed. Noel B. Reynolds (Provo, Utah: Religious Studies Center, Brigham Young University, 1982), 34–52, especially 49–51; and Tate, "Typology," 254–55, where a number of typological connections between Alma's words to Helaman and the Exodus are reviewed.

32. While the results of obeying and disobeying are spelled out in various passages of Deuteronomy, the list of promised blessings is collected in Deut. 28:1–14, and the curses or penalties for disobedience appear conveniently in 28:15–68. To these latter are to be added the curses that were to be recited by the Levites (27:14–26). In this connection, the entire issue of the Deuteronomic flavor of the Book of Mormon is yet to be tested, especially in light of the fact that the book of the law discovered in the temple in 621 B.C. (2 Kgs. 22:8–23:3), which led to a major religious reform (2 Kgs. 23:4–24), was likely Deuteronomy or an abbreviated version of it and would have been both known to Lehi and recently included with the plates of brass (implied in 1 Ne. 5:11). Categories that should be involved in any thorough investigation are promised blessings and threatened cursings that are prominently connected in the Book of Mormon with the Nephites' possession of a promised land. See Ellis T. Rasmussen, "Deuteronomy," in *Encyclopedia of Mormonism*, ed. Daniel H. Ludlow (New York: Macmillan, 1992), 378–79.

33. The theme of deliverance is woven tightly into the story of Israel's exodus. In Alma 36, the verb "to deliver" appears three times, all of which fall in the verses that summarize Israel's Exodus (36:2, 28). In the Old Testament, the Hebrew root translated "to deliver" (*naṣal*) occurs regularly in the Exodus narrative (Ex. 3:8; 12:27; 18:8–10; Deut. 23:14; cf. Ps. 18:48; 34:7, 17, 19; 97:10).

34. Deut. 6:21–24; 26:5–9; Josh. 24:2–14; cf. Amos 2:9–10; 3:1–2; 1 Ne. 17:23–42.

35. Tate has already drawn attention to these reports ("Typology," 254–55).

36. The phrase comes from verse 2, where the forceful emphasis is on the absolute inability of Israel to deliver herself: "For they were in bondage, and *none could deliver* them except it was the God of Abraham . . . and *he surely did deliver them* in their afflictions" (emphasis added). The other bracketing passage, verses 28–29, emphasizes the Lord's continual and continuing care both for individuals, such as Alma, and for his people as a whole, whoever they are: "And I know that he will raise *me* up at the last day . . . for he has brought *our fathers* out of Egypt . . . by his power . . . yea, and he has delivered *them* out of bondage and captivity *from time to time*. Yea, and he has also brought *our fathers* [Lehi's family] out of the land of Jerusalem; and he has also, by his everlasting power, delivered *them* out of bondage and captivity, *from time to time even down to the present day*" (emphasis added).

37. An examination of the biographical account in Mosiah 27 exhibits connections between Alma's experience and the Exodus which are, in some ways, even more impressive than those visible in the first-hand report of Alma 36. Though one must bear in mind that Alma's experience included only himself and his four friends, while an entire people was involved with Moses, the similarities are nevertheless rather impressive. The compelling circumstances arise out of the apparition of the angel, the description of which bears stronger resemblances to the experience of the Israelites at Sinai than to other similar experiences such as the Lord's call of Jeremiah (Jeremiah 1), Isaiah (Isaiah 6), Lehi (1 Nephi 1), or even Ezekiel (Ezekiel 1–3). For instance, the angel who confronted the five young men "descended" to meet them (Mosiah 27:11); in a similar way, "the Lord *came down* upon mount Sinai" (Ex. 19:20, emphasis added). Second, the angel appeared to the youths "as it were in a *cloud*" (Mosiah 27:11, emphasis added) as the Lord had come before both Moses and the people. Third, the angel spoke as if "with a *voice* of *thunder*, which caused the earth to *shake*" (Mosiah 27:11, emphasis added). Likewise, the voice of the trumpet from the holy mount was "exceeding loud" (Ex. 19:16; also 20:18) and "sounded long, and waxed louder and louder" (19:19). At the sound of God's voice (19:19), all of the Israelites "trembled" (19:16) and "stood afar off" (20:18), requesting that God not speak to them "lest we die" (20:19). Further, at God's presence on the mount, "there were thunders and lightnings" (19:16; also 20:18) and "the whole mount quaked greatly" (19:18). Fourth, the angel mentioned specifically the "bondage" of Alma's forebears (Mosiah 27:16), a clear recollection of terms used to describe the plight of the Israelite slaves. Fifth, this very point raises one of the clearest links between the Exodus and the Atonement. All of the words describing Israel's bondage derive from the root *'bd*. It is also a noun from this same root which is translated "servant" in Isaiah 53, which Abinadi had quoted at length and then immediately linked to Jesus' ministry. What is clear here is that Jesus is the expected servant (*'ebed*) who, by paying the price of redemption, frees all those who will follow him from bondage (*'abōdāh*), the very term used in the Exodus account. One could, of course, further echo Exodus themes.

38. It also appears twice in the following verse (2 Ne. 9:13) and is used of the new exodus in Isa. 50:2 (= 2 Ne. 7:2).

39. Of at least thirty-three allusions to the Exodus which appear both in Jacob's words (2 Nephi 6, 9–10) and in Isa. 50:1–52:2 (= 2 Nephi 7–8), I list the following: (a) Israel is to "return again" (2 Ne. 6:9); (b) the Lord God is to "manifest himself," a self-disclosure which echoes the self-disclosures on the holy mount (6:9); (c) the scattered of Israel are to "come to the knowledge of their Redeemer" (6:11, 15, 18); (d) they will return "to the lands of their inheritance" (6:11; 10:7–8); (e) the Lord is to "be merciful" to his people (6:11); (f) the Messiah is "to recover them" a second time (6:14); (g) "pestilence" is mentioned, recalling the plagues (6:15); (h) the phrase added to Isa. 47:25, that appears in 2 Ne. 6:17, clearly points to the Exodus: "The Mighty God shall deliver his covenant people"; (i) the Lord is able to redeem (7:2) and

"the redeemed of the Lord shall return" (8:11); (j) the Lord is able to deliver (7:2; 9:11–13, 26); and (k) the Lord is able to dry up "the sea," "rivers," and "waters" (7:2; more explicit in 8:10; cf. "waves" in 8:15).

40. Taking his lead from others, Tate has drawn attention in rapid fashion to the echoes of the Exodus not only in the gospel accounts of Jesus' ministry but also in the recitation of his visit to the people in Bountiful ("Typology," 255–57 and columns 2 and 7 of the chart on 258–59).

41. The picture of loss and disruption is tremendous, and all forms of life must have been left in tatters: "The whole face of the land was changed" and "the face of the whole earth became deformed" (3 Ne. 8:12, 17). The entire infrastructure was ruined: "The highways were broken up, and the level roads were spoiled, and many smooth places became rough . . . and the places were left desolate" (8:13, 14).

42. I sense that the entire matter of Jesus' quotations from Old Testament sources, when properly reviewed, will reveal that the passages cited point consistently to the period of either the new exodus or the end time. For example, all of the following passages—taken in the order in which they are quoted by the Savior—have to do with the new exodus: Isa. 52:8–10 (3 Ne. 16:18–20); Micah 5:8–9 (3 Ne. 20:16–17); Micah 4:12–13 (3 Ne. 20:18–19); Isa. 52:9–10 (3 Ne. 20:34–35); Isa. 52:1–3 (3 Ne. 20:36–38); Isa. 52:7 (3 Ne. 20:40); Isa. 52:11–15 (3 Ne. 20:41–45); Isa. 52:15 (3 Ne. 21:8); Isa. 52:14 (3 Ne. 21:10); Micah 5:8–14 (3 Ne. 21:12–18); and Isa. 52:12 (3 Ne. 21:29). Chapters 3 and 4 of Malachi, quoted by Jesus in 3 Nephi 24–25, can also be understood as anticipating the new exodus. For instance, reference to the way prepared by the expected messenger (Mal. 3:1 = 3 Ne. 24:1) can be seen as an allusion to "the way of the Lord" to be prepared in the desert (Isa. 40:3). Further, the reference to purifying "the sons of Levi" as a preparatory step before they "offer unto the Lord an offering in righteousness" (Mal. 3:3) finds clear echoes in the selection and setting apart of the Levites in the desert (Num. 3:41, 45; 8:6–22).

43. See Tate, "Typology," 257.

44. During the second day, we are told only that "the multitude had all eaten and drunk" and were thereafter "filled with the Spirit" (3 Ne. 20:9). But the text seems plain enough. In the case of the first day, the statement is clearer. We learn that the disciples were the first to partake of the bread and be filled, afterwards giving the bread to the multitude of twenty-five hundred people until they were filled (18:3–5). The same condition resulted from drinking the wine (18:8–9). One must recall further that by this point in the day the crowd had been without food for several hours, having (a) gone forward "one by one" and felt Jesus' wounds (11:15), (b) listened to his "sermon on the mount" address (3 Nephi 12–14), (c) listened to Jesus' further words (3 Nephi 15–16), (d) seen him heal the infirm among them (17:5–10), and (e) witnessed Jesus blessing their children (17:11–24). Hence, when the record says that the multitude was "filled"—whether on day one or day two—by partaking of

the bread and wine, it is to be understood at least in terms of satisfying their hunger and thirst.

45. One important dimension that still must be explored in the Book of Mormon concerns the social and legal bases for the Lord's acts of deliverance. Such links are clearly visible in the Exodus account, as Daube has pointed out: "God was seen as intervening, not like a despot, but in the faithful exercise of a recognized privilege—which would, in turn, impose lasting obligations on those on whose behalf he intervened" (*Exodus Pattern*, 13). One example of a direction to pursue this sort of tie between the Lord and all the descendants of Lehi would be to investigate the notion that they were the Lord's people whose relationship was rooted in covenant (Mosiah 24:13). Other passages which exhibit this feature and are also connected to the Exodus theme consist of 2 Ne. 8:4 (= Isa. 51:4) and Mosiah 7:29–31; see also Mosiah 11:22; 12:1, 4; 14:8; 24:13, 14; 26:17, 18, 30, 32; Alma 5:57; 10:21; cf. Ex. 6:7.

46. The whole issue of slavery abroad is reviewed by Daube, *Exodus Pattern*, 39–41.

47. Daube, *Exodus Pattern*, 40. Even the ages of Moses and Aaron, 80 and 83 respectively, may have been an important factor, for "envoys were . . . carefully selected for their distinction and fitness for the task. . . . A minimum age was sometimes required."

48. 3 Ne. 20:23, where Jesus applies to himself Moses' prophecy recorded in Deut. 18:15, with slight variation: "Behold, I am he of whom Moses spake, saying: A prophet shall the Lord your God raise up unto you of your brethren, *like unto me*" (emphasis added). See also my study in this book, chapter 10, "Moses and Jesus: The Old Adorns the New."

49. Daube, *Exodus Pattern*, 40.

50. Moses learned that God's name was I AM (Ex. 3:14) and also bore the three signs of (a) the rod that would turn into a serpent, (b) his hand that could be made leprous, and (c) the power to turn water to blood (Ex. 4:1–9). See the relevant remarks of Daube, *Exodus Pattern*, 40.

51. 3 Ne. 9:21, where the "voice heard . . . upon all the face of this land" (9:1) says: "Behold, I have come unto the world to bring redemption unto the world, to save the world from sin." Samuel the Lamanite's words underscore the point: "Behold, the resurrection of Christ redeemeth mankind . . . and *bringeth* them *back* into the presence of the Lord" (Hel. 14:17, emphasis added). It is important to note that the verb "to bring back," or its counterpart "to bring out," often appears describing God's actions in the Exodus (see Daube, *Exodus Pattern*, 31–35). The verb "to bring out" is especially used in the Book of Mormon to summarize the Exodus (1 Ne. 17:25, 40; 2 Ne. 25:20; Mosiah 7:19), to outline Lehi's departure (1 Ne. 17:14; 2 Ne. 1:30; Mosiah 2:4), and to describe the Atonement (3 Ne. 28:29). Compare Jesus' impassioned words to the survivors in 3 Ne. 10:4–6.

52. Even though no captor is mentioned, except perhaps the devil and his angels (3 Ne. 9:2), one recalls that Jesus quoted a key passage from Isaiah that bears on the issue: "For thus saith the Lord: Ye have sold yourselves for naught, and ye shall be redeemed without money" (3 Ne. 20:38 = Isa. 52:3), a passage that is surrounded by Isaiah's prophecies of the second exodus. Plainly, there was no captor to whom Jesus could come, as the quoted passage observes. Even so, Jesus presented himself to the fallen survivors almost as if he were presenting his credentials to one with whom he must negotiate for the release of captives (see 3 Ne. 9:15–18; cf. 11:14–16). Speaking of Jesus during his earthly ministry, Daube observes: "From Jesus sent by God to save mankind, from his legitimation, or refusal to furnish legitimation, before adversaries and followers, from the insistence on the necessity of belief in him, one line of many . . . leads back across the centuries to the practices of international commerce in the matter of prisoners of war" (*Exodus Pattern*, 41).

53. One may object to this interpretation. But the matter, in my view, is settled by the general consensus of New Testament scholarship that, when Jesus is quoted—particularly in John's gospel—using the phrase "I am," he is employing the name revealed to Moses on the holy mount (John 4:26 [the KJV obscures this]; 6:35, 48, 51; 8:12). To hold that the mortal Jesus used the phrase of himself in clear reference to the divine name and then, when he visited the Americas as resurrected Lord and King, used the phrase only in the sense of a grammatical copula, seems to strain one of the plain senses of the text. Jesus' words to the New World survivors resemble the language of the gospel of John more than that of the Synoptics (3 Ne. 9:13–22; only the sayings in 3 Ne. 10:4–7 are clearly stamped as being from the Synoptic gospels). In addition, his opening words to those in Bountiful are clearly Johannine in character (3 Ne. 11:10–11).

6

Marriage and Treaty in the Book of Mormon: The Case of the Abducted Lamanite Daughters

Biblical law and custom must have persisted among Book of Mormon peoples. The account of the abducted Lamanite women offers an unusually clear view into legal and social norms among Nephites. Perhaps surprisingly, the report hints strongly that some of these norms also survived among Lamanites.

Marriage seemingly receives little attention in the Book of Mormon. The earliest notice, that of the marriage of the sons of Lehi and Sariah to the daughters of Ishmael, rates no more than a single verse (1 Ne. 16:7). In the following generation, the prophet Jacob condemns certain men in his society for seeking to introduce the practice of plural marriage (Jacob 2:22–35), a practice that seems not to have been continued.[1] The regent Lamanite king Lamoni, in a much later scene, proposes to marry his daughter to Ammon, a Nephite prince, a proposal that Ammon respectfully declines (Alma 17:22–25). In a celebrated case, the traitorous Nephite Amalickiah deceitfully "obtained the kingdom" of the Lamanites and "took [the queen] unto him to wife" (47:35).[2] Oddly, perhaps, the most interesting, complex, and complete account of marriage in the Book of Mormon is that of the fugitive priests of king Noah to young Lamanite women whom they had abducted (Mosiah 20:3–5), rupturing a treaty in the process.

These priests of Noah, part of a Nephite colony in the midst of Lamanite territory, had abandoned their homes and families in an effort to avoid death at the hands of an invading Lamanite army (Mosiah 19:9–23). Two years later (19:29), the priests crept back to the outskirts of their former colony and, presumably in order to stay alive, "carried off [fellow colonists'] grain and many of their precious things," coming "by night"—which, if caught at night, made their thievery a capital crime (21:21).[3] It was while these priests were in the neighboring wilderness that they stumbled upon "a place in Shemlon where the daughters of the Lamanites did gather themselves" (20:1). After discovering "the daughters of the Lamanites, they laid and watched them; and when there were but few of them gathered together to dance, they came forth out of their secret places and took them and carried them into the wilderness" (20:4–5).

The sudden disappearance of the young women led to an immediate rupture in the treaty—a suzerain–vassal relationship between Lamanite overlords and the subject Nephite colony then under the leadership of Limhi—a rupture that brought a military reprisal against the Nephites (20:6–11).[4] The Lamanite king and his people suspected that the Nephites were responsible for the wrong.[5] When both parties grasped that it was the renegade priests who had kidnapped these young women (20:17–19, 23–24), they set out to discover the whereabouts of the priests and their captives in order to punish them, but without success.[6] When a disoriented Lamanite army accidentally located them many months later, the priests craftily escaped punishment by obliging their "wives" to intercede on their behalf, thereafter easing themselves into Lamanite society and even taking positions of responsibility (23:30–39; 24:1, 4).[7]

"Wives" and "Husbands"

A number of legal and social issues stem from the narrative. The most important is the fact that at the end of this series of events, the women are called "wives" and the priests "husbands" (Mosiah 23:33–34). The terms are most significant, for they establish the legal framework for the outcome of the story. Perhaps just as important is the observation that the editor of the account, Mormon, has accepted the terminology of his source. Plainly, by so doing he demonstrates that in his culture—though he lived much later—the women were thought of as legally married. One of the complicating issues that does not arise in the narrative has to do with the legal status of the priests' previous wives whom they had abandoned, although their children are discussed.[8]

The terminology not only interprets the outcome of the situation but also invites us to enter the world of the Old Testament, where laws deal rather extensively with marriage, including that of a master to a captive woman. As we shall soon see, a number of elements in the account can be understood best in light of either the Mosaic code or Old Testament events that established legal norms.[9]

In the situation at hand, the text features verbs that point to the captive status of the Lamanite women: the priests "took them and carried them" away (20:5; cf. 20:15, 23).[10] But the captivity was illegal, because those who subsequently accused the priests said that they had "stolen" the young women—a term with severe legal implications (20:18; 21:20–21).[11]

Two issues come immediately to the fore: (a) taking the daughters as captives—an illegal act in both the Lamanite and Nephite societies, as the responses illustrate (20:6, 16), and (b) the consequent depriving of each woman of a marriage performed with the "consent" of her parents, particularly of her father—"there is a complete break with her family."[12] In this latter instance, such marriages were allowed between Israelite males and foreign women whose cities, lying at a distance "very far off," had been sacked by an Israelite army (Deut. 20:10–15). But of course, the Lamanite daughters were not foreigners in the sense that they were non-Israelites—hence, the enormity of the priests' actions: abducting the young women, forcibly separating them from their families while intending to take them as wives, forcing their will on Israelite women, and carrying out marriages that were illegal under the Mosaic code because they did not result from war. But in the end, astonishingly, the marriages were honored, at least in Lamanite society.

The decree of death pronounced upon the priests, issued by both the Lamanite king and the Nephite ruler Limhi (Mosiah 20:7, 16), seems to suggest that some of the young women were already betrothed to be married—and therefore were considered to be under a marriage obligation—and that their kidnappers were thought of as rapists. In such a situation, the men are to die.[13] In contrast, in the case of an unmarried virgin, biblical law holds that the rapist must pay a fine, marry the woman, and never divorce her (Deut. 22:28–29). Hence, had none of the young women been engaged—that is, if none were under a marriage contract—the severity of the reprisal sought by the Lamanite king might be thought of as excessive,[14] unless one could demonstrate that he acted solely on emotion and not according to law.[15]

Another possible legal component is at play here, that of "humiliating" a woman.[16] In the Bible this issue is closely associated with that of a woman forced to marry without the consent of her father. The meaning of the humiliation remains an open question. David Daube believes that the matter is identical to taking a woman "without the correct formalities" and arises when a woman is treated as if she comes from a social class that does not deserve a wedding with all the trimmings, so to speak.[17] But the humiliation may rather have to do with treating a woman as a harlot, as was done in the case of Shechem forcing Dinah, daughter of Jacob and Leah. It was this defiling of Dinah that led to the murderous response of her two brothers against Shechem and his fellow townsmen (Genesis 34).[18] From this viewpoint, even though the Lamanite women were later reckoned as wives of the renegade priests, the route to their marriages was through defiled beds, thus humbling the women.[19] In fact, it is the story of Dinah that provides some of the most striking parallels with the experience of the Lamanite daughters, except that in the end Dinah did not marry the man who "took her, and lay with her, and defiled her" (34:2).[20]

Ruptured Treaty

The broken treaty, at least as it was perceived by the Lamanite king, is the next feature to draw our attention. It is important not only because a lot of space is granted to it—underscoring its value to both sides, including mention of the treaty ceremony itself[21]—but also because its apparent rupture lay at the heart of the king's decision to send his armies "to destroy the people of Limhi." It is also important to the story to note that "even the king himself went before his people" into battle (Mosiah 20:7). Apparently the king felt that he had invested a good deal of effort in bringing the treaty about[22] and, as a result, was hurt and angered that the agreement had apparently been broken by the Nephite colonists and Limhi, his negotiating partner.[23]

Beyond question, the making of the treaty is to be understood as a very serious and sacred matter.[24] On the human side, it had become the basis for an era of peace, even though the peace benefitted chiefly the Lamanites (19:25–27, 29).[25] According to Old Testament law, the breaking of an agreement that had been concluded between two parties led to whatever consequences were spelled out in the "curses" which accompanied the oaths, the classic example being the covenant between the Israelites, who were about to possess the promised land, and the Lord.[26] As is plain from the response of the Lamanite king, his promise that "his people should not slay" the people of Limhi (19:25) was reversed as one of the penalties for breaking the treaty.

In the end, the king's decision to destroy the Nephite colony must have rested on a combination of considerations, one of which was his feeling of anger. In general, when a treaty has evidently been broken, the question is, "How flagrant must a violation be before the sovereign could legitimately muster his military forces and attack the recalcitrant vassal?"[27] The Lamanite king must have seen a series of misdeeds in the abduction of the young women. First, it was an act of stealing—a clear breach of law; the people there were not in a state of war or national tension. Second, any marriages that might result would consequently be illegal or, at the very least, extremely odious. Third, the kidnaping was evidence, as he perceived the matter, of the breaking of solemn pledges made only two years earlier.[28] It would appear that he had no choice except to bring down the weight of the Lamanite army on the Nephite colonists.

Status of the Marriages

Now we come to a key question. Why were these marriages between the priests and the abducted women recognized? Clearly the priests broke the law and thus distanced themselves from custom as understood in both the Nephite and Lamanite societies. Yet in the end the marriages were not only more or less legitimized according to the terminology used in a Nephite record—"wives" and "husbands"—but were also allowed to stand in Lamanite society, where the couples came to live and raise families.

The answer must be that an array of factors brought about a favorable resolution of the issue for the priests. First, on the legal side, we have already seen that under Mosaic law a man can marry a captive woman if certain procedures are followed, particularly because the marriage takes place without the consent of her father and without the normal wedding celebrations (Deut. 21:10–14). The law stipulates that the woman must be a prize of war and a citizen of a city "very far off" (20:15). But for the renegade priests, such stipulations—even if honored in the larger society[29]—would have made little difference. Moreover, it was evidently possible in Book of Mormon society, as it was in societies in the ancient Near East,[30] to make a woman a wife by engaging in sexual relations, an action particularly repugnant to the woman's family. Hence, the priests may have been partially, if weakly, justified—in their own eyes at least—in holding onto the Lamanite daughters as wives.

One cannot prove directly that the particular stipulations of the Deuteronomic code, noted above, were known and observed among Book of Mormon peoples. But the account does exhibit clues of a serious legal difficulty in resolving the status of the marriages, clues that invite one to examine the only legal texts that were available to Book of Mormon societies early on.[31]

The second set of circumstances surfaced when the wandering Lamanite army came upon the new settlement founded by the priests and their new wives. Essentially, the priests made a deal. We note before anything else that typical soldiers in antiquity would not be literate and therefore acquainted with legal niceties.[32] But the army that discovered the settlement was well aware that these priests were deserving of death.[33] As a result, the priests did everything they could to escape being killed. The leader of the group, a man named Amulon,[34] adopted a two-pronged approach. First, he himself "did plead with the Lamanites" that they not destroy the members of the settlement. Then "he also sent forth their wives, who were the daughters of the Lamanites, to plead with their brethren, that they should not destroy their husbands" (Mosiah 23:33). His own efforts seem to have failed. But the efforts of the women paid off: "And the Lamanites had compassion on Amulon and his brethren, and did not destroy them, because of their wives" (23:34).[35]

Simply stated, Amulon's tactic to throw himself and his fellow priests on the mercy of the Lamanite army worked because it spared their lives. But there is more. To all appearances, the wives were willing to intercede for their husbands. There was no visibly abusive compulsion on the part of the former priests, forcing the women to come forward and beg on their behalf in a demeaning way, an action that would surely have given the Lamanite soldiers an excuse to execute the husbands.

Negotiations, however, also meant that the priests were required to abandon their new settlement, to return to the homeland of the Lamanites, and to "join the Lamanites," although the text does not specify what this latter means (23:35).[36] The results for the priests were that they would keep both their lives and their wives, a decision that was not subsequently overturned by the Lamanite king because, afterward, he appointed Amulon to serve as a regent king over the colony of Alma, "his [Amulon's] people" (23:39).

Epilogue: The Fate of the Children of the Priests

In a somber aftermath, we learn of the terrible fate of the former priests and their sons.[37] A generation after the priests were allowed to keep their wives, and following a series of remarkable successes by Nephite missionaries preaching among the Lamanites which led to a split in the society along religious lines, a Lamanite army—chiefly out of frustration—attacked the Nephite frontier city Ammonihah and destroyed all life in it (Alma 16:1–3).[38] Of the events that followed, we possess two accounts. One is that of the Nephite army which tracked the Lamanite force "into the wilderness" because this latter group had taken captives from neighboring settlements whom the Nephites sought to rescue. Rescue them they did. The commanding general consulted with Alma, the prophet of the church, who gave inspired instructions about where the Nephite army could intercept the Lamanites with their captives, which they did without loss of life to any of the prisoners. The first account ends with the notation that the former prisoners "were brought by their brethren to possess their own lands" (16:4–8).

It is the second account that fills in the picture about the fate of the priests and their sons who, as it happened, were part of the invading Lamanite army that destroyed the city of Ammonihah. This record originated with the sons of king Mosiah whose successful missionary work had raised anger and fear in certain Lamanite circles, an anger that spilled over into a civil conflict between nonbelievers and newly won believers in the message of Mosiah's sons. Because the believers, called Anti-Nephi-Lehies (23:17), refused to take up arms in self-defense, and because their attackers became frustrated and angry with themselves for slaughtering fellow citizens who were believers, the nonbelievers "swore vengeance upon the Nephites" and subsequently attacked the city of Ammonihah. It was this force that the Nephite army intercepted, freeing the prisoners. But there was more. When the Nephite force ambushed the Lamanite army, it both killed "almost all the seed of Amulon and his brethren, who were the priests of Noah," and drove the remainder deeper into the wilderness where a rift occurred among the Lamanite soldiers (25:4–5). Some had begun to doubt the worthwhile character of making war, having seen the pacifist stance of their fellow countrymen, the Anti-Nephi-Lehies. At this point, the remaining priests and "the children of Amulon" executed those who had begun "to disbelieve the traditions of their fathers, and to believe in the Lord." After an ensuing mutiny, termed a "contention in the wilderness," "the Lamanites" began "to hunt" and kill "the seed of Amulon and his brethren."[39] As a grim ending to this episode, the record observes that "they are hunted at this day by the Lamanites" (25:1–9).

In a postscript, other "descendants of the priests of Noah" (43:13)—presumably not only children of the priests who were too young to participate in the attack on Ammonihah but also grandchildren of the former priests[40]—participated in the protracted wars between Lamanites and Nephites (Alma 43–44; 49–62). From this point on, we lose sight of them in the record. But at last glance, we see them again joining those whose hatred for the Nephites was almost insatiable, and dealing in death.

NOTES

1. Legalized polygamy is not commented on again, with one possible exception. It concerns Amulek, who, in referring to blessings received during the extended visit of Alma to his home, said, "He hath blessed me, and my women" (Alma 10:11). However, the reference may be to his wife and his mother, not to multiple wives. Even though Amulek mentions "my father and my kinsfolk," the nature of the text does not allow a decisive judgment.

2. The legal and social dimensions of this case are intriguing but go beyond the scope of the present study.

3. The seemingly unnecessary notation of the night as the time of crime may suggest Nephite knowledge of this stipulation of the Mosaic code. On theft "by night" (Mosiah 21:21) as a capital crime, see J. Coert Rylaarsdam, *The Book of Exodus* (New York: Abingdon, 1952), 1002–3; and Samuel Greengus, "Law," in *Anchor Bible Dictionary*, ed. David N. Freedman (New York: Doubleday, 1992), 4:249. According to Ex. 22:2, a thief who comes by night can be killed without attaching a "bloodguilt" penalty to the executioner.

4. For a discussion of this treaty and its connections to the Bible and the ancient Near East, see Mark Davis and Brent Israelsen, "International Relations and Treaties in the Book of Mormon " (Provo, Utah: F.A.R.M.S., 1988), 14–16.

5. The Lamanites were aware that the crime was kidnapping, and possibly worse, for the king told Limhi that "thy people did carry away the daughters of my people" (Mosiah 20:15). Hence, either there were witnesses, or one or more of the young women successfully escaped the priests.

6. At first, the kidnappers' identity remained unknown (Mosiah 20:16); according to Mosiah 21:21, the punishment was to be for other crimes, such as theft of grain. For each crime, kidnapping and theft "by night," the punishment was to be death. Cf. Mosiah 20:7, wherein the Lamanite king seeks to "destroy" Limhi's people for the kidnapping; and Mosiah 21:23, wherein Limhi, at first thinking "Ammon and his brethren" to be "priests of Noah," would have "put [them] to death."

7. For one approach to the theft of the Lamanite daughters, see Alan Goff, "The Stealing of the Daughters of the Lamanites," in *Rediscovering the Book of Mormon*, ed. John L. Sorenson and Melvin J. Thorne (Salt Lake City: Deseret Book and F.A.R.M.S., 1991), 67–74. Goff draws attention to connections between this story and accounts in the book of Judges about the people of the tribe of Benjamin. John W. Welch, in *Reexploring the Book of Mormon* (Salt Lake City: Deseret Book and F.A.R.M.S., 1992), 139–41, suggests that the dancing was an annual event. Not incidentally, the narrative in Mosiah 20–23 gives the impression of a significant passage of time.

8. There must have been laws that governed the standing of a wife who found herself in such straits, possibly allowing her to divorce the man who had abandoned her and their children and to not be responsible for his debts. Concerning the status of abandoned children, in the case at hand we read that the children adopted a patronymic that would not identify them with their biological fathers: "The children of Amulon and his brethren, who had taken to wife the daughters of the Lamanites, were displeased with the conduct of their fathers, and they would no longer be called by the names of their fathers, therefore they took upon themselves the name of Nephi, that they might be called the children of Nephi" (Mosiah 25:12). It is not clear how this sort of action might affect, for instance, the legal claim of the children to the property of their fathers. In later Jewish law, these kinds of issues were dealt with, for instance, in the Mishnah, *Yebamoth* 10.1–5; 15.1–16.7; *Shebuoth* 7.7.

9. We know that Nephites appealed to biblical events for legal and social precedents. See Jacob's spirited condemnation of those who appealed to "things which were written concerning David, and Solomon his son" (Jacob 2:23).

10. Understanding the verb *to take* as meaning "to take under one's control" (as Hebrew *lqḥ*) or "to take away by theft" (as Hebrew *gnb*); and "to carry" as connoting "to carry away that which does not belong to one" or, in a broadly legal sense, "to deprive." The Hebrew verb *lqḥ* also appears with the meaning "to take [a wife]" (e.g., Gen. 4:19; 6:2; cf. 1 Ne. 7:1; 16:7). See David Daube, *The Exodus Pattern in the Bible* (London: Faber and Faber, 1963), 73.

11. According to Mosaic law, kidnaping an Israelite was to be punished by death (Ex. 21:16; Deut. 24:7). See Muhammad A. Dandamayev, "Slavery: Old Testament," in *Anchor Bible Dictionary*, 6:63.

12. Daube, *Exodus Pattern*, 65; also Phyllis A. Bird, "Women: Old Testament," in *Anchor Bible Dictionary*, 6:956. The account presumes something like the law found in Deut. 21:10–14. See also Ex. 22:17; Num. 30:16.

13. For biblical law, see Deut. 22:23–27. "In the case of the betrothed . . . woman, the penalty is death for the rapist and the woman goes free if one can presume that she struggled and was coerced." Greengus, "Law," 4:247.

14. The "excessive" character of the reprisal must have to do with the fact that two peoples were living side by side under a treaty. If events had taken place entirely within either the Lamanite society or the Nephite colony, and if all of the young women were not betrothed, a more measured response might be expected. But when a treaty is involved, the king of the wronged party would see himself as pursuing the interests of his people and their god by gathering an army and pursuing the breaker of the treaty. (According to Deut. 28:20–22, even the Lord punishes "with the sword" of another; cf. Jer. 1:13–16.) See Michael L. Barré, "Treaties in the Ancient Near East," in *Anchor Bible Dictionary*, 6:655.

15. Speaking of the Lamanites in general, the text does say that "they were angry with the people of Limhi" (Mosiah 20:6). Further, the Lamanite king admits that "in my anger I did cause my people to come up to war" (20:15). But there is nothing to suggest that the warlike response did not conform to established custom or law. See Michael L. Barré, "Treaties," 6:655, who maintains that "in suzerain–vassal treaties, this [effort to punish] often took the form of a punitive campaign by the suzerain against the transgressor."

16. For example, Deut. 21:14; 22:24, 29.

17. Daube, *Exodus Pattern*, 65–66.

18. Cf. also Lam. 5:11.

19. One must keep in mind that in the ancient world, women and children were often treated as a man's possessions, though not strictly as property (cf. Ex. 20:17; Deut. 5:21); see Phyillis A. Bird, "Women," 6:956.

20. For example, Dinah was initially spotted by Shechem in the company of other women (Gen. 34:1). He in effect abducted her ("he took her"—34:2). His act was judged to be a wrong that needed a strong response, a wrong that had "humbled" Dinah, e.g., Deut. 22:29 ("which thing ought not to be done"—Gen. 34:7; "Should he deal with our sister as with an harlot?"—Gen. 34:31). In this light, the brothers of Dinah sought death for Shechem and those who harbored him (34:25–26). A deal was struck, deceitfully in this case (34:13), that would allow Shechem to retain Dinah as wife. Note the proposed fine in Gen. 34:11, and the required circumcision in Gen. 34:14–17. In the present case, the priests of Noah were required to abandon their new settlement (Mosiah 23:31) and to "join the Lamanites" (23:35).

21. Indicated by the term "granted" in Mosiah 19:15, 22; cf. Gen. 9:12; 17:2 (Hebrew *ntn*, "give" or "grant"; KJV renders "make"; on words used to describe ceremonies, see Michael L. Barré, "Treaties," 6:654). Also present are: the terms of the treaty, confirmed by oaths of ratification on both sides (Mosiah 19:15, 25–26); the elevation of Limhi—"having the kingdom conferred upon him"—who then represented the Nephite colonists in making the agreement (19:26); the Lamanite effort to assure compliance through the stationing of guards (19:28); the benefits of the agreement—peace for two years (19:29); the complaint of breaking the treaty (20:14–15); the Lamanite response to the apparent breaking of the treaty—sending an invasion force "to destroy" the colonists (20:7); and the Nephite military response (20:8–11). Nothing is known of the place where the treaty was concluded—possibly the temple—or whether a written copy was made.

22. It appears that the tribute of "one half of all" was to be paid "unto him" personally (Mosiah 19:26). Clearly, the king was a major figure in the negotiations, providing more than merely the expected oath (19:25).

23. The colonists would eventually break the treaty by flight and particularly—in an echo of the Israelite exodus—by taking their "flocks" and

"herds," in addition to "all their gold, and silver, and their precious things, which they could carry" (Mosiah 22:11–12), half of which belonged to the Lamanites under the agreement. But the Nephites had the law on their side: they had been vassals for a number of years. Hence, their Lamanite-Israelite masters owed them freedom and gifts (Deut. 15:12–15). Cf. also Jacob and Laban (Genesis 29–31). See Daube, *Exodus Pattern*, 47–61.

24. Quite naturally, God becomes involved in the language of oaths sworn in making treaties. Regularly in treaties of the ancient Near East, "the deities before whom the oath was taken were thought to act as guarantors of the treaty"; Michael L. Barré, "Treaties," 6:654.

25. According to Mosiah 19:15 the agreement held that the lives of the colonists would be spared and that they would be allowed to "possess the land" again. In Mosiah 19:25–26, the Lamanite king pledged "that his people would not slay" the Nephites, but Limhi promised that "his people should pay tribute . . . [of] one half of all they possessed." This level of payment had been established in an earlier accord (7:22; 19:15, 22).

26. Deut. 28:1–13 enumerates the "blessings" of the covenant from the Lord, and Deut. 27:15–26 and 28:15–68 list the "curses." One of the consequences of Israelite disobedience to the covenant is, "Thou [shalt] serve thine enemies . . . until [they] have destroyed thee" (28:48). Note the additional phrase, "which the Lord shall send against thee," clear proof that the Lord is the guarantor of the agreement.

27. George E. Mendenhall and Gary A. Herion, "Covenant," in *Anchor Bible Dictionary*, 1:1182.

28. In a moving scene, after he had learned that the guilt rested on the renegade priests, the Lamanite king restores the oath that he thought had been broken and then "did bow himself down" before his army, pleading that they "not slay [the Nephite] people" (Mosiah 20:24–26).

29. Lamanites do not seem to have married female prisoners of war. For example, in the exchange of letters between Moroni and Ammoron about swapping prisoners of war, Moroni seems to expect that he can get most of the women back (Alma 54).

30. In both biblical and ancient Near Eastern law, a dichotomy apparently existed between the divine imperative that an adulterer be punished by death and the right of pardon that could be exercised by the injured husband or, one infers, the injured fiancé. Joseph acts thus for Mary (Matt. 1:18–19). See Elaine Adler Goodfriend, "Adultery," in *Anchor Bible Dictionary*, 1:82–83. In the present case of the abducted daughters who were betrothed, such a dichotomy in Lamanite law would have allowed their former fiancés to forgive them, thus freeing them from penalty. One must remember, of course, that at least three years had passed before the women, now "wives," were discovered by the Lamanite army (Mosiah 23:30–31); some of the former fiancés may have married other women in the meantime.

31. The later legal reforms of king Mosiah do not come into play in the case here (Alma 1:1, 14). The Nephite system then current is described as "the law which has been given to us by our fathers" (Mosiah 29:15, 25); in addition, "the law [of Moses] was engraven upon the plates of brass" (1 Ne. 4:16), which the Nephites possessed.

32. An entire complex of issues has to do with literacy in the wider Nephite and Lamanite societies. To make reasonable judgments about Lamanite levels of education is especially difficult because of the nature of the sources. The Lamanites' regular acceptance of Nephite dissenters and the elevation of them to high places in Lamanite society, particularly in the military, may well stem from the higher levels of education that Nephites seem to have enjoyed (e.g., Mosiah 24:1, 4).

33. The verb "to destroy," meaning to kill, appears twice in Mosiah 23:33–34.

34. In an obvious coloration from the Exodus story, Amulon is usually mentioned in the phrase "Amulon and his brethren" (Mosiah 23:34–35; 24:1; 25:12; Alma 25:4, 8), who stand as a substitute for Pharaoh and his people whom God punishes, even their children eventually being slain (Ex. 12:29–30; Alma 25:4, 8). On the opposite side stand "Alma and his brethren" (Mosiah 23:35–37; 24:8, 15), or "Alma and his people" (Mosiah 24:12, 17–18, 20, 23), who recall Moses and his people whom the Lord delivers from bondage by leading them into the wilderness, onto God's path, all preparations having been made the previous night (Ex. 12:1–13, 21–23; Mosiah 24:18–20). See Daube, *Exodus Pattern*, 75–77. In this vein, in a source with a decided Lamanite connection, Amulon and his followers are routinely called "Amulonites" (Alma 21:3–4; 23:14; 24:1, 28–29). In one passage, one finds the phrase "the people of Amulon" (21:2), which seems to designate this group before it became well established.

35. The successful pleading of the women continues a pattern found elsewhere in the Book of Mormon (1 Ne. 7:19; Mosiah 19:13) that finds echoes in the Exodus story (Ex. 3:21–22; 11:2–3). See Daube, *Exodus Pattern*, 55–61.

36. It is possible that the men, who were Nephites, were obliged to swear an oath of allegiance to the Lamanite nation, or the like. For they were to go with the army to the "land of Nephi," the Lamanite homeland, when they were diverted by the discovery of the people of Alma (Mosiah 23:35–38). Moreover, they raised their children within the Lamanite society, establishing a colony in cooperation with Lamanites and other dissident Nephites, as later accounts indicate (Alma 21:2–3; 25:4). On an oath of allegiance administered by Nephites, see Terrence L. Szink, "An Oath of Allegiance in the Book of Mormon," in *Warfare in the Book of Mormon*, ed. Stephen D. Ricks and William J. Hamblin (Salt Lake City: Deseret Book, 1990), 35–45.

37. Abinadi, who was convicted unjustly by king Noah and these same priests (Mosiah 17:6, 12), had prophesied that both the priests and their "seed" would "be smitten on every hand, and shall be driven and scattered

to and fro, . . . and in that day ye shall be hunted, . . . and then ye shall suffer . . . the pains of death by fire" (17:17–18).

38. The "utter destruction" of the city had been prophesied by Alma the Younger, former chief judge of the country (Alma 9:12, 18, 24; cf. 10:18, 22). The complete ruin was so devastating that the date is repeated twice in introducing the account (16:1). Evidently, it was a date remembered for decades afterward.

39. The distinction between "the Lamanites" and "the seed of Amulon and his brethren" (Alma 25:8) must reflect accurately the Lamanite point of view in this matter (see especially Alma 24:29; also the pointed phrase "his people," meaning Nephites, in Mosiah 23:39). As one might infer, the children of the priests must have looked different from other Lamanites because they came from a Nephite father and a Lamanite mother. It is also possible that, unhappily, those children had also suffered certain kinds of discrimination as they grew up. Of course, the whole issue of social discrimination has yet to be explored. In this connection, one needs to consider the Lamanite "custom . . . to slay [Nephites], or to retain them in captivity, or to cast them into prison, or to cast them out of [the] land" (Alma 17:20). Hence, not all Nephites were welcomed among Lamanites.

40. Over time, people settled an area known as the "land of Amulon" (Alma 24:1) in Lamanite territory, a place name that likely goes back to the leader of the defrocked priests. One can perhaps assume that it was descendants and family members of these former officials who were among the prominent colonists who came to live in this area.

Alma's Conversion: Reminiscences in His Sermons 7

Alma's sermons—formal and informal addresses alike—brim with references to and applications from his personal conversion experience. Whether warning the people of Ammonihah, counseling his sons, or dealing with ordinary matters, Alma uses his conversion experience as a persuasive teaching tool. The three-day period during which he received a visit from an angel and underwent a remarkable change enabled him later to speak from experience as he preached repentance and the cleansing power of the word of God. Not only did he illumine the dark, awful state in which persons find themselves if they do not repent, but he could especially beam light on the indescribable joy that accompanies forgiveness of sin. At base, he sought earnestly that others be born of God as he had been.

The sermons of Alma deserve at least a fraction of the centuries-long attention that the epistles of the Apostle Paul have received. Alma's recorded sermons, whether formal or spontaneous, weave a tapestry of complex and variegated colors, of rich imagery, and yet of a bold and simple unity which holds in tight focus the unspeakable blessings of accepting the atonement of Jesus Christ. This chapter looks at only one of the colorful strands woven into Alma's sermons, that of reminiscences of his conversion experience: the three days during which he appeared to be completely unconscious after the unexpected appearance of the angel of the Lord to him and several friends (see Mosiah 27; Alma 36). To be sure, students of the Book of Mormon have long recognized that Alma's three-day, life-changing experience stood at the foundation of all that he did and said for the rest of his life. But unlike Moses and Isaiah, who almost never referred to their life-changing experiences, Alma's memory of that remarkable ordeal remained with him to the point that all his sermons are infused with allusions to it.

The passage which describes Alma's conversion experience in most detail, beginning with the appearance of the angel and recounting events of the next three days, is chapter 36 of his book. Importantly, we possess a second narration of the angel's words and the resulting impact on Alma in chapter 27 of the book of Mosiah. Moreover, this same passage records some of the words that Alma spoke immediately following his experience (Mosiah 27:24–31). Because the angel's utterance is important for our study, and because by his own admission Alma did not hear all that the angel said—"the angel spake more things unto me, which were heard by my brethren, but I did not hear them; . . . I fell to the earth and I did hear no more" (Alma 36:11)—I shall borrow from the account in Mosiah 27 to fill in the picture.

Alma's Conversion Story: Alma 36

Alma's personal recollection, recounted to his oldest son, Helaman, exhibits a number of features that appear in Alma's later sermons and extemporaneous addresses. Let me briefly summarize Alma 36 since it forms a principal key to understanding what I see as a pattern of reminiscences in Alma's sermons and sermonettes. One significant element consists of his emphasis on God's deliverance of his people, whether they be the children of Israel from Egypt, Lehi's family from Jerusalem, or others (36:2, 28–29). A second element, which borrows language from the first, is Alma's emphasis on God's deliverance of the individual soul from the bondage of sin (36:17–18). A third ingredient, related to the second, consists of a set of expressions which describe Alma's own troubled and sinful state before he received forgiveness of his sins. In this instance, he describes himself as "racked with eternal torment," "tormented with the pains of hell" (36:12–13), and "encircled about by the everlasting chains of death" (36:18). Associated directly with his torment, and evidently a part of it, was his feeling of "inexpressible horror" at the thought of standing "in the presence of my God, to be judged of my deeds" (36:14–15). A fourth component turns out to be the exact reversal of the third: indescribable joy and enlightenment at receiving forgiveness of sins through Jesus' atonement (36:19–21). A fifth feature is his persistent description of his experience as being "born of God," a phrase distinctive to Alma among Book of Mormon authors (Mosiah 27:25, 28; Alma 5:14; 36:5, 23–24, 26; 38:6); he is also unique among Book of Mormon writers in using "born of the Spirit" (Mosiah 27:24–25) and "born again" (Alma 5:49; 7:14). A sixth element arises from his actions as a preacher of salvation, which followed his extraordinary experience, bringing others to taste "as I have tasted" and to see "eye to eye as I have seen" (Alma 36:26).

Sermon in Zarahemla: Alma 5

The initial test as to whether these observations had an impact on Alma's preaching comes in his first recorded sermon (Alma 5), a long and carefully articulated address delivered, presumably over a period of time and on various occasions, to "the people in the church which was established in the city of Zarahemla" (5:2), possibly consisting of seven or more congregations (Mosiah 25:23). As one might expect, most of the elements listed above are present in the opening segment of Alma's discourse. After establishing his divine authority for preaching (Alma 5:3), he noted that the Exodus-like deliverances of his immediate ancestors were illustrations of God's "mercy and long-suffering" and that it was important to remember these divine acts (5:4–6). On this note, he next asked his hearers, "Have ye sufficiently retained in remembrance that [God] has delivered their souls from hell?" (5:6). In framing this question, Alma effectively shifts the focus of his listeners from the Exodus and other such events to the Atonement. For this purpose he borrows the language of the Exodus to describe the Atonement. Specifically, his use of the verb *deliver* in this context forms a firm bridge between Alma's reference to the Exodus and his recounting of the blessings that flow from accepting the Atonement, a discussion of which immediately follows (5:7–27).

As a further illustration of a pattern of reminiscences in this sermon, Alma's vocabulary in his discourse on the Atonement exhibits clear ties to his account of the aftermath of his encounter with the angel given in Alma 36. There he spoke initially of being "racked with eternal torment," "tormented with the pains of hell" at the memory of his sins (36:12–13), and of being "encircled about by the everlasting chains of death" (36:18). Because the "thought of coming into the presence of my God did rack my soul with inexpressible horror," Alma had wished to "become extinct both soul and body, that I might not be brought to stand in the presence of my God, to be judged of my deeds" (36:14–15). Then, as he described his feelings at receiving a remission of sins, he spoke in opposite terms of the "joy, and . . . marvelous light I did behold," as well as of a vision of "God sitting upon his throne, surrounded with numberless concourses of angels, in the attitude of singing and praising their God." Alma exclaimed, "My soul did long to be there" (36:22). Moreover, he talked of being "born of God" and wanting to share the joy and happiness he had received (36:23–24). Importantly, the early part of his Zarahemla speech follows a similar pattern. After noting God's deliverance of his people, the children of Israel, Alma then described the ancestors of his hearers as being "encircled about by the bands of death, and the chains of hell, and an everlasting destruction did await them" (5:7). In counterbalance, he next affirmed that these forebears were not destroyed or lost; rather, the "bands of death" and "chains of hell . . . were loosed, and their souls did expand, and they did sing redeeming love" (5:9; see also 8, 10). Then speaking of his father, Alma noted that there had been "a mighty change wrought in his heart," as there had been in his own (5:12, 14), and he asked the congregation whether they themselves had been "born of God" (5:14), a phrase that he had used to describe himself. His mentioning the "song of redeeming love" (5:9, 26) seems to be tied to the vision of God and His angels that he had seen and heard at the end of his three days of torment. His desire to join in the singing is evidence of this change (36:22).

Sermon in Gideon: Alma 7

Alma's next recorded sermon appears in chapter 7. It is much shorter and less formal than the one in Zarahemla. He delivered it in the land of Gideon, which was apparently settled by the faithful people from the colony of Limhi whom he had known as a child. Even though the tone throughout Alma 7 is generally warm and informal, certain elements do exhibit formal language which, in Alma's words, came at the behest of the Spirit. For instance, the phrases "the Spirit hath said this much unto me" (7:9) and "for the Spirit saith" (7:14) clearly set out the authority and necessity for Alma's commanding words in verses 9 and 14–16. Because the sermon is chiefly an address to faithful friends, a clear patterning of reminiscences does not emerge as it does in the first section of the Zarahemla sermon; however, elements that echo Alma's experience do appear. For example, when speaking of the necessity of repenting he said that one must "be born again" (7:14), a phrase that uniquely characterizes Alma's messages elsewhere. Further, he says that the Lamb of God is "mighty to save" (7:14), a phrase that recalls similar language describing God's redeeming power manifested in the exodus of the children of Israel (e.g., Ex. 32:11; Deut. 4:37; 7:8; 9:26). In another place, he speaks of looking forward "for the remission of your sins . . . which is to come" (Alma 7:6), possibly a recollection of his own remission of sins (36:19–21).

Sermon in Ammonihah: Alma 9–13

Alma's third recorded sermon, which occupies most of chapter 9, was delivered under contentious conditions in the city of Ammonihah. In an effort to postpone arrest (Alma 9:7), he opened his address by scolding his listeners for not remembering "that our father, Lehi, was brought out of Jerusalem by the hand of God" (9:9). The same point is made twice in Alma 9:22. The description of the Son of God as one who will be "quick to hear the cries of his people" (9:26) also exhibits ties to the exodus of the Israelites from Egypt: God heard the cries of the children of Israel (Ex. 3:7, 9; cf. Ex. 6:5). That he raised the issue of remembering "the captivity of thy fathers" illustrates that Alma was obedient to the angel's command that he remember it (Mosiah 27:16) and that he felt it important to observe this instruction in his preaching (e.g., Alma 36:2, 28–29). His subsequent reference to "a state of endless misery and woe" for the unrepentant and his warning that God "will utterly destroy you from off the face of the earth" (9:11–12) both recall the misery that Alma had felt and the destruction that he had feared during his three-day ordeal (36:11–16). Moreover, the reason for warning the people of Ammonihah of impending divine annihilation was the same as the destruction threatened by the angel against Alma: so that they would no longer lead others astray, a notion also at home in the Exodus (Deut. 20:17–18). The words of the angel to Alma were: "If thou wilt of thyself be destroyed, seek no more to destroy the church of God" (Alma 36:9; see also 11). To the people of Ammonihah Alma said in turn, "If ye persist in your wickedness . . . ye shall be visited with utter destruction. . . . For [God] will not suffer you that ye shall live in your iniquities, to destroy his people" (9:18–19).

In contrast, God's wondrous power to deliver was not only apparent in the orchestrated escapes of his people in the past but also in "the salvation of their souls" which comes about "according to the power and deliverance of Jesus Christ" (9:28). Once again, the focus on terms such as "power" and "deliverance" recollects Exodus-like events while at the same time describing the most marvelous of all deliverances: the Atonement of Jesus Christ. Finally, Alma's reference to the Final Judgment recalls another element in his description of his three-day ordeal. To the people of the city he issued this warning: "I say unto you, that it shall be more tolerable for [the Lamanites] in the day of judgment than for you, if ye remain in your sins" (9:15). The sense is clear. For the people of Ammonihah, the Judgment will be terrible. On this matter, Alma could speak with poignant feeling. When he had been forced into a harried contemplation of his own sins, Alma came to wish that he "could be banished and become extinct both soul and body, that I might not be brought to stand in the presence of my God, to be judged of my deeds" (36:15).

On the same day that Alma was obliged to deliver his sermon under contentious conditions to the people of Ammonihah (Alma 9), he spontaneously responded to questions (Alma 12–13) raised by several persons, including Zeezrom, a lawyer and skilled speaker who had openly opposed the preaching of Alma and his companion Amulek (Alma 10:31). While no real pattern of reminiscences emerges from Alma's extemporaneous words, three elements that can be tied to Alma's conversion experience are readily identifiable. One has to do with the prophetic function of angels, clearly recalling the role of the angel of the Lord who confronted Alma and his companions. In an apparent effort to assure his listeners that divine powers were then declaring repentance and salvation among his own people, Alma observed that "the voice of the Lord, by the mouth of angels, doth declare [salvation] unto all nations; . . . wherefore they [the angels] have come unto us" (13:22). Further, "angels are declaring [salvation] unto many at this time in our land" (13:24). Why? Because, said Alma, "at the time of [the Messiah's] coming" his arrival will "be made known unto just and holy men, by the mouth of angels" (13:26).

The second element deals with a notion that one might expect from Alma when one considers the character of his audience in Ammonihah: the terrible, eternal fate that awaits those unrepentant individuals who do not accept Jesus' atonement. On this topic, Alma speaks of the wicked coming to be "bound down by the chains of hell" (13:30; cf. 12:17), echoing the description of his nightmarish vision of being "encircled about by the everlasting chains of death" (36:18; cf. Moses 7:26–27). To the people of Ammonihah, Alma had a good deal to say about such chains. By his words the devil, or adversary, seeks to "encircle you about with his chains, that he might chain you down to everlasting destruction" (Alma 12:6). Alma then spelled out what he meant by the word *chains*. Speaking of those who harden their hearts, he proclaimed that they consequently receive "the lesser portion of the word until they know nothing concerning [God's] mysteries; and then they are taken captive by the devil, and led by his will down to destruction." This situation, Alma disclosed, "is what is meant by the chains of hell" (12:10–11).

Closely related to this second element is a third which concerns the scene at the judgment bar of God. Of his own torment Alma had said that the thought of standing before God "did rack my soul with inexpressible horror" and brought him to wish that he "could be banished and become extinct both soul and body" (36:14–15). To the people of Ammonihah Alma made a similar point: "If we have hardened our hearts against the word, . . . then will our state be awful. . . . And in this awful state we shall not dare to look up to our God" (12:13–14). Moreover, sharing Alma's one-time desire to become extinct, those who persist in their sins "would fain be glad if [they] could command the rocks and the mountains to fall upon [them] to hide [them] from his presence" (12:14). In addition, those who come thus to the judgment bar of God will do so with "everlasting shame" (12:15). As a capstone to this spontaneous address, Alma pled with his audience from the memory of the fearful experience through which he had suffered. Near the end he besought them, "Now, my brethren, I wish from the *inmost part of my heart*, yea, with *great anxiety even unto pain*, that ye would hearken unto my words, and cast off your sins, and not procrastinate the day of your repentance" (13:27, emphasis added). Because of his own ordeal, he knew better than most about the terrible consequences facing those who reject the message of salvation. In the case of the people of Ammonihah, Alma's dire prophecies were fulfilled when an invading Lamanite army destroyed the city and all of its inhabitants in a single day (16:1–3, 9–11).

Alma's Soliloquy: Alma 29

Alma's soliloquy in chapter 29 also exhibits reminiscences of his three-day experience. First, he wishes that he were an angel and, like the angel of the Lord who confronted him, he wishes he could "go forth and speak . . . with a voice to shake the earth . . . as with the voice of thunder" (Alma 29:1–2). The descriptions of the appearance of the angel of the Lord to Alma and his friends are compelling. In his own words, Alma recounted that "God sent his holy angel to stop us by the way. And behold, he spake unto us, as it were the voice of thunder, and the whole earth did tremble beneath our feet" (36:6–7). The account from other witnesses says that "the angel of the Lord appeared unto them . . . and he spake as it were with a voice of thunder, which caused the earth to shake upon which they stood" (Mosiah 27:11). The similarities cannot be missed. They combine mention of the angel with reference to his thundering voice and the resulting earthquake.

The reference to the captivity of his forebears forms a second tie. In his soliloquy Alma says, "I also remember the captivity of my fathers; for I surely do know that the Lord did deliver them out of bondage. . . . Yea, I have always remembered the captivity of my fathers; and that same God who delivered them out of the hands of the Egyptians did deliver them out of bondage" (Alma 29:11–12). At this point, we recall the angel's instructions to Alma: "Go, and remember the captivity of thy fathers . . . for they were in bondage, and [God] has delivered them" (Mosiah 27:16).

Alma's service as a divine instrument in bringing others to God comprises a third connection. In his soliloquy Alma declared: "This is my glory, that perhaps I may be an instrument in the hands of God to bring some soul to repentance; and this is my joy. And behold, when I see many of my brethren truly penitent, and coming to the Lord their God, then is my soul filled with joy" (Alma 29:9–10). Similarly, in his personal recounting Alma told his son Helaman that from the time of his three-day ordeal until that moment, "I have labored without ceasing, that I might bring souls unto repentance; that I might bring them to taste of the exceeding joy of which I did taste" (36:24). He continued by speaking metaphorically of his success in his missionary endeavors as if it were fruit of agricultural labors: "The Lord doth give me exceedingly great joy in the fruit of my labors; for because of the word which he has imparted unto me, behold, many have been born of God, and have tasted as I have tasted, and have seen eye to eye as I have seen" (36: 25–26; cf. 29:13–15).

A fourth component, related to the third, may form the most direct reference back to Alma's three-day trial. In his soliloquy he expresses gratitude for those who had come to the Lord through his efforts in the following words: "When I see many of my brethren truly penitent, and coming to the Lord their God, then is my soul filled with joy" (29:10). Significantly, the next lines form the direct link to Alma's experience with the power of Jesus' Atonement: "Then do I remember what the Lord has done for me, yea, even that he hath heard my prayer" (29:10). In my view, we have the words of this very prayer in Alma's comments to Helaman. Alma says that during his three-day ordeal he recalled his father's prophecies about the coming of Jesus Christ. Then, "I cried within my heart: O Jesus, thou Son of God, have mercy on me, who am in the gall of bitterness, and am encircled about by the everlasting chains of death. And now, behold, when I thought this, I could remember my pains no more; yea, I was harrowed up by the memory of my sins no more" (36:18–19). Because of that unforgettable moment when he received forgiveness of sins from God, Alma says fervently and gratefully, "I remember [God's] merciful arm which he extended towards me" (29:10).

The next two ties are less firm; however, they are worth mentioning. The first has to do with Alma's guilt. From his description of his reaction to his sins, it is clear that he did not see himself as a blameless person before God. For instance, he said that in his three-day experience, "I saw that I had rebelled against my God, and that I had not kept his holy commandments" (36:13). In discussing who is blameworthy before God and who is not, Alma gives the following in the dissertation, a clear characterization of his own situation when confronted by the angel of the Lord: "He that knoweth good and evil, to him it is given according to his desires, whether he desireth good or evil, life or death, joy or remorse of conscience" (29:5). Alma had certainly experienced "remorse of conscience": "My soul was harrowed up to the greatest degree and racked with all my sins. Yea, I did remember all my sins and iniquities, for which I was tormented with the pains of hell" (36:12–13). The second additional component deals with a hint of Alma's state during the three days that he was unable to respond physically but was fully conscious spiritually. In the soliloquy in chapter 29 he speaks of his joy at the accomplishments of his friends, the sons of Mosiah, during their ministries among the Lamanites. And he hints that the joy which he feels at such moments almost overcomes him: "Now, when I think of the success of these my brethren my soul is carried away, even to the separation of it from the body, as it were, so great is my joy" (29:16). Perhaps Alma was thinking of his own ecstatic experience when he wrote these words.

The Trial of Korihor: Alma 30

While we possess a substantial number of words that Alma spoke during the trial of Korihor (Alma 30), because of the nature of the legal interchange, we would normally expect to find nothing linked to Alma's three-day ordeal. But one matter reaches back to that experience: the idea that one soul perishes so that others may live.[1] To illustrate, when the angel of the Lord scolded Alma and his friends, the angel specifically said to Alma: "If thou wilt of thyself be destroyed, seek no more to destroy the church of God" (36:9). This thought led Alma not only to be "racked with eternal torment" because of all his "sins and iniquities" (36:12–13) but apparently to conclude that he "had murdered many of [God's] children, or rather led them away unto destruction" (36:14). In the case of Korihor, Alma tried to warn him simply to repent and not to seek a sign from God. "I am grieved," said Alma to Korihor, ". . . that ye will still resist the spirit of the truth, that thy soul may be destroyed. But behold, it is better that thy soul should be lost than that thou shouldst be the means of bringing many souls down to destruction" (30:46–47). Clearly, Alma had once faced the possibility that his own life might be taken to preserve others; his own experience of coming face to face with this reality seems to underlie his appeal to Korihor not to "resist the spirit of the truth" (30:46).

Sermon to Zoramites: Alma 32–33

About 75 B.C., before the Zoramite people convinced the Lamanites to oppose Nephite interests—an act which led to war the following year (Alma 35:10–13)—Alma and his missionary companions had tried to preach to the Zoramites (31:1–7). Even though Alma spoke frequently and to various groups in his missionary activity among these people, only one of his discourses—to an audience of the poorer class—is preserved (Alma 32–33). In this address Alma touched on several points that link to his three-day experience. One of the most prominent of these points concerns his affirmation that God "imparteth his word by angels unto men, yea, not only men but women also" (32:23). Part of Alma's testimony would have consisted of his knowledge that his missionary companion, Amulek, had been visited and taught by an angel (10:7–10). The mention of women in Alma 32:23 seems important. Depending on who the subject is in Alma 10:11—it is either Alma or the angel—the angel may have also appeared to others of Amulek's household, including "my women, and my children." Alma had received many angelic visitations (see 8:14); however, the first and most important visitation occurred when he and the sons of Mosiah were confronted by the angel of the Lord (Mosiah 27:11; Alma 36:5–6). Thus he was a personal witness that angels were imparting the word of God to his fellow beings.

A second feature is Alma's discussion of the virtues of humility, contrasting being compelled to be humble with the humility that some seek without compulsion. His audience, who were from the poorer classes of the Zoramite people and who had been cast out of their synagogues (Alma 32:5), certainly invited such a comparison because of their circumstances. Nevertheless, in a real sense Alma himself had been compelled by the angel to become humble. Thus, Alma spoke out of his own experience when he made the following observation: "Because ye are compelled to be humble blessed are ye; for a man sometimes, if he is compelled to be humble, seeketh repentance; and now . . . do ye not suppose that they are more blessed who truly humble themselves because of the word? Yea, he that truly humbleth himself, and repenteth of his sins, and endureth to the end, the same shall be blessed—yea, *much more blessed* than they who are compelled to be humble because of their exceeding poverty" (32:13–15, emphasis added).

Alma concluded his discussion by saying: "Blessed are they who humble themselves without being compelled to be humble; . . . yea, without being brought to know the word, or even compelled to know, before they will believe" (32:16). While there may exist other reminiscences to Alma's three-day experience in this discourse, they are more difficult to demonstrate. Two come to mind. The first has to do with Alma's metaphorical use of the verb *taste* in the sense of tasting light (32:35) and tasting joy (36:24, 26). The second possible tie would link the concern for those who seek "a sign from heaven" (32:17) and the fact that Alma was given a clear heavenly sign in the person of the angel of the Lord who appeared to him.

Counsel to His Sons: Alma 38–42

In his counsel to his second son Shiblon, Alma spoke briefly and directly of his experience. After mentioning that during his ordeal he had been "born of God" (Alma 38:6), Alma related the following: "The Lord in his great mercy sent his angel to declare unto me that I must stop the work of destruction among his people. . . . And it came to pass that I was three days and three nights in the most bitter pain and anguish of soul; and never, until I did cry out unto the Lord Jesus Christ for mercy, did I receive a remission of my sins. But behold, I did cry unto him and I did find peace to my soul" (38:7–8).

Another connection exists between Alma's words to Shiblon and those to Helaman. It consists of the tie between Exodus terminology and that used in reference to the Atonement. As I have already noted, the verb *deliver* regularly describes the Lord's actions on behalf of both the Hebrew slaves in Egypt and the Nephite peoples who found themselves in grave circumstances. When he complimented his second son on his patience in the face of persecution, Alma affirmed: "Thou knowest that the Lord did deliver thee" (38:4). He then continued by saying: "Now my son, Shiblon, I would that ye should remember, that as much as ye shall put your trust in God even so much ye shall be delivered out of your trials, and your troubles, and your afflictions, and ye shall be lifted up at the last day" (38:5). The clear connection between God's power to deliver and the resurrection is not to be missed.

In Alma's extended counsel to his third and youngest son, Corianton (Alma 39–42), there are only a few references to Alma's three-day ordeal, such as: "Is it not as easy at this time for the Lord to send his angel to declare these glad tidings unto us as unto our children, or as after the time of his coming?" (39:19). Apparently, the appearance of the angel of the Lord to Alma was in the back of his mind when he discussed God's interest in informing His children in advance about the coming of the Messiah. A second point of contact is Alma's urgent plea that his children not lead others astray. He declared that the "Spirit of the Lord" had directed him to command his children "to do good, lest they lead away the hearts of many people to destruction" (39:12). Likewise, the angel of the Lord had earlier commanded Alma to "seek no more to destroy the church of God" (36:11), effectively accusing Alma of leading others astray and leading him to accuse himself in very serious terms: "I had murdered many of his children, or rather led them away unto destruction" (36:14).

A third feature in Alma's instructions to Corianton is his description of the fearful condition of the wicked. In his review of the "state of the soul between death and the resurrection" (40:11), Alma says of the wicked that "these shall be cast out into outer darkness; there shall be weeping, and wailing, and gnashing of teeth, and this because of their own iniquity. . . . This is the state of the souls of the wicked, yea, in darkness, and a state of awful, fearful looking for the fiery indignation of the wrath of God upon them" (40:13–14). Alma further characterized this period as "that endless night of darkness" (41:7) and the inheritance of the wicked as "an awful death" which is tantamount to drinking "the dregs of a bitter cup" (40:26). If unrepentant, Corianton's evil acts "will stand as a testimony against you at the last day" (39:8). Such words, of course, recall Alma's own horror at the thought of seeing God at the judgment bar: "So great had been my iniquities, that the very thought of coming into the presence of my God did rack my soul with inexpressible horror" (36:14).

Summary

In summary, virtually every one of Alma's recorded sermons, whether they were formal discourses or spontaneous addresses, are characterized by the recollection of one or more features of his three-day conversion experience. The exceptions are his long prayer offered just before he and his companions began their work among the people of Zoram (Alma 31:26–35) and his final words to his son Helaman, which included his dire prophecy about the eventual extinction of their people (45:2–14). Perhaps the element most often alluded to is the appearance of the angel of the Lord. Further, Alma frequently referred to the captivity and deliverance of earlier generations, whether the Israelite slaves or his Nephite forebears, the memory of which was specifically enjoined on him by the angel. An important connection, not made as often, concerns the association of Exodus-like deliverances with the power of deliverance manifested in Jesus' Atonement. In quite a different vein, Alma repeatedly mentioned the fate of the wicked in terrifying language and imagery which he similarly used to describe his own horror at facing God at the final judgment. In addition, almost as a counterbalance, he also regularly noted the unspeakable joy and light that believers would experience if they would accept Jesus' redemption. A final ingredient is his testimony of what had happened as a result of his determination and actions to bring others to accept Jesus' atonement: to be "born of God," to taste "as I have tasted," and to see "eye to eye as I have seen" (36:26).

This article, slightly revised, appeared in a Religious Studies Center publication as "Alma's Conversion: Reminiscences in His Sermons," in THE BOOK OF MORMON: *ALMA,* THE TESTIMONY OF THE WORD, ed. Monte S. Nyman and Charles D. Tate Jr. (Provo, Utah: Religious Studies Center, Brigham Young University, 1992), 141–56.

NOTES

1. The justification is first laid out in Nephi's dramatic encounter with the drunken Laban (1 Ne. 4:11–13). Compare Caiaphas' maxim about the need for Jesus' death (John 11:50; 18:14) that bears the sense of political expediency.

The underlying principle can be seen in 2 Sam. 20:20–22; Jonah 1:12–15. For similar Jewish formulations of the idea, see those cited by Hermann L. Strack and Paul Billerbeck, *Kommentar zum Neuen Testament aus Talmud und Midrash* (Munich: C. H. Beck, 1924), 2:545–46. Most of these instances deal with political reasons for one to die instead of many. Legal and religious grounds are not spelled out.

The Prophetic Laments of Samuel the Lamanite 8

The wide-ranging sermon of Samuel the Lamanite, spoken from the city wall of Zarahemla, exhibits poetic features that recall laments found in the Bible, most notably in the Psalms. Like laments in the Bible, those in Samuel's speech display traits at home in worship settings. But unlike biblical laments, the two poetic pieces in Samuel's sermon unexpectedly contain prophecies, an element that appears elsewhere in the Thanksgiving Hymns of the Dead Sea Scrolls. These prophecies in Samuel's poetry find fulfillment in later periods, including in the woeful days of Mormon, the compiler and editor of the Book of Mormon.

Quite unexpectedly I have discovered that the recorded words of Samuel the Lamanite include two laments, that is, psalms or poems that express sorrow. Measured by the criteria for laments identified by scholars of the biblical Psalms,[1] the two from Samuel do not fit precisely. However, in my view, they exhibit enough characteristics to qualify as lament literature. Samuel himself apparently identifies them as laments, at least in his contemporary terminology, when he introduces the first lament by saying, "And then shall ye lament" (Hel. 13:32). Moreover, a compelling point is made in a mirroring lament uttered some forty years later over the destroyed city Moronihah, a lament that Mormon introduces with the words, "And in another place they were heard *to cry* and mourn" (3 Ne. 8:25, emphasis added). As Richard N. Boyce has noted, not only does one of the bases of the relationship of God and his people lie in their cry to God, but also the cry to God is fundamental to the inspired and inspiring laments of the Old Testament.[2] As I read this passage in 3 Nephi,

Mormon is expressing a similar notion when he notes the cries of lament that followed the destruction of the city Moronihah.

To be sure, we must rely on Joseph Smith's translation of the passage, so we cannot be certain that we are taking account of all of the language nuances that may have been present in the text preserved on the Book of Mormon plates. As a result, we may not grasp the precise balancing that the composer intended between the various parts of the two poems, particularly in the second and longer piece. Even so, the texts of the laments are sufficiently clear, are apparently translated with sufficient literalism,[3] and are bracketed distinctly enough in the text that one can offer a preliminary set of observations, including the fact that formal structural frames exist within each.[4]

The two laments appear near the end of chapter 13 of Helaman and form part of the long haranguing speech that Samuel delivered from the top of the city wall of Zarahemla. Of course, one cannot determine whether he sang, chanted, or spoke these pieces, although the possibility of singing, or perhaps more likely chanting, cannot be ruled out.

One of the more intriguing issues concerns whether these laments may have been composed spontaneously by the prophet. If so, such a composition would match what is known about the uttered and written prophecies of biblical prophets whose works consist substantially or entirely of poetic or hymnic language. We must reckon seriously with the possibility that Samuel had the ability to compose such pieces more or less on the spot, much as biblical prophets did. However, there exist indicators in the second poem, and in later references to it, that he may have depended on a source for that one.[5]

The First Lament

The first poem is very short. Although it lacks the extended development that the second exhibits, it displays fine skill and balance in its conception. This first piece (Hel. 13:32–33), which appears to be an individual lament, can be arranged as follows, repeating Samuel's introductory words that set it off:

And then shall ye lament, and say:

> O that I had repented,
> and had not killed
> the prophets,
> and stoned them,
> and cast them out.

The expression "the prophets," the only noun, seems to constitute the middle element; as such, it is clearly emphatic. Even though Samuel's language is consistent with the fact that he is addressing a crowd in Zarahemla, because of the plural pronoun "ye," the "I" of this piece is abrupt and therefore should probably be understood as a reference to an individual. Moreover, all of the verbs in the passage are in the first person singular, agreeing with the pronoun "I." Hence, we are likely looking at an individual lament, possibly composed for solo recitation.

All individual laments in the Bible envision the Lord as somehow connected to the suffering of the composer, usually by covenant. As a result, there regularly appears either an affirmation of the person's desire to repent, in order to come under the protective umbrella of the Lord, or a defense of the person's innocence, usually using legal terminology.[6] In this first lament, the wish to repent on the part of the poet is broadly assumed.

Although short, the poem exhibits what Robert Alter has called "parallelism of specification," a very common feature of biblical poetry in which the language pattern moves from a generalized statement to one that is more specific or focused. The result is that when "the general term is transformed into a specific instance or a concrete image, the idea becomes more pointed, more forceful."[7] We can see this sort of development in the last three verbs of the lament: the notion of killing the prophets becomes more specific by mentioning the action of stoning them, and this latter is made more graphic by the idea of casting them out, possibly specifying the location of execution and reflecting a legal necessity of taking a convicted person outside a city before execution.[8]

We cannot determine with certainty whether the few preserved lines represent the whole piece. To be sure, in his editorial notes Mormon states that he has not repeated everything that

Samuel had spoken (Hel. 14:1). And it is not clear from the passage in Hel. 13:33 whether Mormon had a longer piece in front of him and therefore has only reproduced a few lines from it.

However, a passage that both echoes and expands the first lament, and also exhibits poetic qualities of its own, may bring us closer to resolving this issue. The piece consists of a lament over the destroyed city of Moronihah.[9] The passage can be arranged as follows, including Mormon's introductory and summarizing words, so that one can see its possible poetic features (3 Ne. 8:25):

And in another place they were heard to cry and mourn, saying:

A. O that we had repented
  before this great and terrible day,
 and had not killed
 and stoned
  the prophets,
 and cast them out;

B. then would our mothers
 and our fair daughters,
 and our children
  have been spared,
  and not have been buried up in that great city Moronihah.

And thus were the howlings of the people great and terrible.

Several similarities and differences with the lament uttered by Samuel immediately present themselves. First the similarities. It is obvious that the same order of verbs appears—"repent," "stone," and "cast out." And the sentiment of the first verset[10] remains as it appears in Samuel. On the other hand, the pronouns have been altered from "I" to "we." Further, the poem has been expanded by the added second line in the first verset. In addition, an entire second verset has been appended which decries the loss of loved ones. In this second verset, one notes the feature observable in the first part of this lament and in the version of the lament in Samuel, namely, parallelism of specification. In the case of the lament over Moronihah, the verbal phrase "have been spared" is sharpened by the words "not have been buried up." Moreover, the noun phrase "the prophets" is one place removed from where it is in the version preserved in the words of Samuel.

I cannot leave the discussion of Samuel's first lament and the *responsum* that is found in the last verse of 3 Nephi 8 without discussing the apparently unusual order of the verbs "stone" and "cast out." It seems that they reverse the order of execution, for usually one first casts out and then stones the condemned. Why would an author reverse them? The answer may come from a narrative passage that preserves this proper ordering of events in the case of executing a condemned person. It is in 3 Ne. 9:10 that we find what seems to be a more natural order, "cast out" and then "stone." The Lord mourns, "I caused [these cities] to be burned with fire, and the inhabitants thereof, because of their wickedness in *casting out* the prophets, and *stoning* those whom I did send" (emphasis added). In light of this passage, I judge that placing "cast out" last in Samuel's lament, and in the lament preserved in 3 Ne. 8:25, constitutes poetic license.[11]

The Second Lament

The second piece, which immediately follows the other in the text, qualifies as a communal lament. As one would expect, it is written in the first person plural, using the pronouns "we," "us," and "our." Moreover, in a passage in which Mormon describes the fulfillment of the prophetic features of this lament among people of his own day, Mormon specifically uses the term "lamentation" to describe the sorrowing that he had witnessed (Morm. 2:10–12).

Once again, Samuel introduces the text of the poem in a way that plainly sets off its beginning and ending (Hel. 13:33–37).

Yea, in that day ye shall say:

A. 1. O that we had remembered the Lord our God
in the day that he gave us our riches,
and then they would not have become slippery
that we should lose them. . . .

B. 5. Behold, we lay a tool here

and on the morrow it is gone;
and behold, our swords are taken from us
in the day we have sought them for battle.
Yea, we have hid up our treasures
and they have slipped away from us,
because of the curse of the land.
C. O that we had repented
in the day that the word of the Lord came unto us;
for behold the land is cursed,
and all things are become slippery,
and we cannot hold them.
D. Behold, we are surrounded by demons,
yea, we are encircled about by the angels of him
who hath sought to destroy our souls.
Behold, our iniquities are great.
O Lord, canst thou not turn away thine anger from us?
And this shall be your language in those days.

Although the two laments recited by Samuel should probably be seen as independent poems or hymns, they clearly bear a relationship to one another. They both point out the estrangement Samuel feels from God, real or imagined. Their independence seems assured, however, because the source of estrangement in the earlier lament comes from not repenting and from actively opposing the agents of the Lord. That opposition, as the poem reads, is the result of not repenting. In the second lament, the community will feel a distance from the Lord because, initially, its members did not "remember" the Lord God and, thereafter, because it did not repent as a group. As a result, the land is to be cursed and, what is worse, the community is finally to become "surrounded by demons" (line 17).

In my mind this piece clearly fits the character of a communal lament. The first person plural is the initial indicator. Further, the expected connection between the actions of the Lord and the suffering of the community is clearly apparent. In addition, such laments typically exhibit a sense of trust that those who recite them will be given a hearing by the Lord. And that is the force of the last line, which assumes that the Lord is listening to the petitioners.[12] Moreover, such laments have customarily been composed in the face of some disaster that threatens the community, such as invasion or famine. Obviously, this lament expects disaster, not only of a physical type but also of a spiritual kind. Insofar as it does not envision a specific incident from the past, it must be seen as prophetic in its forward-looking anticipation of disasters to come. This last detail, incidentally, has to be taken into account in any determination whether Samuel was the author or was borrowing an already-composed lament for the occasion of his prophesying.

Clues exist that this latter lament was composed to be sung or recited in worship. If so, Samuel was reciting it from memory. What are those clues? Perhaps the most compelling observation that Samuel was repeating a known communal lament arises from comments made by Mormon regarding the fulfillment in his day of the part of Samuel's prophecies contained in, and virtually limited to, the second lament.[13] The key passage is the following: "The Nephites began . . . to cry even as had been prophesied by Samuel the prophet; for behold no man could keep that which was his own, for the thieves, and the robbers, and the murderers, and the magic art, and the witchcraft which was in the land. Thus there began to be a mourning and a lamentation in all the land because of these things" (Morm. 2:10–11).

One first notes the generally deteriorating situation that led to complaints that Mormon characterized as "lamentations." In addition, the content of these lamentations coincided with the prophecy of Samuel, a detail that Mormon specifically noted. This observation leads implicitly to the conclusion that these lamentations were verbalized in commonly known expressions of sorrow, and the expression that fits most closely is Samuel's second lament. This lament incorporates a unique set of ideas which appear in only two passages—Samuel's sermon and the lamentations of Mormon's contemporaries.[14] In a relevant study, Walter Brueggemann has noted that the ancients expressed grief in formal ways and that those formal expressions persisted for generations within ancient societies.[15] In the case of Samuel, the formal lament repeated in Hel. 13:33–37 lies at the base of the expressions of grief uttered in Mormon's day, almost 350 years later.

Other clues point in the same direction. In the opening line of the lament, the verb "remember" is one that frequently denotes a recollection that takes place in worship settings at which the oral recitations or physical actions of the celebrants recall certain important events or doctrines. And this sense characterizes "remember" in the Book of Mormon, as well as in the Bible.[16]

Second, the phrase "the Lord our God" in line 1 may point to a worship setting for this lament. In scriptural language, particularly from the Old Testament, the Lord is often petitioned in important celebrations by his title "Lord God," particularly in the making of covenants. One immediately thinks of three crucial moments in the history of the Lord's dealings with his children where this name/title is invoked: in the account of the Garden of Eden (Gen. 2:4–3:24), a series of events that has been celebrated in worship for centuries; in the covenant ceremony at Mount Sinai, at the heart of which was placed the Ten Commandments (Ex. 20:2–17); and in the renewal of the covenant led by Elijah on Mount Carmel in an attempt to turn the hearts of the children of Israel back to the Lord God of their fathers (1 Kgs. 18:30–39).

Walter Brueggemann has called the account of placing Adam and Eve in the Garden of Eden and of their actions that led to expulsion a "drama in four scenes"; Jerome Walsh has termed it a dramatic "series in seven scenes."[17] As Brueggemann has noted, in the prior segment of Genesis "there is no action or development."[18] Only beginning at Gen. 2:4 does one find a narrative that can be acted out by *dramatis personae*, that is, by persons whose acting re-creates the drama in the Garden as a worship celebration of what has been done in the past. Here, for the first time in scripture, the title "Lord God" is introduced, and it appears in Genesis only in this passage. The obvious celebratory and therefore worship traits cannot be missed.[19]

The covenant-making ceremony at the holy mount invokes the name/title "Lord God" as the author and authority of the Ten Commandments, the heart of the law received that day. The Lord identifies himself as "the Lord thy God, which have brought thee out of the land of Egypt, out of the house of bondage" (Ex. 20:2). Obviously, it is the Lord himself who has tied this title to his miraculous act of delivering the Israelites from bondage, an event that has been celebrated in family worship settings for centuries (Ex. 12:1–28). Moreover, it is reasonable to suppose that whenever one spoke of this event and God's role in it, one would mean that it was the Lord God who had performed the feat, even if one referred only to the Lord or to the God of Israel. One need only think of the custom of swearing an oath on the name of the "Lord

God . . . that brought Israel up out of the land of Egypt" (2 Ne. 25:20; cf. Jer. 23:7).[20]

A third passage that bears on the question is found in 1 Kings 18. It is the narrative of Elijah's contest with the priests of Baal, a passage full of references to worship and covenant making. According to the account, after Elijah had made all the necessary preparations for the miracle, he began his prayer by saying, "*Lord God* of Abraham, Isaac, and of Israel" (1 Kgs. 18:36, emphasis added). Besides recalling the name by which the Lord had revealed himself to Moses at the burning bush (Ex. 3:6), Elijah also employed the name/title that the Lord had used of himself when sending Moses to bring the Hebrew slaves out of Egypt, adding a covenantal promise on that earlier occasion (3:15–17). As Elijah continued to pray, he set out the purpose for requesting the miracle: "that this people may know that thou art the Lord God" (1 Kgs. 18:37), emphasizing the connection between "Lord God" and the covenant that Elijah sought to reestablish with his people.[21] In the end, after the fire had fallen from heaven and consumed Elijah's sacrifice and more, the gathered Israelites uttered the words that verified renewing the covenant, "The Lord is God, the Lord is God" (1 Kgs. 18:39, Revised English Bible), a declaration that "re-echoes a cry long established in the cult [worship]."[22] Consequently, this affirmation that the Lord is God clearly offers one of the important covenantal contexts for the use of the name/title "Lord God."[23]

Evidence can be marshalled that a significant number of instances of the use of this name/title among Book of Mormon authors points to worship contexts. For instance, at Alma 13:1, one reads that "the Lord God ordained priests, after his holy order." Moreover, one sees a worship connection in Ammon's establishment of synagogues among the Lamanites, "that they might have the liberty of worshiping the Lord their God according to their desires" (Alma 21:22). A sense of worship and covenant brims in the following words of Alma the Younger: "When I see many of my brethren truly penitent, and coming to the Lord their God, then is my soul filled with joy" (29:10). In another passage, the soldiers of Moroni "cried with one voice [in prayer] unto the Lord their God" when facing a strong Lamanite army (43:49). Examples could be multiplied of both explicit and implicit association of the title "Lord God" with worship and covenant making.[24]

Thus, we conclude that the second lament was composed to be sung or recited during communal worship. While some may not want to rule out the possibility that it was composed on the spot by Samuel, the evidence strongly suggests that Samuel was quoting a known piece that continued to be recited as a formal expression of grief and sorrow.

General Structure

The introductory and concluding observations by Samuel serve as the *inclusio* of the second poem. The frame or outline seems to rest on the three strong wishes, here represented by the words "O" that appear in the beginning, middle, and final lines. The first and second occurrences are clearly parallel, both beginning with the wish, "O that we. . . ." A second frame seems to consist of the two repetitions of the word "behold" in lines 5 and 17, with a third structure tied to the other three occurrences of "behold" in lines 7, 14, and 20. Earlier in his sermon (Hel. 13:17–20), Samuel had pressed home the point that the land, the people, and their treasures would be cursed "because of their wickedness and their abominations." All of the elements that are to be cursed—land, people, treasures—are repeated in this second lament. Further, the references to property that has "slipped away" and to "the curse of the land" at the end of verset B leads by "catchword" association to verset C, which concerns the curse.

Not only do these structural elements support the view of the poetic character of this piece, but the occurrences of the verbal phrase "become slippery" that appear in versets A and C also point to the independent composition of this piece apart from its context. Except for one further occurrence in Morm. 1:18, it is only in this second lament and in a verse immediately preceding it (Hel. 13:31)—which could be expected from Samuel as he was preparing his hearers for this lament—that one finds the verbal phrase "become slippery." In the case of Mormon, the person who edited Samuel's sermon, he was citing in his own book the prophecy that is embedded in the second lament to the effect that property in his day had become slippery because of God's curse on the land, just as Samuel had prophesied (Morm. 1:18–19). Thus the use of this verbal phrase apparently arises in this lament and is found in no other passage in the Book of Mormon except in sections that are directly connected with the lament and its prophecy of coming disasters.

Content

The first verset, of course, deals almost exclusively with possessions or "riches." It is important to note that for Samuel, "riches" or possessions come as a gift from God (Hel. 13:21; and Mormon's words in Hel. 12:2). The fact that they come from God gives him the right to hide them from unrighteous custodians, as the lament spells out.

One can also sense a crescendo building through the poem, beginning on a low level and rising to a pitch. It has to do with the concept of the loss of riches set out in verset A. The composer first notes that the Lord God was the giver of "riches" (line 2), a term that is general in its application. Then the poem becomes more specific when it mentions the loss of "a tool" (lines 5–6). Next, it is "our swords" (line 7) that disappear. In this movement from tools to swords, I sense a slight heightening of the drama of the lament. In general, a tool is not critical for one's well-being. Even the loss of a tool used to support life, such as a plow or scythe, is not critical since a person has a "season" in which to plant or harvest and thus can acquire another tool within the "season" to replace the one lost. But a sword, under certain circumstances, can be very critical for protecting life and property. And one such circumstance of needed protection is noted in line 8: "in the day we have sought them for battle." Here one senses the desperation of those whose swords have disappeared. After swords, the next item to be lost consists of "our treasures" (line 9). To be sure, a treasure may not be critical for preserving life, but it may be necessary for sustaining it. In addition, depending on the nature of the treasure, it may be the kind of possession that helps to give a person his or her identity or place in society. Moreover, the loss of treasure may not only doom the individual to an ill fate but also have a debilitating effect on one's extended family. Furthermore, the word itself implies a loss of much more than a tool or sword.

After treasures, it is "all things" (line 15) that are lost. While we cannot know the sweep of this concept in the mind of the composer, we can safely assume that it must include the totality of one's personal wealth. Finally, the last loss consists of the loss of "our souls" (line 19), the most tragic loss of all. Thus, the poem has led us from the concepts of God's gift, and our loss of his gift of riches, to the loss of "all things," and finally to the forfeiture of "our souls."

Parallelisms

One of the important characteristics of Hebrew poetry and psalmody is the general balancing of component parts. Usually, this feature will appear in the form of parallel language, either stating the same idea in similar terms or setting out opposite concepts. This trait can be seen in both laments. As I have noted in the first, one sees a "parallelism of specification" in the sequence of the verbs "to kill" and "to stone."

The second lament, on the other hand, exhibits what may be termed synonymous and antithetic parallelisms, expected counterparts that characterize Hebrew psalmody. We have already seen an example of what has been called a specifying or intensifying parallelism, that builds from one concept to another, in the series of items lost, beginning with the general idea of "riches" and concluding with the loss of "our souls." In verset A one sees antithetic parallels between the following clauses: "[God] gave us our riches" and "we should lose them." The expression has to do with riches, but the point of view alternates. On the one hand, God is the one who gives riches; on the other, it is humans who lose them.

In verset D one discerns an instance of synonymous parallelism, an expression that complements another by saying essentially the same thing but alternating the images. One can see that the following clauses express similar ideas: "we are surrounded by demons" (line 17), and "we are encircled about by the angels of him who hath sought to destroy our souls" (lines 18–19). However, it may be more accurate to say that these balancing ideas represent another instance of "parallelism of specification," coupled with a circumlocution that defines more clearly the meaning of the second of two general terms. The word "demons" seems rather general (line 17). But the balancing term "angels" (line 18), while also general, is immediately defined more closely by the added phrase, "of him who hath sought to destroy our souls" (lines 18–19).

A similar phenomenon occurs in verset B. The mention of "the morrow" in line 6 is rather vague. Two lines below, one reads of "the day we have sought them for battle" (line 8), a much more specific reference which implies deeper consequences.

Versets B and C are tied together by an instance of chiasmus, a literary ordering in which the first and last constituents match, and the components immediately adjacent to the extremes also match, and so on to the middle of the piece (i.e., a, b, c, c′, b′, a′). In the case of versets B and C, there are three elements that tie the two versets together directly, arranged in a chiastic structure. First, something is said about the slippery character of property (lines 10, 15). Within these, one sees that the last line of verset B reads "the curse of the land" (line 11). Three lines down in verset C we find the following: "the land is cursed" (line 14). The order of the components of these particular phrases is curse, land, land, curse. Taking account of the fact that the notion of slipperiness stands at the extremes, within which the idea of cursing appears, and within which mention of "the land" occupies the center spots, one sees the following chiastic arrangement: slippery, curse, land, land, curse, slippery.

Between versets A and C there is a clear parallelism in language. One need only notice the reiterated opening words, "O that we . . ." (lines 1, 12), whose verbs "had remembered" and "had repented" are roughly equivalent in Louis Midgley's view.[25] A further parallelism consists of the subsequent repeated phrase "in the day that . . ." (lines 2, 13). Further, as we have already noted, the final lines of these two versets both use the unique verbal phrase "become slippery," followed by short refrains that are roughly equivalent and form something of a synonymous parallel: at the end of verset A, "that we should lose them" (line 4), and at the end of verset C, "and we cannot hold them" (line 16).

Between versets B and D the parallelism breaks down. As one can see from the arrangement above, each segment is introduced by the word "behold," followed by another "behold." Moreover, each incorporates a clause of explanation that begins with the word "yea." However, there is no balance in the arrangement of the clauses associated with these terms. The "yea" clause in verset B comes after the second "behold," whereas the corresponding "yea" clause in verset D precedes the second "behold." Part of the explanation for the differences between versets B and D may well arise from the differing subject matters, concern for the loss of property in B and concern over the gripping power of the destroyer in D. In this case, however, we should not claim that no connections exist between versets B and D. In fact, we may be looking at what is termed an "emblematic" parallelism, in which the first subject has to do with the physical world (e.g., treasures, riches, etc.) and the second uses a metaphorical device to point to spiritual realities (e.g., demons, angels, etc.). A good example of this kind of parallelism appears in Ps. 42:1: "As the hart panteth after the water brooks, so panteth my soul after thee, O God."

Conclusions

In this brief foray into the world of Book of Mormon poetry, it should be clear that my focus has been narrow. I have looked at only two pieces incorporated within the prophecies of Samuel the Lamanite. But from my investigation, I believe that I can conclude with some confidence that Samuel was a poet. It is the first and shorter lament that leads me to this view. It seems to be his own composition. In the case of the second and longer piece, Samuel was likely quoting a hymn that was already known. I arrive at this observation principally because the formal expression of the hymn was known by a later generation that lamented the loss of properties, and secondarily because of the indicators of a worship context that appear in the opening lines, namely, the use of the verb "to remember," which is associated with the title "Lord God."

As one might expect, one also sees features in these pieces that mirror traits found in Hebrew poetry. My notations about these features have been anticipated in the work of several others who have turned their attention to poetry in the Book of Mormon. But the one element that has struck me most forcibly is the prophetic character of these laments. The first lament, set off in prophetic language by Samuel, finds fulfillment in the *responsum* recorded by Mormon which followed the destruction of the city of Moronihah. The second, of course, was fulfilled, as Mormon reminds us, in his own day. This prophetic character reminds me of certain Dead Sea Scroll Thanksgiving Hymns that also cast prophetic words about the last days in hymnic dress.[26] But that is a subject for another study.

This article, now revised, was first published as "The Prophetic Laments of Samuel the Lamanite," JOURNAL OF BOOK OF MORMON STUDIES 11 (fall 1992): 63–80.

NOTES

1. The standard work has been Hermann Gunkel's *Die Psalmen* (Göttingen: Vandenhoeck and Ruprecht, 1926), in which he identifies the chief characteristics of laments among the biblical Psalms. These are summarized both by Gunkel, in *The Psalms: A Form-Critical Introduction* (Philadephia: Fortress, 1967), and A. R. Johnson in his important article, "The Psalms," in *The Old Testament and Modern Study*, ed. H. H. Rowley (Oxford: Clarendon, 1951), 162–209, especially 169–70. See also the acclaimed work by Claus Westermann, *Praise and Lament in the Psalms* (Edinburgh: Clark, 1965). A recent study that challenges many of the assumptions and observations of earlier studies on psalmic literature is that of Robert Alter, *The Art of Biblical Poetry* (New York: Basic Books, 1985).

2. Richard N. Boyce, *The Cry to God in the Old Testament* (Atlanta: Scholars Press, 1988), 1–5, 68–69. A similar point is made by Westermann, *The Praise of God in the Psalms* (Richmond, Va.: Knox, 1965), 75. Walter Brueggemann, "The Costly Loss of Lament," *Journal for the Study of the Old Testament* 36 (1986): 63, has noted that "it is the cry of Israel (Ex. 2:23–25) which mobilizes Yahweh to action that begins the history of Israel."

3. Judging the character of the translation of the Book of Mormon text is largely a subjective matter. In the instance of the two poems under review, the balanced poetic themes and other elements lead me to be confident that Joseph Smith's translation was faithful to the text of the hymns.

4. According to Robert Alter, *The Art of Biblical Poetry*, 6, one need only have the frame of a formal structure to have a poem, at least in Hebrew poetry.

5. From a brief examination, it is apparent to me that some prophetic discourses in the Book of Mormon incorporate poetic features. I have not yet determined how much of this kind of psalmic writing and speech is due to the prophet who is speaking and how much lies in the words of the Lord, or in words quoted by one of his agents, say, an angel. Three persons who have produced studies that deal with poetic characteristics appearing in the Book of Mormon text are Angela Crowell, "Hebrew Poetry in the Book of Mormon," parts 1 and 2, in *Zarahemla Record* 32 and 33 (1986): 2–9, and 34 (1986): 7–12; Donald W. Parry, "Poetic Parallelisms of the Book of Mormon," Work-

ing Paper, F.A.R.M.S., 1986; and Richard Dilworth Rust, *Feasting on the Word: The Literary Testimony of the Book of Mormon* (Salt Lake City: Deseret Book and F.A.R.M.S., 1997), chapter 4; and "Poetry in the Book of Mormon," in *Rediscovering the Book of Mormon,* ed. John L. Sorenson and Melvin J. Thorne (Salt Lake City: Deseret Book and F.A.R.M.S., 1991), 100–13.

6. Johnson, "The Psalms," 171.

7. Alter, *The Art of Biblical Poetry,* 20–21. Johnson, "The Psalms," 17.

8. Whether the last line of the lament mirrors a requirement that a person must be taken outside of a city or village for execution must remain unresolved. However, we must be open to the possibility that Samuel's words reflect such a legal necessity, already spelled out in the Old Testament and elsewhere (Num. 15:35; cf. Lev. 24:14; Luke 20:15; John 19:17, 20; Acts 7:58).

9. Donald W. Parry, *The Book of Mormon Text Reformatted according to Parallelistic Patterns* (Provo, Utah: F.A.R.M.S., 1992), 393–94, has demonstrated that this lament is joined to another in the prior verse concerning Zarahemla (3 Ne. 8:24).

10. I have adopted the terminology of Robert Alter, *The Art of Biblical Poetry,* 9, in calling units "versets" rather than "colons" or "stanzas," terms that are more appropriate for the study and description of Western forms of poetry. In his parlance, a verset designates "the line-halves, or the line-thirds" found in the semantic parallelisms of Hebrew poetry.

11. On the basis of Ether 8:25, a note of warning added by Moroni, one could argue that the expected order would place "cast out" in the last spot. For in this passage Moroni complains that the Jaredites, and others, "have *murdered* the prophets, and *stoned* them, and *cast them out* from the beginning" (emphasis added). However, it is just as possible that this order in the expression is influenced by, or dependent on, the form found in the lament of Samuel. Walter Brueggemann has pointed out that formal poetic expression, especially that associated with lamentation, continues to influence speech; "The Formfulness of Grief," *Interpretation* 31 (1977): 263–75.

12. These characteristics of laments are noted in a variety of works; see, for instance, Duncan Cameron, *Songs of Sorrow and Praise* (Edinburgh: Clark, 1924), 125, 132, 136; and Johnson, "The Psalms," 166–67.

13. Just before quoting the two laments in verses 33–37, Samuel declared that "the time cometh that [the Lord] curseth your riches, that they become slippery, that ye cannot hold them; and in the days of your poverty ye cannot retain them" (Hel. 13:31). But this passage clearly depends on the second lament for its inspiration, as the verbal phrase "become slippery" illustrates, a phrase that is otherwise unique to this lament.

14. One set of ideas associated with the second lament is that of the loss of tool and sword, which is specifically tied to the notation that this loss was due to "the curse upon the land" (lines 5, 7). Significantly, this arrangement

of concepts is also combined in Moroni's summary of events that occurred in the last generation of Jaredite history: "If a man should lay his tool or his sword upon his shelf, . . . behold, upon the morrow, he could not find it, so great was the curse upon the land" (Ether 14:1). It is not clear whether Moroni's language here is influenced by that of Samuel or whether Moroni is saying that this set of observations was present in his copy of the translation of the Jaredite record, and consequently that he is simply summarizing what he found there in terms already present in the translated copy. If the former, then one could conclude that Moroni has adopted concepts expressed by Samuel in the second lament in order to depict the Jaredite situation. If the latter, it may be that the link between these ideas was already known to Samuel, or the composer of the lament, through the general knowledge of the Jaredite record that was had among Nephites and Lamanites (see Mosiah 28:11–13, 17–19; Alma 37:21, 27–30; 63:12), and therefore may have served as a source of inspiration for the vocabulary of the lament. Unfortunately, it is impossible to determine which alternative is closer to the truth.

15. Brueggemann, "The Formfulness of Grief," 265–67, 273–74.

16. Louis Midgley, "The Ways of Remembrance," in *Rediscovering the Book of Mormon*, ed. Sorenson and Thorne, 168–76.

17. Walter Brueggemann, *Genesis: A Bible Commentary for Teaching and Preaching* (Atlanta: Knox, 1982), 44–50; Jerome T. Walsh, "Genesis 2:4b–3:24: A Synchronic Approach," *Journal of Biblical Literature* 96 (1977): 161–77.

18. Brueggemann, *Genesis*, 44.

19. Two important studies on ritual in the ancient Near East are those of Theodor Gaster, *Thespis: Ritual, Myth, and Drama in the Ancient Near East* (New York: Gordian, 1961), and Ivan Engnell, *Studies in Divine Kingship in the Ancient Near East*, 2d ed. (Oxford: Blackwell, 1967). Engnell followed his disputed but valuable volume with an important essay, "'Knowledge' and 'Life' in the Creation Story," in *Wisdom in Israel and in the Ancient Near East*, ed. Martin Noth and D. Winton Thomas (Leiden: Brill, 1955), 103–19, in which Engnell dealt with ritual elements in the Garden of Eden account. But see the cautioning words of Howard N. Wallace concerning some of Engnell's assumptions in *The Eden Narrative* (Atlanta: Scholars Press, 1985), 161–63.

20. In Jer. 23:7, and in the secondary passage at Jer. 16:14, the oath runs, "The Lord liveth, which brought up the children of Israel out of the land of Egypt." But it appears that the more complete name for God in the oath is preserved by Nephi, a contemporary of Jeremiah.

21. To be sure, the Hebrew text could be translated "that thou, Jehovah, art the God," a translation suggested by J. Hammond in *I Kings, The Pulpit Commentary* (Grand Rapids, Mich.: Eerdmans, 1950), 5:426. But the definite article that precedes the word for God ("Elohim") should not blind us to the fact that in this covenant context it is the name/title "Lord God" that carries

both authority and power in the minds and hearts of the participants. After all, the Lord has been addressed thus a few verses earlier in 1 Kgs. 18:36.

22. John Gray, *I & II Kings: A Commentary, The Old Testament Library,* 2d ed. (London: SCM, 1970), 402. Gray suggests that the precedent for covenant renewal in this form is as old as Joshua (Josh. 24:18).

23. Other important passages, of course, consist of the restatement of the Decalogue, in which God says of himself, "I am the Lord thy God" (Deut. 5:6). In Deut. 5:2, Moses makes the following point, using the title "Lord God": "The Lord our God made a covenant with us in Horeb." In the Pearl of Great Price, one can also compare the worship dimensions implied in the command, "Choose ye this day, to serve the Lord God who made you" (Moses 6:33).

24. One may ask why I have argued at length about the name/title "Lord God." To be sure, this title appears in contexts that have little or nothing to do with worship (e.g., Judg. 11:21, 23). The point is that at crucial junctures in God's relations with his children, which involve worship and/or covenant making, the title "Lord God" has been the appellation by which he has been addressed. See the suggestive list of passages associated with worship in Umberto Cassuto, *A Commentary on the Book of Genesis, Part I* (Jerusalem: Magnes, 1961), 97–100 (Ex. 9:30; 2 Sam. 7:22, 25; 1 Chr. 17:16–17; 2 Chr. 6:41–42; Ps. 84:8, 11).

25. Midgley, "The Ways of Remembrance," 170, 176.

26. See, for instance, Bonnie P. Kittel, *The Hymns of Qumran* (Chico, Calif.: Scholars Press, 1981), 56–80, especially 71–73, on the hymn that appears in the Dead Sea *Thanksgiving Hymn* scroll in column 3, lines 19–36, particularly her stanza D. This hymn is number 5 in the numbering of Geza Vermes, *The Dead Sea Scrolls in English,* 4th ed. (London: Penguin, 1995), 197–99, and appears in column 11 in the numbering of Florentino García Martínez, *The Dead Sea Scrolls Translated,* 2nd ed. (Leiden: E. J. Brill, 1996), 332–33.

9

When Did Jesus Visit the Americas?

Conflicting views exist about when Jesus appeared to his New World disciples. Did he appear directly after his ascension to the Father? Some believe that his appearance followed the forty days with his disciples in Palestine, while others believe that an entire year had passed after the resurrection when he appeared in the Americas. Observations from the text suggest that he mercifully waited for the people to recover from the destruction that attended his crucifixion. Compelling details help us approach an answer to this puzzling question.

Even in the bright light of written commentary and artistic depiction, a question persists about the dating of the risen Jesus' visit to the Americas. One view holds that approximately one year had passed following the severe destruction that attended Jesus' death.[1] A second view suggests that the Savior's visit occurred in connection with or soon after his initial appearance to his disciples in Jerusalem following the resurrection (see Luke 24:28–43; John 20:11–18).[2] A third view, which stands between these two, maintains that the Savior's manifestation occurred only following his forty-day ministry (see Acts 1:3–4).[3]

Among those who either avoid the question or take an ambiguous stand are George Reynolds and Janne M. Sjodahl, who wrote, "Some time after the terrible events which denoted His death, exactly how long we know not, a multitude assembled near the temple, which was in the land Bountiful."[4] Daniel H. Ludlow did not attempt a solution but simply stated that he was aware of the three views.[5]

Among artistic representations that depict Jesus as arriving directly after the destruction of the Nephite cities and the subsequent period of total darkness is Arnold Friberg's well-known painting, now reproduced in virtually all inexpensive copies of the Book of Mormon and once featured on the cover of the Gospel Doctrine manual for 1967–68. The original painting was part of a series done during 1952–57, now hanging on the lower floor of the South Visitors' Center on Temple Square in Salt Lake City. We note especially the portrayal of recent destruction in the right foreground and the fallen posture of some of the people—as if they were struggling to their feet just after spending the past three days in darkness (see 3 Ne. 8:23).

A painting by Ronald Crosby exhibits a similar posture toward the question of whether a substantial period of time had elapsed. From 1967 to 1991, the Joseph Smith Building on the Brigham Young University campus was home to Crosby's painting of Jesus' visit to the Nephites. In that painting Crosby has depicted recent destruction, particularly in the left background. In a telephone conversation, the artist said that he had tried to capture the scene of Jesus' appearing to the Nephites "as soon after" the destruction and darkness as possible.

Calendar Issues

In seeking a solution to the question, we must first review two passages in 3 Nephi that seem to chronicle the relative timing of Jesus' death and subsequent visit. The first passage informs us that "in the thirty and fourth year, in the first month, on the fourth day of the month, there arose a great storm" which brought the destruction and period of darkness (8:5). We note particularly that it was at the beginning of the thirty-fourth year by Nephite calendrical reckoning that these events occurred.

The second key passage observes that "in the ending of the thirty and fourth year . . . soon after the ascension of Christ into heaven he did truly manifest himself unto them [Nephites and Lamanites]—showing his body unto them, and ministering unto them" (10:18–19). Here we note that it was apparently at the end of the same year, the thirty-fourth, that Jesus appeared to those assembled at the temple in the land of Bountiful (11:1).

But much depends on how we understand the meaning of the phrase "the ending."[6] The calendrical system that the Nephites used at Jesus' visit dated from the ninety-first year of the reign of the judges (3 Ne. 1:1; 2:8), the year of the appearance of the sign of Jesus' birth (1:15–21). In this connection at least two problems of the Nephite calendar remain unsolved: (a) whether the Nephites employed a solar or a lunar calendar, and (b) whether the new calendrical sequence dated from the very day, night and day when the sign appeared, or whether the Nephites merely retained the existing annual cycle, renumbering it from ninety-one to one.[7] In any case, it is evident from 3 Ne. 2:4–8 that they may have used as many as three calendars concurrently during the years immediately following the sign of Jesus' birth.

Thus far, the chronology seems clear. According to the Book of Mormon, the destruction and associated darkness had occurred at the opening of the year, and the subsequent appearance of the risen Jesus evidently came at its closing. But as we mentioned above, this chronological sequence has not been accepted everywhere. To date, discussion has focused on two items—chronometrical notations and circumstantial evidences. Let us now examine these two matters.

Expressions of Time

Concerning the chronological notes, the first potential difficulty arises from the fact that the prophet Mormon, while abridging the record of 3 Nephi, interrupted his work for an indefinite period just before copying the report of Jesus' visit: "An account of his [Jesus'] ministry [among Nephites and Lamanites] shall be given hereafter. Therefore for this time I make an end of my sayings" (3 Ne. 10:19). We must ask whether the interruption of Mormon's work could have impaired his sense for the timing of this most important moment for his people. Joseph Fielding Smith noted the interruption in Mormon's work, as did Sidney Sperry.[8]

It seems highly unlikely that Mormon became careless—even with the interruption in his editing—in handling an event that he chose to place at center stage in his abridgment. We have only to recall that Mormon's work exhibits throughout a thorough care in treating details of sequence and place.[9] In reviewing Mormon's huge effort represented in the Book of Mormon, we have to be impressed with his consistent attention to detail as he rewrote large segments of the material that came into his hands, particularly the large plates of Nephi. These sections have always exhibited a steady consistency. If we were to urge that Mormon erred in his chronological note in 3 Ne. 10:18, we would have to accept the consequent view that he committed a totally unexpected blunder while introducing the risen Jesus' ministry, the major event narrated in his literary work.

Consequently, since we can fault none of Mormon's efforts at chronological accuracy, there is no reasonable cause for questioning his remarks regarding the events associated with the beginning and the ending of the Nephites' thirty-fourth year.

The second chronometrical issue concerns Mormon's note that the Lord's special manifestation came "soon after the ascension of Christ into heaven" (10:18). The ascension itself has been understood variously as that which took place on the day of Jesus' resurrection or that which followed his forty-day ministry (see Acts 1:3).[10] Whichever the case, Mormon's notice that Jesus' manifestation fell "soon after the ascension" would seem to place the event earlier rather than later. The reply consists first in pointing to Mormon's single chronometrical observation—doubtless trustworthy, as noted above, and made in the same verse—that the visitation occurred at "the ending of the thirty and fourth year," that is, well into its latter half. This position is the one taken by Elder Bruce R. McConkie in *The Mortal Messiah*: "Then 'in the ending' of that [thirty-fourth] year (see 10:18–19), several months after the Ascension on Olivet, Jesus ministered personally among the Nephites for many hours over many days."[11] An earlier view expressed by Elder McConkie seems to indicate a belief that Jesus' visit to the Nephites occurred simultaneously with his forty-day ministry among his disciples in Palestine,[12] a position which he later abandoned. Additionally, Mormon's expression "soon after" (10:18), especially when compared to his rather clear chronological remark about "the ending" of the year, may lack sufficient precision upon which to build a firm case one way or the other.

In this connection we must consider one further chronological notation in a passage far removed from the action of 3 Nephi. Although it may shed little light on our topic, we read in a note made by Moroni several hundred years after the fact that "Christ showed himself unto our fathers, after he had risen from the dead; and he showed not himself unto them until after they had faith in him" (Ether 12:7).[13] This passage seemingly points to a rather substantial period between the Savior's resurrection and his appearance in America; but undue weight should not be placed upon it. The primary purpose of Moroni's statement in Ether 12:7 was to illustrate his prior instruction to his readers: "Dispute not because ye see not, for ye receive no witness until after the trial of your faith. For it was by faith that Christ showed himself unto our fathers, after he had risen from the dead" (12:6–7).

In dealing with chronometrical statements in the Book of Mormon, nothing has so far impelled us to abandon the literal meaning of Mormon's statement concerning "the ending" of the thirty-fourth year. We now turn to evidence that is largely circumstantial in character. We can rely upon such features only to tell us whether the drift of our interpretation is tending in the proper direction.

Circumstantial Evidences

On behalf of the view that Jesus came early to the Nephites, the most compelling observation is that the Savior would not have caused those faithful Nephites and Lamanites to wait an entire year for his appearance, especially because his instructions—momentously— brought the era of the law of Moses to a close.[14] This view possesses an interesting merit. Even the response that one year does not represent much time may seem a bit weak. We might suggest, however, the likelihood that the people, having just suffered through severe destruction and loss of loved ones, may not have been physically and emotionally able to receive the Savior. Is it not reasonable to suppose that the Lord knew the Nephites' spiritual and physical state following such a calamity and thus delayed his visit so that their minds would be relatively free of pain and anxiety? While we cannot speak with certainty, this seems to be a reasonable assumption.

The second view is less strong. It is apparently based on the remark that, just before the Savior appeared at the temple, the survivors "were marveling and wondering one with another, and were showing one to another, the great and marvelous change which had taken place" (3 Ne. 11:1). It may be natural to suppose that this verse described a scene not one year after the destruction, by which time the alterations in the landscape would have become somewhat familiar, but reported a situation directly following the great catastrophe. The answer to this interpretation is rather straightforward. In the first place, the usual human response to catastrophe is not to gather quickly to discuss the changes resulting from the event. Instead, people are thrown immediately into deep mourning for the lost (cf. 8:23–25; 10:8). Second, we must surmise, the able-bodied survivors went straight to work not only to rescue others buried in the debris of buildings[15] but also to recover the bodies of loved ones in order to provide them with proper burial. Next must have come the tremendous efforts required to rebuild and refurbish in order to protect self and loved ones both from natural elements and from enemies. Such a process would slowly return life to a level of normalcy. It is difficult, therefore, to imagine people conversing in groups at the temple, as described in 3 Ne. 11:1, if the catastrophe had occurred but recently. Moreover, discussions concerning the changes in life and circumstance would have been fittingly natural—especially if an entire year had passed since the destruction—simply because people had to respond to the tremendous human problems posed by the catastrophic events and would not likely have found an earlier opportunity to gather at the temple. This lack of opportunity would certainly have been the case if travel there involved significant distances for many. Consequently, when people finally did congregate, they had a lot to discuss. Thus it is reasonable to assume a lengthy period between the destruction and the gathering at the temple if only because the conversation was rather casual.

Buttressing the view that substantial time had passed and life had returned to some normalcy is the remark that, at the end of the Savior's first day among the Nephites, all the people went to their homes and were able to contact friends and discuss the day's events (19:1–3). Such a "settled condition could scarcely have existed immediately following the great destruction at the time of the Savior's death."[16] But there is more. The evidence now takes the form of seemingly tiny points in the account of Jesus' appearance. We refer to several small but significant details of circumstance that stand together to demonstrate that a long time had passed before the Savior's manifestation.

The first two particulars form an integral part of Jesus' introduction of the sacrament of bread and wine. We note with considerable interest that, during the first day of his visit, "Jesus commanded his disciples that they should bring forth some bread and wine unto him" (18:1). Later, after "the disciples had come with bread and wine" (18:3), Jesus hosted a banquet in which those present were filled (18:3–9)—all of this taking place on the same day. Where, we naturally ask, did the disciples obtain the bread and wine, especially on such short notice? The answer, I suggest, bears directly on our question.

In the case of the wine, while it is possible that some jars and skins survived the three destructive hours described in 3 Ne. 8:5–19, it is more likely that virtually every storage facility and instrument suffered damage, if not total ruin, since according to the account the desolation was severe.

While "there was a more great and terrible destruction in the land northward" (8:12)—implying less severe damage in the south—and while "there were some cities which remained" (8:15), even in the areas least affected "the damage thereof was exceedingly great, and there were many [of the inhabitants] in them who were slain" (8:15). The catastrophe was so widespread that "the face of the whole earth became deformed" (8:17). Moreover, if we assume a recent collapse of buildings and homes, could anyone be expected to dig through tons of rubble in a matter of minutes in order to find sufficient uncontaminated, unspilled wine for a large crowd? One may argue, of course, that the wine stored in the temple at Bountiful miraculously escaped harm. But such a suggestion lacks substantiation from the text. Rather, in the passage we clearly sense that Jesus' request for wine was not extraordinary and did not require an extensive search for a cache unexpectedly preserved. This conclusion is strengthened by the simple observation that it was not until the second day of his visit that Jesus' own supernatural powers came into play when he miraculously provided the wine and bread: "Now, there had been no bread, neither wine, brought [on the second day] by the disciples, neither by the multitude; but he truly gave unto them bread to eat, and also wine to drink" (20:6–7). We are thus led to deduce that the ready accessibility of wine on the first day points not to a moment almost directly after the destruction but rather to a time substantially later when people had tended and harvested the remaining vineyards and refurbished the means to store the processed wine.

While the previous point is essentially circumstantial in character, the following tightens the knot. It concerns the bread and its ready availability on the first day. We note that the Nephites and Lamanites must have made bread daily, as did all known ancient cultures, because of the lack of preservatives. Consequently, the fact that bread was within reach on request illustrates the likelihood that, on the day that Jesus appeared, bread had been baked—unless it was Sabbath. From all indications, that day began like any other day—without any special expectations on the part of those assembling at the temple.[17]

If we were to insist, in this connection, that Jesus had come almost immediately after the destruction, we would need to explain how kilns and ovens used for baking escaped the terrible ruination that devastated the whole society. The answer, in my view, lies in a different direction. The bread blessed by the risen Jesus and then consumed during the ensuing meal had probably been prepared and baked in the early-morning hours of the first of Jesus' three-day ministry. Bread could not have been prepared from contaminated water and scattered flour supplies—if any survived—nor baked in crushed ovens. Once again, if we were to hold that Jesus' appearance followed almost directly after the wreckage, we would have to argue for a miraculous preservation of supplies of water and flour as well as kilns, in addition to an amazingly rapid return to normality in the daily routines of those who had suffered so severely.

A third passage sheds further light on the chronometric issue. When the risen Jesus turned to the matter of "other scriptures . . . that ye should write, that ye have not" (23:6), he specifically drew his disciples' attention to a prophecy of Samuel the Lamanite concerning "many saints who should arise from the dead" (23:9). For our discussion, the following exchange between Jesus and his disciples is key: "And Jesus said unto them [the Twelve]: How be it that ye have not written . . . that many saints did arise? . . . And it came to pass that Jesus commanded that it should be written" (23:11–13). In addition, the text affirms that "Nephi remembered" when Jesus recalled that many had arisen and had appeared "unto many and did minister unto them"—probably comforting the survivors of the destruction at their loss (23:11–12). These events were obviously associated with Jesus' own resurrection and thus must have followed almost immediately after the lifting of the darkness (10:9). Clearly, Nephi the record keeper had simply forgotten to include in his account this notable proof of the resurrection. In correcting this oversight, Jesus reminded both him and the rest of the Twelve that such an important feature was to be recorded. Moreover, Jesus' remarks indicate that enough time had passed to make this notation in the record. To summarize, then, the language of the passage plainly leads us to conclude that Jesus was referring to an unrecorded series of events in the reasonably distant past rather than to recent occurrences.

Finally, Daniel H. Ludlow has suggested two more convincing evidences for Jesus' appearance several months after his resurrection. When the Savior selected his twelve disciples on the first day, all twelve of them were present in the congregation of twenty-five hundred people. Such a circumstance would have been highly unlikely unless the meeting were an important gathering of the Church, or at least a meeting of the faithful from throughout the whole land. Such a meeting could not have been called and held immediately after the great destruction. The roads and terrain were then simply impassible (8:13, 17). Further, when the Savior commanded the multitude to gather the remainder of the people together on the following day, his hearers knew exactly where to go—that is, they knew which cities had been destroyed and which had not—and people were able to gather back the next day. Thus, the roads must have been repaired.[18]

Conclusion

The cumulative evidence reviewed here weighs in the direction of the Savior having come to the Nephites only after a substantial period of time. That period must have extended well into the latter half of the year—presumably between October and April—if we correctly understand Mormon's chronological notations concerning the timing of both the destruction (3 Ne. 8:5) and the manifestation of the Savior (10:18). The one serious consideration that weighs in favor of only a brief interlude is the supposition that the Lord would not have left his faithful followers so long without a personal visit. But it is at least as reasonable to hypothesize that, given the situation following the destruction, it was more timely that the Savior delay his visit. Moreover, in terms of the internal evidence from the text, the heft of the documentation suggests that life had returned to some normalcy. This conclusion derives from a series of notations in the text, including remarks that, after the first day of the Lord's ministry, people returned home and discussed the events of the day with friends (19:1–3) and that bread and wine were readily available at Jesus' request (18:1–3). Implied in the concept of a substantial period is the notion that enough time had probably passed to allow a new harvest, which would resupply stores both of grain and of produce from the vine lost in the catastrophe. Thus, Mormon's chronological note that the risen Jesus appeared "in the ending" of the thirty-fourth year is confirmed by particulars connected with Jesus' first day among Nephites and Lamanites in the Americas.

This article has been revised from its first appearance as "Jesus among the Nephites: When Did It Happen?" in A SYMPOSIUM ON THE NEW TESTAMENT *(Salt Lake City: Church Educational System, 1984), 74–77.*

NOTES

1. See Sidney B. Sperry, *Book of Mormon Studies* (Salt Lake City: Deseret Sunday School Union Board, 1947), 101; *The Book of Mormon Testifies* (Salt Lake City: Bookcraft, 1952), 294; *Book of Mormon Compendium* (Salt Lake City: Bookcraft, 1968), 401; Joseph F. McConkie and Robert L. Millet, *Doctrinal Commentary on the Book of Mormon* (Salt Lake City: Bookcraft, 1987–92), 4:50; see also J. N. Washburn, *Book of Mormon Lands and Times* (Bountiful, Utah: Horizon Publishers, 1974), 186.

2. See Milton R. Hunter, *Christ in Ancient America* (Salt Lake City: Deseret Book, 1959), 97–98.

3. Reid E. Bankhead and Glenn L. Pearson, *The Word and the Witness: The Unique Mission of the Book of Mormon* (Salt Lake City: Bookcraft, 1970), 34; James E. Talmage, *Jesus the Christ*, 3d ed. (Salt Lake City: Deseret Book, 1916), 724. On Jesus' forty-day ministry, see S. Kent Brown and C. Wilfred Griggs, "The Postresurrection Ministry," in *Studies in Scripture, Vol. 6: Acts to Revelation*, ed. Robert L. Millet (Salt Lake City: Deseret Book, 1987), 12–23.

4. George Reynolds and Janne M. Sjodahl, *Commentary on the Book of Mormon* (Salt Lake City: Deseret Book, 1955–61), 7:133.

5. See Daniel H. Ludlow, *A Companion to Your Study of the Book of Mormon* (Salt Lake City: Deseret Book, 1976), 260.

6. In the other two instances wherein Mormon employs the phrase "in the ending of the [such and such] year," the context points to the very end of the

year since Mormon notes events of the following year immediately thereafter (Alma 52:14–15; Hel. 3:1–2).

7. These complexities are noted by John L. Sorenson, "Seasonality of Warfare in the Book of Mormon and in Mesoamerica," in *Warfare in the Book of Mormon*, ed. Stephen D. Ricks and William J. Hamblin (Salt Lake City: Deseret Book and F.A.R.M.S., 1990), 445–77, especially 448–53; and by John P. Pratt, "Book of Mormon Chronology," in *Encyclopedia of Mormonism*, ed. D. H. Ludlow (New York: Macmillan, 1992), 169–71.

8. Joseph Fielding Smith, *Answers to Gospel Questions* (Salt Lake City: Deseret Book, 1957–66), 4:27; Sperry, *The Book of Mormon Testifies*, 295; *Book of Mormon Compendium*, 401.

9. See Eldin Ricks's summary of Mormon's literary work in *Story of the Formation of the Book of Mormon Plates*, 3d ed. (Salt Lake City: Olympus Publishing, 1966); Grant R. Hardy speaks of "Mormon's honesty as a historian"; "Mormon as Editor," in *Rediscovering the Book of Mormon*, ed. John L. Sorenson and Melvin J. Thorne (Salt Lake City: Deseret Book and F.A.R.M.S., 1991), 15–28.

10. See also Ludlow, *A Companion to Your Study of the Book of Mormon*, 260; Bankhead and Pearson, *The Word and the Witness*, 34; Ora Pate Stewart, *Branches over the Wall* (Salt Lake City: Bookcraft, 1950), 129; and Talmage, *Jesus the Christ*, 724.

11. Bruce R. McConkie, *The Mortal Messiah* (Salt Lake City: Deseret Book, 1981), 4:307.

12. See Bruce R. McConkie, *Mormon Doctrine* (Salt Lake City: Bookcraft, 1958), 52.

13. See also Sperry, *Book of Mormon Compendium*, 401.

14. Smith, *Answers to Gospel Questions*, 4:28–29.

15. The collapse of buildings during the devastation was foreseen by Nephi (2 Ne. 26:5; cf. 1 Ne. 12:4).

16. Sperry, *The Book of Mormon Testifies*, 294, n. 4; repeated in Sperry, *Book of Mormon Compendium*, 401, n. 4.

17. The question has to be asked why the people had gathered. Was it a festival? We can speculate that if the end of the thirty-fourth year had indeed come, then the occasion for assembling may have been a New Year festival. But we lack evidence from the text.

18. Report of the Church Correlation Committee, 5 April 1984.

10

Moses and Jesus: The Old Adorns the New

Scriptures draw on the experiences of Moses to teach about the Savior and his mission. For example, the gospel writers illumined ties between Moses and Jesus through their depiction of events such as the Sermon on the Mount. In 3 Nephi, the risen Lord himself cites Isaiah's prophecies of a "new exodus" to instruct his audience about the gathering of Israel in the last days. By miraculously providing bread and wine, and by identifying himself as the law and the light, the Savior established himself as one greater than Moses. On a deeper level, the Book of Mormon links together the deliverance of the children of Israel through the intervention of Jehovah and the freeing of the Nephites and Lamanites from spiritual bondage through the visitation of the resurrected Christ.

Reading the pages of 3 Nephi leads one naturally to conclude that the resurrected Jesus regularly and consciously drew the attention of his hearers to Moses. But Jesus' attention to Moses was not intended merely to tell us what an important and wonderful prophet Moses had been. Rather, it is evident that Jesus' chief intent was to say that the ministry of Moses had foreshadowed or anticipated his own. Indeed, Jesus quoted an important prophecy of Moses and applied it to himself. The prophecy is recorded in Deuteronomy 18 and speaks of a future prophet, like Moses, whom the Lord would raise up among his people. In 3 Ne. 20:23, the resurrected Savior says: "Behold, I am he of whom Moses spake, saying: A prophet shall the Lord your God raise up unto you of your brethren, like unto me; him shall ye hear in all things whatsoever he shall say unto you. And it shall come to pass that every soul who will not hear that prophet shall be cut off from among the people" (see also Deut. 18:15, 18–19).

Moses as a Type of the Savior

With these words, Jesus established the connection between Moses and himself. Moses had prophesied that a notable prophet would arise among his people. Moreover, that prophet would be like Moses himself. By quoting this passage, Jesus made it clear that Moses had been speaking of him. Thus, there exists an obvious prophetic connection between the two, including the fact that Jesus would somehow be like Moses. Hence, we are justified in speaking of Moses as a type of the Savior.[1]

In a related vein, ancient authors, including the New Testament gospel writers, have noticed the resemblances between Jesus' ministry and that of Moses. For instance, Matthew recounts that like Moses, who ascended the mount to receive the law, Jesus ascended a mount where he dealt with the law (Matt. 5:1). But in contrast to Moses who went up *to receive* the law, Jesus went up *to give* a new law, a law which is incorporated into his Sermon on the Mount (Matthew 5–7). In addition, in his gospel account Matthew seems to have consciously divided the teachings of Jesus into five segments, thus emphasizing the similarity between Jesus' teachings and the five books of Moses, which are the repository of the Mosaic law. To achieve this purpose, at five key points in his narrative Matthew used the following phrase, or a similar one: "And . . . when Jesus had ended these sayings," thus arranging Jesus' teachings into five sections (see 7:28; 11:1; 13:53; 19:1; 26:1).

Having said this much, I would like to point out a subtle distinction between the treatment of Jesus' ministry and teachings in the New Testament and that which we find in the Book of Mormon. In the case of Matthew's gospel, to which I have made brief reference, Jesus himself is partly responsible for making the connection between Moses and himself. After all, it was Jesus who went up on the mount to deliver his sermon that is recorded in Matthew chapters 5 through 7, an action which consciously imitated the act of Moses ascending Mount Sinai. Moreover, we can recall that Jesus specifically addressed issues in his Sermon on the Mount that are subjects of the Mosaic law—subjects such as how one responds to one's enemies, what the definition of adultery is, and under what circumstances one properly swears an oath. For drawing these connections to Moses and to the Mosaic law, Jesus himself was responsible. However, Jesus did not write the gospel of Matthew. Matthew did. And it is Matthew who was responsible for making the further comparison between Moses and Jesus in his gospel by arranging the teachings of Jesus into five segments in imitation of the five books of Moses. As a result, we can conclude that not only Jesus but also those who wrote about him in the New Testament drew analogies between him and Moses. And, using the Sermon on the Mount as an example, the intent of those analogies seems to have been to underscore the notion that in the person of Jesus one greater than Moses had come.

Greater Than Moses

Let us now leave the New Testament and return to 3 Nephi. I believe that we have said enough in these brief examples from the New Testament to grasp the point that both Jesus and the authors of the New Testament were interested in making comparisons between Jesus and Moses. In the Book of Mormon the case is different. In every instance that I have found in 3 Nephi, it was the resurrected Jesus, either by word or action, who drew attention to connections between Moses and himself. Certainly Mormon, the compiler of the work, did not. We have already seen—in the prophecy Jesus quoted from Deuteronomy concerning the prophet God would raise up "like unto" Moses—that the resurrected Jesus consciously linked himself to Moses (3 Ne. 20:23). But there is much more.

I shall next draw attention to prophecies about the last days that were uttered by Isaiah, specifically those found in chapter 52, a chapter from which the resurrected Jesus quoted extensively when he was speaking of the house of Israel and the Gentiles in the last days (3 Nephi 16, 20–21).[2] Isaiah 52 is known as a chapter dealing with the so-called "new exodus" or "second exodus," that is, the gathering of the house of Israel in the last days. In its own way, the new exodus of Israel is to resemble the old exodus under Moses because of its miraculous character and because the results will be the same: a return to the land promised to Israel's forebears and a return of the covenants that the Lord had made with them. If one were to read Isaiah 52 with care, one would see allusions in almost every verse to the exodus that took place in the days of Moses.[3]

A third ingredient, in addition to the prophecy in Deuteronomy 18 and the quotations from Isaiah on the new exodus, consists of Jesus' role as lawgiver in his sermon at the temple in the land of Bountiful. Clearly his words disclose a close connection between himself and Moses. But they also communicate the fact that he is greater than Moses. Let us consider the following: "Behold, I am he that gave the law, and I am he who covenanted with my people Israel; therefore, the law in me is fulfilled, for I have come to fulfil the law; therefore it hath an end" (3 Ne. 15:5). Moses was chiefly the transmitter of the Law, its recipient. Jesus, on the other hand, was its giver, its author. Further, it was only the divine Jesus who could fulfill the law which he himself had given, a task that Moses could not perform as the bearer of the law, carrying it as he did from the premortal Jesus—known as Jehovah—to his people who were camped at the base of Mount Sinai.[4]

As if this were not enough, the resurrected Jesus said more: "Behold, I am the law, and the light. Look unto me, and endure to the end, and ye shall live; for unto him that endureth to the end will I give eternal life" (3 Ne. 15:9). The connections here to Moses and the Exodus of the children of Israel are compelling. First, Jesus identified himself as the law. But he was and is much more. He is also the light. What does this recall to our minds from the Exodus? Does it not remind us of the pillar of fire that was visible at night above the sacred tabernacle during the years of Israel's wandering and camping in the wilderness? (see Ex. 13:21; 14:24; Num. 14:14; cf. Ex. 14:20). Further, Jesus says that we are to look to him, and if we endure well, we shall live. What do these concepts recall? On one level, they recall the brass serpent on a pole that was lifted up for all who had been bitten by serpents to see. Moreover, it was the Lord's promise through Moses that those who looked to the raised serpent would live and not die (Num. 21:4–9; 1 Ne. 17:41; 2 Ne. 25:20; compare the following passages in which the brass serpent on the pole is likened to Jesus on the cross: John 3:14–15; Alma 33:19–22; Hel. 8:14–15). We can see, therefore, that virtually every word that Jesus said in this verse recalls a dimension of Israel's experience while under the leadership of Moses.

A fourth element arises from Jesus' miraculous provision of bread and wine to the multitude on the second day of his visit. This event is thrown into relief by the fact that on day one he had asked the disciples to bring bread and wine to feed the multitude (3 Ne. 18:1–4). On the second day it was different. The scriptural record recounts that "there had been no bread, neither wine, brought by the disciples, neither by the multitude; but he [Jesus] truly gave unto them bread to eat, and also wine to drink" (20:6–7). Can one miss the connection back to the experience of Moses and the children of Israel? We first note that the Lord had preserved the lives of the Israelites by miraculously providing water for them when Moses struck a rock in the desert. Actually, a similar miracle took place three times (see Ex. 15:22–25 for the healing of the waters of Marah; 17:1–7 and Num. 20:2–11 for instances of Moses striking a rock in order to bring forth water). Second, the book of Exodus informs us that after the Israelites had spent two weeks in the desert and had run out of food, the Lord generously provided bread, or manna, in the desert for the entire period that they wandered and camped there (see Ex. 16:1–6). Third, if we are not convinced that the bread and wine exhibit a link backwards in time to the period of the Exodus, then we should consider the New Testament account of Jesus breaking the bread and blessing the wine during the Last Supper with his twelve apostles, an event during which Jesus instituted the emblems of the sacrament among his followers in the Old World. At this point, two questions are in order. Was not the Last Supper a Passover meal? Although the gospel of John seems to hold that the Last Supper was not a Passover meal, the Synoptic gospels are unanimous in affirming that it was (see Matt. 26:17–19; Mark 14:12–16; Luke 22:7–13). Further, does not the Passover meal celebrate the deliverance of Moses and the children of Israel from bondage? The answers to these questions, of course, are affirmative. In this light, then, we readily see the connections between Jesus' actions among the Nephites and Lamanites and the earlier actions of the Lord for the children of Israel in preserving them from thirsting and starving in the desert.

Recovering One Enslaved Abroad

A final, and perhaps the most intriguing, component of our comparison is grounded in an important and rather common legal function in the ancient world, that of one person sending an envoy or representative to recover a third person who has been enslaved in a distant place. The opening of the Exodus account brims with the legal essentials required in cases wherein one seeks the release of another. In this instance, it was the Lord who sought the release of the children of Israel through his agent Moses.

In all such cases, the agent had to bear credentials from the sender in order to prove who he was and whom he represented. The reasons were twofold. First, the captor had to be convinced that the agent had authority to negotiate the release of the one held captive. Second, the captive too had to be reassured that the agent represented the person who was seeking the release, particularly if the agent was not known to the captive. Hence, we see the need for the agent to bear credentials which prove that he or she is an authorized representative of the one seeking the release of the captive. In the case of Moses, it is clear that he understood the need for such credentials. On the Lord's part, he willingly provided them. For as soon as Moses had been called at the burning bush to "deliver [the Israelites] out of the hand of the Egyptians" (Ex. 3:8), he asked to know the Lord's name, a name that would be recognized by the Hebrew slaves. As the account says, the Lord revealed to him the name "I AM THAT I AM." Then the Lord instructed Moses, "Thus shalt thou say unto the children of Israel, I AM hath sent me unto you" (3:14). But the Lord gave to Moses more than his name, because the name would only serve to convince the Hebrew slaves of Moses' authority, and Pharaoh certainly would not accept the name as an indicator of legal or divine prerogatives. Hence, Moses was given power to cast down his staff, turning the staff into a snake. This miraculous power was exhibited both to the children of Israel (4:1–4, 30) and later to Pharaoh (7:9–12). For the enslaved Israelites, however, Moses received other powers or credentials from the Lord that were designed to convince them of his authority, namely, the power to make his hand leprous and the power to turn water to blood (4:6–9). This latter power, of course, was subsequently exhibited to Pharaoh and the Egyptians (7:19–21). In the end, then, Moses bore credentials both to Pharaoh—the captor—and to the Hebrews—the captives—in the form of extraordinary powers from the Lord, who sought the release of the captives.

When we turn to the scene described for us in 3 Nephi, we are able to see rather quickly that all of the required elements are present. We first must ask who the envoy was. In one sense, there was none. In another sense, we find the most important envoy ever to come to this world. In the first sense, the resurrected Jesus came for himself. He sent no one as his representative or ambassador. In the second sense, it was the Father who sent the Savior as envoy on his errand to the Nephites and Lamanites (see 3 Ne. 11:11; 17:4; 18:27).

A second question concerns the identity of the captor in 3 Nephi. Two possible answers appear. One consists of the devil and his angels. In this connection, one should contemplate the following passage: "Wo, wo, wo unto this people; wo unto the inhabitants of the whole earth except they shall repent; for the devil laugheth, and his angels rejoice, because of the slain of the fair sons and daughters of my people" (9:2). These words were spoken by the voice that was heard throughout the land during the terrifying three days of darkness that followed the three hours of devastating storm and earthquakes. If one is looking for a living captor, one need look no further than the devil himself. But there is a second answer which may make more sense. A hint of it is found in the words that we have just read. When the voice used the verb *repent*, it brought its hearers to the other captor, namely, their sins. For in the same passage, speaking of those who had been slain, the voice went on to say, "And it is because of their iniquity and abominations that they are fallen!" In this light, perhaps a better way to ask the question is, *what* is the captor? As a partial response and for more light on this subject, we should examine a passage which the Savior quoted from Isaiah 52. It reads, "For thus saith the Lord: Ye have sold yourselves for naught, and ye shall be redeemed without money" (3 Ne. 20:38; see also Isa. 52:3). Here it becomes clear that those who are to be "redeemed without money" had "sold" themselves for nothing of value. Knowing the general tenor of Isaiah 52 to be that of the second or new exodus, one chief meaning would be that such persons had sold themselves into bondage, a bondage not unlike that of the Hebrew slaves in Egypt. On a spiritual level, the reference would be to persons who had sold themselves into spiritual bondage, or sin.

The case is clinched by Jesus' words spoken on day two of his visit and recorded in 3 Ne. 20:26. The resurrected Lord declared that the reason the Father had sent him was "to bless you [Nephites and Lamanites] in turning away every one of you from his iniquities." In light of this understanding and the earlier one about the devil and his angels, one must conclude that the captor or captors consisted of the devil and one's sins. It is from these that Jesus came to deliver his Nephite and Lamanite brothers and sisters.

If, then, Jesus was the envoy or representative who came in his own name and in that of the Father, and if his purpose was to rescue his people from both Satan and their own sinful state, what, we might ask, did he bring as his credentials? We need not look far. He bore the proofs of his rescue mission in his own body. One need only repeat his words of invitation to the spellbound crowd who had gathered at the temple in Bountiful on the first day of his visit: "Arise and come forth unto me, that ye may thrust your hands into my side, and also that ye may feel the prints of the nails in my hands and in my feet" (3 Ne. 11:14). It is important to notice that it was the scars of the wounds inflicted during his crucifixion that the resurrected Jesus wanted the crowd to feel. Why? There was a reason, and he spelled it out in his next words: "That ye may know that I am the God of Israel, and the God of the whole earth, and have been slain for the sins of the world" (11:14). Let me suggest that what the crowd would learn when they touched his old wounds, if the spirit of testimony were not present, would be that he had some deep scars. Nothing more. However, because of the spiritual dimension of the experience, Jesus' hearers would gain the testimony that he was who he said he was, namely, "the God of Israel, and the God of the whole earth" and that he had "been slain for the sins of the world." From the account in 3 Nephi we learn that it happened as he said it would. For after "they had all gone forth, and did see with their eyes and did feel with their hands," they "did know of a surety and did bear record, that it was he, of whom it was written by the prophets, that should come" (11:15). It therefore becomes clear that Jesus carried two sets of credentials, as it were. One set was embedded in his body and consisted of the scars of his crucifixion. The other was evidently the power of the Spirit that brought testimonies to those who went forward and touched him—who "witnessed for themselves" (11:16). As I read the narrative, the overwhelming character of this physical and spiritual experience led those in the crowd to do the only thing that they could do in such a sacred setting: to sing. Now I realize that verse 16 says that "they did cry out with one accord." Why do I conclude, then, that they sang? I do so for two reasons: context and unison. In my view, the sacred moment described here would invite song, even if it were loud singing, rather than calling out in a loud voice. Hebrew verbs of speech, even of loud speech, can be translated as references to singing, depending on the context. And I personally believe that the context warrants this understanding. Further, the context is defined by the implication that the crowd spoke in unison, for we are told that it was "with one accord" that they voiced their feelings. While it is possible that they simply recited aloud the words recorded in verse 17, it seems just as likely that they sang them. Perhaps significantly, indicators exist in the Book of Mormon that songs and hymns formed an important part of Nephite worship.[5]

The credentials of the resurrected Jesus included more than the physical and spiritual dimensions that his hearers experienced that day. They also included a name, the same name that Moses carried from the holy mount into the Hebrew slave camps. It was the name I AM. Please notice the words with which Jesus began his visit in the New World: "Behold, I AM" (3 Ne. 11:10, capitalization added). Of course, the fuller statement is, "Behold, I AM Jesus Christ" (capitalization added). Observe a few statements of Jesus about himself in 3 Nephi that sound very much like what we read in the gospel of John: "And behold, I am the light and the life of the world" (11:11); "I am the God of Israel" (11:14); "Behold I am the law, and the light" (15:9); "Behold, I am the light" (18:16); "Behold, I am he of whom Moses spake" (20:23; see also 12:1–2; 18:24; 20:19, 31, 39; 27:27). Scholars of John's gospel agree that the so-called "I am" sayings of Jesus, which are quoted in that gospel, are all references back to the divine name that was revealed to Moses at the burning bush. That is to say, whenever Jesus used the "I am" clause of himself—whether to say that he was the light of the world, the resurrection and the life, or the true bread come down from heaven—he was consciously recalling the divine name and applying it to himself. He was therefore saying that one of his names is I AM and that he was the same person who had called Moses to be a prophet at the burning bush. In this light, I suggest that the same concepts apply in what Jesus said to his Nephite and Lamanite hearers.[6] In my view, the case is clinched by Jesus' words in 3 Ne. 15:5: "Behold, I am he that gave the law, and I am he who covenanted with my people Israel." Who else could this have been except Jehovah, the great I AM, the premortal Jesus?

Conclusion

Let me offer some concluding remarks. As a person who grew up on the Bible, so to speak, I have been deeply impressed—even astonished at times—by what I have found in the pages of the Book of Mormon. By focusing on a single thread, that of the connections between Moses and Jesus, we have been able to explore the meaning of a number of passages whose depth and richness continue to unfold. The broad ties with the Old Testament, particularly with those of the era of Moses and the continuities with Jesus' ministry in Palestine, form a luxurious tapestry which portrays the spiritual strength and consistency that the resurrected Jesus brought to his Nephite and Lamanite brothers and sisters. Perhaps the best reward of all for studying 3 Nephi is that we are permitted to see the resurrected Lord and hear his words in a firsthand, personal manner. For me, in 3 Nephi, more than in any other scriptural source, Jesus becomes alive, real, and complete, with his wondrous quality of divine love, a love which brought him to rescue all of us from the grasp of Satan and from our own sinfulness, a rescue mission which we all desperately need. And the power of the resurrected Savior to deliver us from all bondage, physical or spiritual, is real.

This article, slightly revised, appeared in a Religious Studies Center publication as "Moses and Jesus: The Old Adorns the New," in THE BOOK OF MORMON: 3 NEPHI 9–30, THIS IS MY GOSPEL, ed. Monte S. Nyman and Charles D. Tate Jr. (Provo, Utah: Religious Studies Center, Brigham Young University, 1993), 89–100.

NOTES

1. Because Jesus does not quote the passage precisely as it reads in the present text of Deuteronomy, the question arises: Was Jesus quoting the passage verbatim from the version preserved on the plates of brass or was he merely citing the passage as he knew it from the Hebrew Bible and then adjusting it to suit his present purposes? The issue is impossible to resolve. However, for an example of Jesus' use of the latter technique, see his composite quotation of passages from Isa. 61:1–2 and 58:6 in Luke 4:18–19.

The issue naturally arises whether Deuteronomy, or a version of it, was part of the collection of scripture on the plates of brass. The answer must be affirmative. Jesus quotes a passage here as if it were already known to his hearers. Moreover, in connection with the disappearance of Alma (Alma 45:18–19), there is discussion of the account of the death of Moses, an account that appears only at the end of Deuteronomy (34:5–7).

2. In addition, Jesus quoted from Micah 4–5, chapters that also speak of the "second exodus" or "new exodus."

3. For instance, Isaiah 52:2 speaks of "the bands of thy neck," clearly a reference to enslavement. Verse 3 continues the same imagery of slavery by reference to selling oneself "for nought," a condition of servitude that poor people frequently faced when they were unable to pay their debts. Moreover, the reference to redemption "without money" in the same verse echoes the rescue of the Hebrew slaves by the Lord. The command to depart in verse 11 recalls the departure of the Israelites from Egypt. Further allusions could be multiplied. The only verses not quoted by the resurrected Jesus are Isa. 52:4–5, verses wherein the enslavement of the Israelites in Egypt is described. While not all of the following match exactly our present Old Testament texts, the passages quoted by Jesus in 3 Nephi chapters 16, 20 and 21 are Isa. 52:8–10 (3 Ne. 16:18–20); Micah 5:8–9 (3 Ne. 20:16–17); 4:12–13 (3 Ne. 20:18–19); Deut. 18:15 (3 Ne. 20:23); Isa. 52:8 (3 Ne. 20:8), 9–10 (3 Ne. 20:34–35); Isa. 52:1–3 (3 Ne. 20:36–38), 6–7 (3 Ne. 20:39–40), 11–15 (3 Ne. 20:41–45), 15 (3 Ne. 21:8).

4. A summary of this topic can be found in David R. Seely, "Jehovah, Jesus Christ," in *Encyclopedia of Mormonism*, ed. Daniel H. Ludlow (New York: Macmillan, 1992), 720–21.

5. See "The Prophetic Laments of Samuel the Lamanite," chapter 8 in this book.

6. James R. Harris, "The 'I Am' Passages in the Gospels and in 3 Nephi," in *The New Testament and the Latter-day Saints*, ed. H. Dean Garrett (Orem, Utah: Randall, 1987), 89–114.

Scripture Index

Old Testament

Leviticus

Numbers

Jeremiah

Lamentations

Ezekiel

Amos

Jonah

Micah

Nahum

2 Nephi

Jacob

Omni

Words of Mormon

Mosiah

Alma

Helaman

3 Nephi

4 Nephi

Mormon

Subject Index

A

B

C

D

E

M

R

S

T

W

Y

Z